D0502553

4444 00043 3227

LOSING OUR VIRTUE

LOSING OUR VIRTUE

*Why the Church Must Recover
Its Moral Vision*

David F. Wells

William B. Eerdmans Publishing Company
Grand Rapids, Michigan / Cambridge, U.K.

© 1998 Wm. B. Eerdmans Publishing Co.
255 Jefferson Ave. S.E., Grand Rapids, Michigan 49503 /
P.O. Box 163, Cambridge CB3 9PU U.K.

Printed in the United States of America

03 02 01 00 99 98   7 6 5 4 3 2 1

Library of Congress Cataloging-in-Publication Data
Wells, David F.
Losing our virtue: why the church must recover its moral vision /
David F. Wells
p.   cm.
Includes bibliographical references and index.
ISBN 0-8028-3827-8 (alk. paper)
1. Christianity and culture — United States.
2. United States — moral conditions.
3. Christianity — United States — 20th century.
4. Christian ethics.
I. Title.
BR115.C8W43   1998
241'.0973 — dc21   97-32963
                                                    CIP

Unless otherwise noted, the Scripture quotations in this publication are
from the Revised Standard Version of the Bible, copyrighted 1946, 1952
© 1971, 1973 by the Division of Christian Education of the National
Council of Churches of Christ in the U.S.A., and used by permission.

To
my faculty colleagues
and
to our students
at
Gordon-Conwell Theological Seminary

Contents

Preface

In 1989, I was the recipient of a generous grant from the Pew Charitable Trusts. The purpose of the grant was to allow Mark Noll, Neal Plantinga, and myself the opportunity to explore the reasons for the decay of evangelical thinking, and not least in theology. My own contribution to that enterprise, *No Place for Truth*, began a line of inquiry for me that has continued into this present volume. I remain grateful for that original grant as well as for the half sabbatical granted to me for the purpose of writing this volume.

Because this book has sought to explore terrain that is not commonly traversed by theologians, I have been especially grateful for the help I have received from a number of people. Initially, I sought some guidance from Kaye Cook on postmodern psychology and from Paul Kennedy on current sociological research on evangelicalism. In due course, portions of the manuscript were read by Greg Beale, Os Guinness, Ray Pendleton, Dick Keyes, and Richard Lints. In addition, I met with the Dead Theologians Society, made up of post-D.Min. pastors, who offered many helpful suggestions on a chapter that I had circulated. I am grateful for the help I received in these various ways, though of course I alone am responsible for whatever errors and blemishes remain.

During the writing of this book, I had the opportunity to deliver material that I had been working on in lecture form. It was my privilege to give the Pedersen Lectures at the Lutheran Brethren Schools, the Centennial Lectures at Trinity Evangelical Divinity School, to be the Pinecrest Lecturer at South Florida Center for Theological Studies, and to be a speaker at the annual New England Reformed Fellowship conference. All of this interaction with my material was very helpful.

Part of chapter II appeared in an earlier version as "Our Dying Culture" in James Montgomery Boice and Ben Sasse, eds., *Here We Stand: A Call from Confessing Evangelicals* (Grand Rapids: Baker, 1996), 25-42. It is published here with permission.

Finally, I wish to express my gratitude to the remnant of serious readers without whom I, for one, would have no audience.

Introduction

Old ways of belief are dying within millions of minds.

Walter Truett Anderson

This book is about the disintegrating moral culture in American society and what this now means for the Church. This disintegration is, of course, a well-worn theme. It is the subject of editorials, books, and television commentary. It is a cause of concern among many people, and it has occasioned quite a lot of political posturing. Pronouncements are easy to make on such matters. It is easier still to exploit what is of genuine national concern for private gain, but understanding what is happening is far harder and far more important. Without this understanding, there will be no durable solutions. Nor will there be an effective Christian presence in society.

In this book, I have tried to understand. More than that, I have tried to think about the face-off between Christian faith and our morally disintegrating culture. What has this breakdown done to our understanding of ourselves as *moral beings*? For if this understanding is being lost, and I believe that it is, the consequences are large for how Christian faith will be seen and for how it needs to think about itself and its responsibilities in society.

I should say straight away that what I have done in this book will be irritating to those who do not wish to hear theological truth, and many in the evangelical world do not. They have already washed their hands of it. As little as I wish to wave red rags before bulls and further provoke those who took offense at my earlier books, the fact is that the

1

enculturation of the evangelical world and its self-betrayal through its
theologically emptied-out faith is the reason why the Church has no
answer to the national crisis of character. It is also the reason why the
postmodern world is not hearing, as it should, a Word from God. For
this is what theology is really about. I am understanding theology, then,
as the work of bringing the truth of God's Word into lively intersection
with the life of the Church, as it exists in its own culture, with the
intention of seeing Christian understanding, character, and behavior
made more authentic. It is also the work of readying the Church to
speak effectively to its world, to speak in ways that are germane to that
world. As innocent and as time-honored as my intentions are in this
book, the evangelical Church today has little appetite for this kind of
thing. That, I must insist, is a mistake. In the generation to come,
unfortunately, evangelicals will learn just how costly that mistake has
been, because the seeds are now being abundantly sown out of which
a new liberalism is already arising that will be as destructive to biblical
faith as was the older liberalism.

Changing Terrain

Twenty-five years ago, I am quite certain, I could have cheerfully used
the word *theology* without having to reach for the smelling salts. For
then I was a young professor, a sapling in an evangelical world filled
with large trees. It was a time when evangelical beliefs were more certain
than they are now, theology was a more honorable word, and there was
a sense of mission that was infectious.[1] That was the day when the trees
that stood so tall in this world were usually made so by their theological
conviction and not simply by their money, the size of their church, or
the expansiveness of their organization. Then, the leaders in evangel-

---

1. In its early years, the National Association of Evangelicals (NAE), which
gave voice to the emerging movement, was not fully representative of those who
later identified with it. It was dominated by fundamentalists then, but its credo,
"Cooperation without compromise," indicated a willingness to go beyond the more
narrow fundamentalist concerns. Cooperation there was in the years that followed,
though it was also limited by in-house fragmentation, some scandals, and leadership
that went beyond the core items on the evangelical agenda. The compromise
mentioned here is less in consciously transgressed doctrinal boundaries than in
unconscious bartering with the culture. On some of these issues in the NAE, see
John Stackhouse, "The National Association of Evangelicals, the Evangelical Fellowship of Canada, and the Limits of Cooperation," *Christian Scholars Review* 25, no.
2 (December 1995), 157-79.

icalism were often its pastors and biblical scholars; today, its leaders are its entrepreneurs and managers, and an increasing number of its pastors are indistinguishable from business people whose skills in finding market niches have been honed to a fine edge.[2] In 1996, *Christianity Today* identified the most noteworthy evangelical leaders who were under forty. Pastors, biblical scholars, theologians, and other kinds of scholars amounted to less than a third of the constellation, but forty-two percent were leaders of organizations.[3]

It would be a mistake to think, though, that a golden age has passed or that the flow of events has only been downhill. If we can look still further back, to the early postwar years, and compare this day with that, it will soon be discovered that evangelicals today do, indeed, enjoy many of the fruits of success. In many ways they are better off today than they were then. Evangelical churches have grown in numbers and size, ministries have been developed that did not exist, scholars abound, libraries have expanded, seminaries are numerous, politicians take note, and the theological liberalism that looked so formidable then looks quite forlorn now. Along with this astounding growth — indeed, we might even say, conquest — there has nevertheless come a hollowing out of evangelical conviction, a loss of the biblical Word in its authoritative function, and an erosion of character to the point that today, no discernible ethical differences are evident in behavior when those claiming to have been reborn and secularists are compared. When evangelicals were small in number in the immediate postwar years, it seems that they were larger in stature, but now that they have become large in number they have been diminished in stature. It is not inevitable that success should take such a toll, but this startling dialectic should not catch us unawares. Even in apostolic times there were those who said, "I am rich, I have prospered, and I need nothing." The reality was that they were "wretched, pitiable, poor, blind, and naked" (Rev. 3:17). Lukewarm, their inward condition lost to them because of their outward success, they were disgorged from Christ's mouth.

2. This change in the style and type of leadership is to be explained by the diminished theological character in the evangelical world and by the growing professionalization of its pastors. See my *No Place for Truth; or, Whatever Happened to Evangelical Theology?* (Grand Rapids: Eerdmans, 1993), 218-57. It is also part of the transition that movements typically undergo as they move from the "charisma" of the founders into the "structure" of those who follow when the movement becomes institutionalized (to use Max Weber's analysis).

3. "Up & Comers: Fifty Evangelical Leaders 40 and Under," *Christianity Today* 40, no. 13 (November 11, 1996), 20-30.

From Augustine to Postmodernity

In 1993, my book *No Place for Truth; or, Whatever Happened to Evangelical Theology?* appeared. In that volume, I sought to show how the assumptions of modernity had intruded on the evangelical Church. The loss of theological thinking in the pew, as well as the pulpit, could best be explained, I argued, by the way in which modernity refocuses our interests, displacing the moral by the therapeutic, the divine by the human, truth by intuition, and conviction by technique. As a result, we have not only secular humanism in our society but also secular evangelicalism. And in the volume that followed in 1994, *God in the Wasteland: The Reality of Truth in a World of Fading Dreams,* I sought to show that what we today know as modernity is, in many ways, giving contemporary expression to what the New Testament pejoratively calls "the world." Worldliness is that system of values, in any given age, which has at its center our fallen human perspective, which displaces God and his truth from the world, and which makes sin look normal and righteousness seem strange. It thus gives great plausibility to what is morally wrong and, for that reason, makes what is wrong seem normal. It is this spiritual reality that is pervasive in modernity and that has caused the evangelical world to stumble so badly. I concluded that what is most put in jeopardy, and what most needs to be recovered with respect to God, are our understanding of his moral nature and his sovereign providence. And without this recovery, evangelical faith would lose — if it has not already lost — its moral pungency and its spiritual authenticity.

In these two books, however, as well as this present book, my angle of vision has been different from what has become conventional in theological writing. Although each of these books assumes the Reformation's principle of *sola Scriptura,* I have also insisted that part of the theological task must always be to ask what it means to have this Word in this world at this time. The only way to answer that question is to engage in careful, rigorous, and sustained analysis of the culture.

This I have attempted to do while following a traditional theological sequence in these studies.[4] In most systematic theologies, Karl

4. At the turn of the century James Orr addressed a problem that was felt to be more vexed than it is now, though it was far less serious then than it is now in our postmodern context. "What our age chiefly feels the need of," he said, "in the midst of the confusions which beset it, is some way of bringing theological doctrines to a higher test than the individual judgment" (James Orr, *The Progress of Dogma: Being the Elliot Lectures, Delivered at Western Theological Seminary* [London: Hodder and Stoughton, 1901], 14). This was the very issue that Newman had addressed in

Barth's being a notable exception, the work typically begins with a section devoted to prolegomena. This serves as an introduction to the body of theology that is to follow. It explains what kind of knowledge this is, what its relationship to philosophy is, what role reason plays, what place experience should have, and so on. The prolegomenon I have written is *No Place for Truth*. It is not, of course, a traditional prolegomenon but a cultural one. I have not asked what the rational assumptions are for the doing of theology, but what the conditions are, given the nature of this particular culture, that will best serve the cause of theology by allowing it to become deeply rooted in the life of the Church. My question has not been what we must understand about the subject if we are to do theology but what we must understand about ourselves if that theology is to engage our lives.

In traditional theologies, the prolegomenon is usually followed by the doctrine of God. Here his nature as triune is discussed, as are his attributes, his character of holy-love, and his acts in creation and providence. The second of these two books, *God in the Wasteland,* follows my cultural prolegomenon, in much the same way as it would in a traditional systematic, and it contains some of the same themes treated in the doctrine of God. However, it is far from being a full treatment because, once again, I have not only asked what biblical teaching should be believed but where that teaching is being placed in jeopardy by modernity and what it is we need to understand about ourselves if that teaching is to take root in the center of our lives and actually shape the way we live in our world.

The doctrine of God, in a conventional theology, is typically followed either by Christology or by anthropology. And so it is that my *God in the Wasteland* is here being followed by this study on the contemporary person. I am, then, following a traditional sequence without formulating a traditional theology.

My task would probably be simpler if I were writing a traditional theology. Over the last two thousand years, the Church has left behind

---

his *The Development of Doctrine.* And like Newman, Orr developed some tests for judging doctrinal authenticity. The bulk of his book, however, was a discussion of the parallel he saw between the traditional systematic sequence — prolegomena, God, anthropology, Christology, objective soteriology, subjective soteriology, ecclesiology, and eschatology — and the way the Church has concentrated on these topics in this order and then moved on when a definitive formulation has been given. I am not concerned with the merits of this argument here but simply with Orr's observation that there is a natural sequence in which theological topics call to be addressed, a sequence that I have chosen to follow here.

an extraordinarily rich repository of theological works. Anyone entering this field today benefits from the fact that the terrain has already been carefully and deeply plowed. Much of the work in a traditional systematic theology, then, is one of retrieval, of reclaiming what has been part of the Christian tradition even if that ownership must take place, in our case, within the circumstances of modernity.

The terrain I am attempting to enter is not laid out at all because modernity and postmodernity are too fresh, too many-sided, and too complicated to have produced a clear consensus on what has happened. When one enters this world of cultural analysis, one is entering a murky swamp in which little is settled and much is unexamined or unexplained.

The model I have in mind in my own work, therefore, is rather different from conventional works of theology. In none of these books have I worked out in a complete and systematic way the various strands of Christian doctrine. That, I must leave to others. I have been on a different errand, and for this I have had a different model in mind.

My concern is with the Church. The erosion of its theological character, its unwitting worldliness, its inability to think clearly and incisively about the culture, and the growing barbarism of that culture, have all reminded me of a much earlier period. It was the time in which Augustine wrote his *City of God* when faced with the calamity that befell Rome in A.D. 410. The barbarians, who had swept down out of Europe, leaving behind them nothing but smoking ruins, finally presented themselves at the gates of Rome, the Eternal City. This was an utterly inconceivable circumstance, at least to the pagans. They had comforted themselves that Rome would never be conquered, that it would always be protected by their gods. No one was prepared for what befell this corrupted society during three days of ruinous invasion and pillaging led by King Alaric.

The reaction to Rome's conquest was instant. Pagans turned on the Christians, charging that it was their presence that explained the desertion of Rome by the gods. These gods were obviously displeased that Roman society was tolerating the presence of Christians. Not only so, but Christian doctrine, pagans said, demanded that they renounce the world. That meant that Christians could not be good citizens since they had to be disengaged from society. Was it any surprise, then, if Rome, thus abandoned by so many, had fallen to the barbarians in its moment of need? Christians, apparently, were at a loss to know how to explain this tragedy, a circumstance that seemed to be simply incomprehensible, and they were also unsure how best to combat the pagan charge on citizenship. They did, however, send emissaries to Augustine in North Africa asking that he help them understand what had happened from within a Christian framework. And over the next twenty-two years, Augustine formulated his answer. He turned the pagan argument on its head by saying that Rome had collapsed, not because of Christian morality but pagan immorality. How could pagans object to the Christian desire for redemption from the vice latent in all human nature? The last twelve books of his work, however, move from this particular tragedy to thinking more generally of the presence of the two cities, the City of God and the City of Man, in all of human history. It was thus that he came to formulate an understanding of providence, and of the relation of Christ and culture, that framed all of life. For him, it was this cultural tragedy that cried out for an answer and that provoked his thought about the relationship of God to the world and to the Church. Now, many centuries later, I find myself wanting, in some very small way, to do something along the same lines, given the vastly destabilizing consequences of modernity. There are, however, large differences.

My agenda is clearly more modest. In these volumes, I have been mainly concerned with the business of retrieval, of preserving and reclaiming those riches of our classical spirituality that are especially in danger of being lost. Mine has been a task that is subsidiary to the major business of developing a theology for this time. I have worked at it in a limited and piecemeal fashion, and not with the comprehensiveness that the urgency of our time demands and that others will have to accomplish.

Augustine's work is an instructive case study of one person's reflection on his own culture, but ancient Rome also offers an equally interesting case study of cultural collapse in general. The conquest of Rome has always been a perplexing matter to historians, for on the surface it should not have fallen like a pack of cards before the barbarians. This has raised a question that cannot be answered definitively but that nevertheless remains a tantalizing consideration. What role did the slow, inexorable dissolution of Roman character play in this defeat? Would it be correct to surmise that in some ways Rome was not so much defeated by outsiders as by its own hand? And, if this surmise has any validity at all, should we not view our own deeply destructive social pathologies and the rotting of our national character with some alarm? America seems so strong, so invincible as it bestrides the world, its technology unmatched, its economic system robust and virile, its government stable, and the validity of its laws uncontested. Rome, however, once occupied a comparable position in the ancient world, and against every human calculation and expectation, it fell. Indeed, when the barbarians arrived outside the gates of Rome, their hair dressed down in rancid butter, their breath heavy with garlic, and their tongues clattering away with primitive sounds, they found no one at home. They simply walked into the city and began their conquest. A fate as improbable as this is not beyond repetition, even for America, if this nation cannot address its own disintegrating life, for no civilization will endure forever.[5]

Some, in fact, see the process of final dissolution as already having begun. The art critic, Robert Hughes, for example, draws a direct parallel between Rome in its final stages of decomposition and America in the 1980s and 1990s. Then as now, many were skeptical of authority and became easy victims of superstition. Political language began to disintegrate, even as it has today, though in our case one of the main causes is that it has to carry the burdens of a fake piety, which is what political correctness has become. Hughes speaks of "the corruption and verbosity of its senators," of foolish old emperors whose extravagant wives also consorted with astrologers, of Rome's dependence upon its geese to protect it from unseen enemies, the geese today having been transmuted into pollsters. The gladiatorial games, which were put on as a distraction for a populace ever more restless, are now superseded by the high-tech blood letting in our movies and on television.[6]

---

5. In his lengthy study of civilizations, Arnold Toynbee gives considerable space to why they disintegrate. What are the signs that they are coming apart? Especially pertinent to the West at present is his discussion of the "schism of the soul." He sees in disintegrated cultures the emergence of patterns of behavior that belong together but have very different expressions depending upon whether it is the active or passive form, though it is the latter that we see predominantly today. In its passive form, cultural demise is preceded by moral decay, lawless abandon in which "antinomianism is accepted — consciously or unconsciously, in theory or in practice — as a substitute for creativeness" (Arnold Toynbee, *A Study of History* [12 vols.; London: Oxford University Press, 1934-61], 5:399). This is accompanied by the desire to break away from existing structures, by a sense of drift, which "is the passive way of feeling the loss of the *élan* of growth" (ibid., 5:412). This drifting "has the effect of an opiate in instilling into the soul an insidious acquiescence in an evil that is assumed to reside in external circumstances beyond the victim's control" (ibid., 5:432). This is also accompanied by a kind of promiscuity that "takes practical effect in an act of self-surrender to the melting-pot" (ibid., 5:439), by which Toynbee meant the declining moral and spiritual consensus rather than an ethnic melting pot. It is not difficult to hear in this delineation echoes of much of our own contemporary life in America. See also the useful discussion in Jim Nelson Black's *When Nations Die: America on the Brink: Ten Warning Signs of a Culture in Crisis* (Wheaton, Ill.: Tyndale House, 1994).

6. Robert Hughes, *Culture of Complaint: The Fraying of America* (New York: Oxford University Press, 1993), 4-5.

Irving Kristol, a fellow of the American Enterprise Institute, has also seen a parallel between Rome in its declining years and America, though he works this parallel from a politically conservative angle. The similarity he sees lies in the decadence that obtained then and that has become ubiquitous now, a theme to which I will return in chapter two.

Fifty years ago, Kristol argues, the welfare state was created in America to provide cradle-to-grave security. It was expected to eliminate the social diseases that have become so destructive in our own time, such as violent crime, illegitimacy, drugs, and the decay of marriage. A tacit trade was made. Responsibility for much of life was handed over to the government, and private life became dominated by the belief that each citizen had the unencumbered right to individual autonomy (a theme that I will explore in chapters two and three). "The transfer of major areas of responsibility to the welfare state," Kristol writes, "combined with a bland permissive toleration of moral irresponsibility among the citizenry is about as fair a description of national decadence as one can imagine."[7] And this decadence has crossed over into much of our religion, which has become a largely internal and private matter, disconnected from the public square. "But religion that is a merely private affair," he counters, "has been, until our time, unknown in the annals of mankind. . . . Such religion quickly diminishes into an indoor pleasure, a kind of hobby of one or more individuals, like reading a book or watching television."[8] Beneath the collapse of Rome was a spiritual failure, and Kristol sees a comparable failure, brought about by different means, happening in America. If we abandon our moral obligations and indulge our "right" to do and say whatever we want, we will have to live in a society that is trivialized, emptied out, and increasingly more dangerous and inhospitable.

Alasdair MacIntyre, the philosopher and ethicist, also suggests that we have reached a "turning point" comparable to what happened in Rome and that today, amidst the moral disintegration of our society, we should begin "the construction of local forms of community within which civility and the intellectual and moral life can be sustained through the new dark ages that are already upon us."[9] That may be the only path toward survival at some point in the future, but should

7. Irving Kristol, "The Welfare State's Spiritual Crisis," *The Wall Street Journal* 229, no. 23 (February 3, 1997), A6.

8. Ibid.

9. Alasdair MacIntyre, *After Virtue: A Study in Moral Theory* (Notre Dame: University of Notre Dame Press, 1981), 245.

we be so ready to surrender this territory at this point in time? Might it not be possible that this cultural chaos, so painful and disorienting, is itself the soil for a new planting of faith? Could it be that evangelical faith, once again made serious, once again possessed of biblical truth and moral fiber, could serve America today as it did England in the eighteenth century, when slavery was abolished and that nation was turned back from its barbarism?

I believe that this question should be the constant preoccupation of theologians and Church leaders. One of the striking developments today is the emergence of a renaissance in the writing of systematic theologies at the very time when the Church, both evangelical and otherwise, has been disengaging itself from theological substance. So what does this development mean? It surely points to the reality that what preoccupies theologians is remote to most people in the Church. And the reason is only partly that theologians are more intellectually disposed whereas most people in the Church are less so. More importantly, theologians in the writing of their systematic theologies are in far more earnest conversation with the academic guild than they are with the life of the Church and with that of our culture. If there is a payoff for the Church from these volumes, it is mostly only in the crumbs that fall from the tables in the learned guild. These volumes are largely written by professors for students; with few exceptions, they are not written by those who want to engage the Church as it lives out its life in the postmodern world. This task would require that theology understand the life of the Church as well as the way life in the postmodern world works, and not simply orient itself to the preoccupations of the academic guild. However, those who have attempted to orient themselves to culture as well have found that this is hard to pull off without losing their theological bearings. That, in fact, has often happened. Theology of this kind, moral philosopher Jeffrey Stout writes, "has often assumed a voice not its own and found itself merely repeating the bromides of secular intellectuals in transparently figurative speech." But what is the alternative? Those who have something distinctive to say — and, not least, something distinctively Christian to say — are apt, he says, "to be talking to themselves — or, at best, to a few other theologians of similar breeding."[10]

The task of shaping the Church's mind has therefore been left to the purveyors and makers of popular theology. Popularizing theology

---

10. Jeffrey Stout, *Ethics after Babel: The Languages of Morals and Their Discontents* (Boston: Beacon Press, 1988), 163.

— that is, making its truth accessible to a wide number of people — is an honorable undertaking. What comes to mind when the words, *popular theology*, are heard, though, is usually something different. Popular theology is a hybrid in which what is popular so often eclipses what is theological, because what is popular typically owes far more to the habits and mental conventions of modernity than it does to biblical truth. The result is that the evangelical Church, whose taste for what is popular appears to be insatiable, is in danger of being destabilized by the cultural captivity of some of its popular "thinkers," as well as by the academic captivity of some of its scholars.

Those who are oblivious to the past are, indeed, condemned to repeating its mistakes. In this case, the mainline denominations and their theologians have just completed walking this road of cultural accommodation with disastrous consequences. Historian Douglas Sloan has described how mainline theologians attempted to penetrate the university. The three most prominent in the postwar years were Reinhold and H. Richard Niebuhr, and Paul Tillich. They sought, on the one hand, to describe and circumscribe the way in which knowledge flourished in the academic world and, on the other, to argue for the necessity of faith as a way of knowing that was deeper and more encompassing of reality than secularized ways of knowing. Their work was highly influential and, against all expectations, the study of both theology and religion gained in respectability on the campuses.

This conquest was, however, short-lived because the "twentieth-century Protestant theological renaissance failed to penetrate the cognitive center of the modern university." Why was this so? The answer, according to Sloan, is that these proponents of faith imagined "that it is possible to be at once a committed person of faith and thoroughly modern."[11] As cognitive ground was conceded to the prophets and proponents of modernity, Christian faith left itself nowhere to stand. The collapse that followed was as inevitable as it was swift.

Throughout this century, the mainline denominations have been vulnerable to dalliances with high culture, in this particular case that part of it which has flowered in the academic world. And throughout this century, evangelical faith has been vulnerable to dalliances with popular culture. These may seem very different on the surface, for one is elitist and the other is not, one is sophisticated and the other is not. Yet they are no different at the point where the dalliance occurs, for

---

11. Douglas Sloan, *Faith and Knowledge: Mainline Protestantism and American Higher Education* (Louisville: Westminster/John Knox Press, 1994), 212.

modernity has cultural expressions that are high as well as those that are popular. And for evangelicals drinking from the popular end of the trough of modernity, the collapse will be as inevitable and swift as for those who have drunk from the high end of that same trough. Those who are serious about maintaining an authentic biblical theology "must come to terms with the scope, impact, and significance of popular theology," Quentin Shultze, Calvin College's communications professor, has written, because this "increasingly establishes the cultural context for the religious communities that academic theologians serve."[12]

Our culture is in trouble today, and the weakness of the evangelical Church, the evisceration of its theological character, is therefore all the more troubling. How is it going to address the large questions that have arisen over the meaning of our life? These questions have many points of focus beside the obvious ones of abortion and euthanasia. One of the telltale signs of our trouble, for example, is that we are dealing awkwardly with our conquest of the world. While we feast on the largesse of modernity, enjoying the enormously enlarged capabilities that technology has bestowed upon us, linking us with everyone everywhere in a twinkling of an eye, and while we are laden with the fruits of our abundant economic system, and while we strut the world as its sole super power, benign as our conquest may be, and though we know everything (almost) and are everywhere (at least psychologically), we have become incomprehensible to ourselves. And central to this internal mystery is that we are losing our moral imagination, our capacity for seeing ourselves as moral beings. We are losing our moral bearings.

The consequences of this are now so distressing that we have embarked on a search for self-understanding that is so far reaching as to be without precedent in the West. The search for self-understanding is not itself, of course, novel. The need for at least some self-understanding is part and parcel of human experience, and every generation has its own language for this pursuit. Today, however, all of the older models of understanding are being shelved, and new models, many of them laden with radical consequences, are being tested. A century ago, the answer to the question, "Who are we?" would have been one thing, but today it is something entirely different. "I am my genes," some say, as they surrender themselves to biological fate. "I am my past," "I am my self-image," "I am my gender," "I am what I have," "I am what I do," "I am whom I know," "I am my sexual orientation," say others

12. Quentin J. Schultze, "Civil Sin: Evil and Purgation in the Media," *Theology Today* 50, no. 2 (July 1993), 233.

who think that there are other kinds of fate or that identity is either something that we do or something that we can construct. And what we once would have said — "I am one who is made in the image of God" — simply does not translate into the language of modernity.[13] Today, our vocabulary is in crisis. This is precisely where theologians should be heard and just where the Church should be stationing itself.

From Virtues to Values

The language we use to understand ourselves and our world is not simply a matter of words. It is the result of the interactions of many other factors: how we understand the world; the particular social pressures to which we are subject; patterns of behavior into which we have settled; how our collective life is shaped politically; how our most deeply felt anxieties and perplexities are understood; how we conceive of our gender and ethnic differences; how we relate to our things, to the past, to ourselves, and most fundamentally, to God. In this sense, our everyday language is the outcome of our engagement with life at very deep, complex, and sometimes painful levels.

It is this engagement, I shall argue, that is now framing life in such a way that the most important part of self-understanding — that we are moral beings — has been removed from the equation. That is the beguilingly simple thesis I shall be pursuing: functionally, we are not morally disengaged, adrift, and alienated; we are morally obliterated. We are, in practice, not only moral *illiterati;* we have become morally vacant. MacIntyre argued this thesis with respect to society, and I will be listening for its echoes in the Church.

Few subjects have received more attention over the last twenty-five years than the declining moral literacy in our society. In our schools, no doubt out of good intentions, we shifted from teaching character formation to values clarification. Now we have moved on to a plethora of new but confused agendas, and we are genuinely nonplused by all of the practical consequences. Our children are not only more lawless in school, as evidenced by the astounding increase in crime, but are too often without any apparent moral consciousness regarding their actions. And this will not be easily remedied, since, as William Kilpatrick, the education specialist, argues, "without the sense that life makes sense,

13. I am indebted for this way of stating the matter to Elaine Storkey's comments at a conference on modernity held in Uppsala, Sweden, in 1993.

all other motives for virtuous behavior lose their force."[14] Life in a postmodern world does not make sense, so the recovery of virtue will, as a result, be constantly frustrated.

Our concern that society is rapidly losing moral altitude, however, goes far beyond our concern about the schools. It is evident throughout the professions, many of which have scrambled to introduce courses in ethics in the universities, and it is evident in our apprehension about the crumbling structures all around us, from the family to the inner city. The problem is not that we cannot discuss moral theory, although even that is rapidly being lost, and it is certainly not that we are unconcerned about our cultural circumstances. The problem is that our talk is now empty.

For over two thousand years, moral conduct was discussed under the language of the virtues. First Plato and then Aristotle talked about the cardinal, or foundational, virtues. These were justice (or rectitude), wisdom, courage (or fortitude), and moderation (or self-control). Subsequently, of course, other lists were drawn up, and the discussion of the virtues has followed numerous paths. However, it is important for us to understand that the change in our language reflects changes in our understanding of what the moral life is about. And that, at a deeper level, reflects changes in who we think we are.

The importance of the classical view of the virtues was that moral conduct was seen to be the outcome of *character*, and it was considered entirely futile to divorce inward moral reality from its exercise in the society or community in which a person lived. In time, this discussion about the cardinal virtues passed into Catholicism, where it was incorporated into a structure of thought in which these virtues were seen to be the basis for, and as becoming finally realized in, the theological virtues of faith, hope, and love. Luther, of course, was quite impatient with this line of thought, because Aristotle, he said, had introduced into the Church a theory of natural virtue that took insufficient account of sin.[15] It allowed

14. William K. Kilpatrick, *Why Johnny Can't Tell Right from Wrong* (New York: Simon and Schuster, 1992), 27.

15. In 1517, before Luther had been catapulted into the role of a Reformer by the posting of his *Ninety-five Theses*, he had already attacked medieval notions of piety and morality. These, he knew, were predicated, to a considerable degree, on Aristotle. Luther's view was that "nothing precedes grace except indisposition and even rebellion against grace" (Martin Luther, *Luther's Works*, ed. Jaroslav Pelikan and Helmut T. Lehman [55 vols.; St. Louis: Concordia Publishing House, 1955-86], 31:11). Man, he said, "by nature has neither correct precept nor good will" (ibid.). Human nature "glories and takes pride in every work which is apparently and outwardly good" (ibid.). The pivotal distinction between what he believed and what

its followers to find in their moral accomplishments and character formation a basis for laying claim to God's salvation. On the Protestant side,
therefore, matters of moral principle were discussed differently. These
were seen as the outcome to a knowledge of God, which was given
independently of any internal moral achievement, through the Word and
by the Holy Spirit. Godliness, it was argued, combined the right beliefs
about God and his Christ (2 Tim. 3:16), a reverential attitude before him
(2 Tim. 3:5; 2 Pet. 1:3), and a sense of obligation to live well before one's
family (1 Tim. 5:4), the Church, and in society. The texture of the
discussion was different, but when Protestant and Catholics talked of
moral conduct they both rooted it in internal spiritual reality that had to
be practiced in external relationships.

In the wider society, during the eighteenth and nineteenth centuries, the classical virtues came under fire from Enlightenment ideology, the Christian virtues in particular came under heavy bombard-
ment, and slowly our language began to change.

These classical virtues had always been thought about in relation to
the community in which a person lived. To act justly was not an internal
attitude but the practice of what was upright in a context where that moral
virtue had been put to the test. When we come into the modern period,
and as communities begin to disappear, the virtues come to stand alone,
out of the social context in which they had formerly been understood.
Thus, as MacIntyre points out,[16] the virtue of honor increasingly comes
to be understood in terms of a social status that is not awarded because of
moral desert but gained through wealth or birth. When the virtues were
thus privatized, when they were disengaged from public life, that life had
to be governed, not by morality but by social rules that became etiquette.
It was these rules that replaced the virtues, and these rules have now been
replaced by governmental regulation and by litigation, a point that will
be developed more fully in chapter two.

By the end of the nineteenth century, the virtues (plural) had also
contracted into virtue (singular). And virtue was an altogether thinner
and vaguer matter; indeed, it was increasingly reduced simply to sexual
matters. To say that a woman had lost her virtue could no longer mean
that she was a habitual liar, or that she had often acted in a cowardly or

---

Aristotle stood for was this: "We do not become righteous by doing righteous deeds
but, having been made righteous, we do righteous deeds" (ibid., 12). The result is
that "virtually the entire *Ethics* of Aristotle is the worst enemy of grace" (ibid.).
"Indeed, no one can become a theologian unless he becomes one without Aristotle"
(ibid.). "Briefly, the whole of Aristotle is to theology as darkness is to light" (ibid.).
16. MacIntyre, *After Virtue*, 211-17.

dishonorable way. It meant that she had lost her virginity. Some of the Victorian voluntary associations concerned with vice, like the Society for the Suppression of Vice, had no interest in suppressing avarice and injustice. Their focus was on prostitution. In the transition from Aristotle to our postmodern world, the language we have used to talk about moral matters shows how withered and diminished our understanding has become.

At the turn of this century, Nietzsche pioneered what, by a different route, has come to be embraced in popular culture today. Gertrude Himmelfarb, whose principal field has been Victorian England, has observed that morality became so thoroughly relativized and subjectified that virtues ceased to be virtues. They had also ceased to be virtue. They had become "values."[17] In Nietzsche, this transition was the deliberate outcome of his belief in the death of all truth and morality. Virtue had to be replaced by values. More recently, as this habit of thought has passed into the wider culture, the change appears to have been more unconscious and inadvertent. Yet it is clear, as Himmelfarb notes, that today values may mean nothing more than a preference, belief, feeling, habit, or convention — "whatever any individual, group, or society happens to value, at any time, for any reason."[18] Thus our values have, in a strange way, become "value-free." That, though, is hardly a surprise, for values can have no universal value if truth has died.

Our society talks of values in this way because relativism has triumphed and because the constant rubbing against postmodern life has had the almost inevitable effect of emptying us out morally. It is because we have lost our virtue that we are left to talk about values. And this has an interesting parallel in the Church. If it is true that values divorced from character become empty in society, it is even more true in the Church. The character of which we speak here is not simply the cultivation of natural virtue but the intensely conscious sense of living morally before God. Without this sense, built into character, our moral conduct disintegrates. That is happening today. We often have little sense of the Holy as something Other that presses in upon us and demands that we give it our most earnest attention. In consequence, the older quest for spiritual authenticity, for godliness, has often been abandoned and been replaced by newer quests for psychological whole-ness. This transition commends itself to us because the outcome, a more

17. Gertrude Himmelfarb, *The De-moralization of Society: From Victorian Virtues to Modern Values* (New York: Alfred A. Knopf, 1995), 9.
    18. Ibid., 11.

whole and psychologically integrated person, seems to us to be far more attuned to the dangerous and jarring world in which we live than are the older concerns about piety. And a more relaxed and amusing atmosphere in church seems like a better compensation for what we find in the world than that older piety which called for seriousness and self-examination in the light of God's Word.

Despite this earthquake, this shifting of the plates beneath our moral world — and the resulting movement in the Church — America continues to exhibit some social virtue. We are certainly more humane and less cruel than most other societies have been. America continues to be generous in so many respects, and its influence is exercised in remarkably benign ways when contrasted with the way other dominant powers have exerted their wills in the past. At the same time, we are probably less honest than many other societies have been and undoubtedly we are more self-indulgent. But in one matter we stand almost alone, along with other parts of the West. This is the first time that a civilization has existed that, to a significant extent, does not believe in objective right and wrong. We are traveling blind, stripped of our moral compass. And this is true, not only in society, but increasingly in the Church as well.

This situation has stolen up upon us so quietly that its real nature is largely obscured. I believe that what Camille Paglia, *provocatrice extraordinaire*, has said with respect to our pop culture is correct. We are witnessing, she asserts, "an eruption of the never-defeated paganism of the West."[19] Her thesis, which she developed in some detail in her

---

19. Camille Paglia, *Sex, Art, and American Culture* (New York: Vintage Books, 1992), vii. "For me," she says elsewhere, "the ultimate power in the universe is nature, not God, whose existence I can understand only as depersonalized energy" (Camille Paglia, *Vamps and Tramps: New Essays* [New York: Vintage Books, 1994], 20). Defying many of the icons of feminist devotion, she then sets out with brilliant and pristine clarity what it means today to be pagan, and she is far more mainstream than the feminist critics who take such pained exception to her. Pornography, for example, she thinks is good. "Porn dreams of eternal fires of desire, without fatigue, incapacity, aging, or death. What feminists denounce as woman's humiliating total accessibility in porn is actually her elevation to high priestess of a pagan paradise garden, where the body has become a bountiful fruit tree and where growth and harvest is [sic] simultaneous." She adds that " 'dirt' is contamination to the Christian but fertile loam to the pagan" (ibid., 66). Paglia, to be sure, is cutting her own path through the world with a rather beguiling swagger, but many of her assumptions, which she rightly calls pagan, are very widely held. The glowing picture of a sexually liberated America that she offers is actually at odds with the results. See Katie Roiphe, *Last Night in Paradise: Sex and Morals at the Century's End* (Boston: Little, Brown, 1997).

Sexual Personae, is that there are always in culture two principles at work — the Apollonian and the Dionysian — one whose urge is to expand and the other whose work is to restrain, one that undoes shape and the other that demands definition. What is now at work, what she believes was recovered in the 1960s, is the pagan impulse to expand, an impulse that commonly meets us wrapped in what is earthy and sensual. This is liberating us from most social taboos, a circumstance that she thinks is very happy. In fact, what it is doing is eviscerating our moral understanding, with the result that the whole of our society is now caught up in a fatal contest: will our moral license be allowed to triumph, or will we have to save ourselves from its consequences by more and more recourse to law and litigation? We are now teetering between these competing impulses, one wanting endless expansion and the other being called upon to provide increasing contraction. Our society will not survive this conflict. This is a theme I explore further in chapter two.

This book, then, is about the changing spiritual topography of our time and about the place of the evangelical Church in it. Can the Church recover its moral character enough to make a difference in a society whose fabric is now much frayed?

In the first chapter, I argue that there are two kinds of spirituality in the evangelical Church; what distinguishes them is not so much different doctrinal belief but the different significance that the moral has in each. In the one, what is moral has weight, while in the other it does not. The inevitable consequence of this is that the one has the capacity to be counter-cultural, while the other does not. In chapter two, I look at contemporary society and explore the strange dynamic at work between license and law, the chief casualty of which is the moral life. In the third chapter, I sketch the ways in which a secular salvation is emerging through such means as style, consumption, fitness, and psychotherapy, producing a form of spirituality bereft of moral understanding. This leads me, in the fourth chapter, to the heart of this contemporary development, which is how the self is conceived. I examine how shame has now emerged as our most distressing emotional problem. I argue that guilt has vanished and that its place has been taken by a distinctly modern sense of shame far more psychological than moral. I suggest that this is really just another indication of how our moral life has become secularized since the dilemmas that rattle us inwardly can now be dissolved, it is thought, internally and relationally. The fifth chapter is an exploration of the contradiction between what we are by creation and how we see ourselves in the midst of this culture.

I argue that the biblical revelation stands so many of our cultural assumptions on their head, not least those concerning honor and shame. In the final chapter I suggest that there is an apologetic which is peculiarly fitted to the circumstances of the postmodern world. It arises from our experience of ourselves as moral agents whose internal contradictions are resolved nowhere but in the Cross. I conclude by returning to the theme of the first chapter. How can our spirituality regain its moral weight? This, I maintain, is where the hope of the Church lies if it is to be effective in this postmodern world. How is the Church to regain its saliency so that, like those of the first century who also lived "in the midst of a crooked and perverse generation," its members will also be able to "shine as lights in the world, holding fast the word of life" (Phil. 2:15-16)?

Our Moment

These chapters are written from the conviction that no time in this century has been more ripe with opportunity for Christian faith. For the first time this century, Christian faith is now without a serious secular opponent, if it can be allowed that postmodernity is now so heavy with its own cynicism as to be unsustainable for very long. Worldwide, Christianity's major religious competitor is probably Islam. Islamic faith in America now has more adherents than the Episcopal Church, the United Church of Christ, the Assemblies of God, or the Presbyterian Church (U.S.A.). However, while this incursion is real, it is not yet massive. It is localized mainly in the Black community, where it has become both the voice of Black rage and, in its countercultural thrust, a voice of hope amidst the shanties of dilapidated modern values.

Outside the Black community, though, Islam is not flourishing. Among the more affluent in particular, the religion *du jour* is the New Age movement, whose roots are both premodern and pagan, though much of it is so intertwined with postmodern relativism as to make it difficult sometimes to distinguish them. Since neither New-Age nor postmodern relativism has a *moral vision*, neither poses a real alternative to Christian faith, though both remain competitors.

Critics of Christian faith used to set themselves in opposition to it on the grounds that this or that tenet was unbelievable. Today, postmodern critics oppose Christianity not because of its particulars, but simply because it claims to be *true*. This situation is radically different from what prevailed even three or four decades ago, but there is no major competitor offering an alternative vision of life in which what is true and what is right are central and defining. And at this very moment when, as it were, the Berlin Wall topples of its own accord, at the very moment when the Church in general sees before it those who have abandoned Marxism and Enlightenment ideologies and have no-where to go, the Church is losing its voice. It should be speaking powerfully to the brokenness of life in this postmodern world and applying the balm of truth to wounds that are fresh and open, but it is not. It is adrift.

This, then, is a book that tries to discern the nature of contemporary culture not for its own sake, but for its significance for the Church. What does the Church need to understand about the culture, specifically its way of thinking about the person, if it is to fulfill its missionary mandate? That mandate calls for it not only to send missionaries to distant places, but also to understand its own cross-cultural situation and to think in cross-cultural ways. Until the Church begins to do so, it can be no more effective than a missionary who travels to a foreign land but neglects to learn the language and customs of that land before attempting to offer a Christian witness. That is our challenge today.

CHAPTER I

A Tale of Two Spiritualities

Long my imprisoned spirit lay
Fast bound in sin and nature's night.
Thine eye diffused a quickening ray;
I woke — the dungeon flamed with light!
My chains fell off, my heart was free,
I rose, went forth, and followed thee.

Charles Wesley

I need you to hold me
Like my daddy never could,
And I need you to show me
How resting in your arms can be so good.

I need you to walk with me
Hand in hand we'll run and play
And I need you to talk to me
Tell me again you'll stay.

Brenda Lefavre

Can the Church Be Reformed?

The Protestant Reformation, which was inadvertently launched by Luther in 1517, came to birth in a world vastly different from our own. It was different because it was still feudal in form, rather than modern, and this gave to life an entirely different texture. That was a religious age, whereas ours is not. Of course there were skeptics then, but life was nevertheless understood for the most part in religious ways, with the Catholic Church a dominant and imposing factor in society. In America, not only has the Church been disestablished, but our modern secularization has stripped the public square of religious reality. Our public discussions and calculations are devoid of the kind of religious considerations that dominated public life in the Reformation era.

That era was a supernatural age in a way that ours is not. It is, of course, true that secularization has not hounded the supernatural out of modern life entirely. What has happened is that it has restricted the supernatural to what is private and internal and has forced it out of the public square. If the supernatural is flourishing privately — and it is — it is often in bizarre ways. We hear its strains in New Agers, channelers, in resurgent witchcraft, as well as in more traditional Christian forms, but the nature of what we hear is more often strange than moral. In these and many other ways the differences between our world and Luther's loom large.

Indeed, these differences also point to the ways in which our modern age is unique. Most generations imagine that they are unique, and sometimes they imagine that what makes them unique is their superiority to all that has come before. It is thus that our devout belief in progress — progress not only in technology and medicine but also in the human spirit — betrays us into a kind of conceit that is as old as the human race. No, we are not unique in our spiritual achievements, but we have produced a culture through which we experience life in ways that are new. Peter Drucker, the business leader, has observed that in no other century have there been so many radical social transformations as in our own. The result is that in "the developed free-market countries . . . work and work force, society and polity, are all, in the last decade of this century, *qualitatively* and *quantitatively* different from . . . what has existed at any other time in history: in their configurations, in their processes, in their problems, and in their structures."[1] And what is so remarkable about this is that changes of lesser magnitude, occurring at less speed, have in other ages produced wrenching upheavals, revolts, and wars. We have taken these changes in stride as if they were matters of little consequence. Their marks upon our time, however, are indelible.

1. Peter F. Drucker, "The Age of Social Transformation," *The Atlantic Monthly* (November 1994), 53.

Modern Differences

First, we are seeing on an unprecedented scale the birth of a world civilization. There have been empires before as well as those who have dreamed of conquering the world. This civilization, however, is not arising on the ashes and blood of conquest but upon the wings of modernization. Our world is rapidly being reshaped, to start with, by urbanization — 93 percent of Americans now live in a city of 50,000 or more — and this is not simply a Western phenomenon. It is increasingly a world phenomenon and we now have over 400 cities of a million or more. This transformation, especially in the West and Asia, is driven by capitalism, for these societies have come to want and to need the goods and services which it so abundantly provides. Capitalism, however, could not work as efficiently as it does without technology which, in its own way, is also transforming the world. Finally, linking it all together are our means of mass communication which enable us to transcend place and local circumstance.

No one could have foreseen how these key elements in modernization would interact with one another, feeding on each other and extending each other, and in time producing an entirely different world. One of the most unforeseen consequences has been the way in which change has been accelerated both by our capitalism and our technology. Not only has the life cycle of products been greatly reduced as new replace old with increasing rapidity in this throw-away society, but most vestiges of permanence in life are also gone. Few people stay in one place for any length of time. Jobs and spouses are changed. Values come and go. In this world, fads and fashions are in and permanence is out. The quotient of what is new to what is old has increased dramatically, and this has profound effects on how we view our world, how we think about life, and what we come to value in it.

Our cities, too, change the way we think about our world. Unprecedented numbers of people have come to live in close proximity to one another. What is so striking about these urban dwellers is how different they are from one another. We are living in one of the great eras of migration. From around the world, people are being drawn to America to find the freedom for which they yearn or the opportunity and promise of plenty of which they have known little. What this means in practice, however, is that our cities bring into close proximity people of different ethnicity, religion, lifestyle, language, and culture. Our Constitution protects this cultural pluralism, this human variety, and America has always taken a certain pride in it, but in a secular context this cultural diversity also breeds relativism. It becomes much more difficult, and it may appear uncivil, to assert that one faith or one set of moral convictions is uniquely true, given that there are so many whose outlook is different and with whom we must continue to work side by side. The compact to which we have now arrived is that beliefs of this kind should be entertained privately, that they can be indulged to the fullest in private, but that they should not be injected into the public domain. Thus it is that secularism, working through our social diversity, has reordered the workings of Christian faith. It thus has shaped a way of looking at life that has our common consent and that also seems to be full of common sense, but the result is a more deeply entrenched and unchallenged secularism.

Nor should we overlook the way in which our constant use of technology tends to shape our perspective on life as a whole.[2] For technology not only greatly enlarges our powers but also suggests that the world can be managed if we can follow the right rational steps. It is not difficult, for example, to see this mind-set manifesting itself in the many popular Christian books that lay out the simple steps by which even the most daunting malfunction in the human spirit can easily be corrected.

Technology also reduces all of life to the productive order, to measurable benefits, to the calculus of cost and profit, and what is most efficient rapidly becomes what is ethically permissible or right. In a technologically dominated world, what is real is what is found along the flat plane of human management, where effects can be strictly controlled by our own causes. The use of technology greatly enlarges the sense of autonomy, of being at the center of one's own world and of pulling the strings of its circumstances, though it is probably also the case that different generations look on technology in slightly different ways. And while technology has had an enormously productive impact on business, it has also extracted a profound cost from the human spirit; it has reduced life to being so much less than it really is. While it is the

2. The way our use of technology shapes the way we see the world was explained most satisfactorily by Jacques Ellul in his two books *The Technological Society,* trans. John Wilkerson (New York: Alfred A. Knopf, 1965), and *The Technological System,* trans. Joachim Neugroschel (New York: Continuum, 1980). More recently Neil Postman has written incisively on this same theme in his *Technopoly: The Surrender of Culture to Technology* (New York: Vintage Books, 1993). For a more compact study, see John Staudenmaier, "U.S. Technological Style and Atrophy of Civic Commitment," in *Beyond Individualism: Toward a Retrieval of Moral Discourse in America,* ed. Donald L. Gelpi (Notre Dame: University of Notre Dame Press, 1989), 120-52.

means of our conquest of the world, it also has played a part in the emptying out of the human spirit. Is it mere coincidence, Theodore Roszak asks, that "in the midst of so much technological mastery and economic abundance, our art and thought continue to project a nihilistic image unparalleled in human history? Are we to believe there is not a connection between these facts?"[3]

What I have been describing is not just true of America but of wherever modernization is reshaping a society. That is why, despite many other differences, life looks about the same in Hong Kong as it does in London, in Cape Town as it does in Bombay. Indeed, in some ways it is exactly the same! As historian James Twitchell has observed, Muscovites are lining up for blocks to buy Big Macs. They avidly watch *Geraldo* and the *Love Boat* (with a voice overlay in Russian), and they listen to American rock music. Coca Cola signs are everywhere in China. Roseanne and Oprah are immensely popular in Britain. Nintendo has made its way into American hearts and pockets. Michael Jackson makes more money touring Japan than America, and everywhere in the world the ubiquity of American culture is signaled by the presence of blue jeans, T-shirts, and expressions like "OK" or "No problem."[4] Everywhere we see the same gadgets, the same cars, and the same entertainment. Whereas cultures were once local and derived their texture from the ethnicity, history, and religion of that people, this civilization owes little to local culture and much to urbanization, capitalism, technology, and telecommunications. And these realities lack the color, depth, and shape of local cultures.

The gathering conquest of the world by the forces of modernization is making politics look impotent by comparison. Those in the center of political power, those whose words and doings occupy reporters on the evening news, are not the ones who have effected the truly significant changes of our time. They have been mere bystanders. And what this means is that, in the future, ideological differences between the nations will probably decline. It is certainly the case that the ideological differences of the Cold War will no longer shape the way that most nations behave. Perhaps what we will see in the future is a contest not between ideologies but between civilizational alliances, with the so-called Christian West competing with Islamic cultures, or

3. Theodore Roszak, *Where the Wasteland Ends: Politics and Transcendence in Postindustrial Society* (Garden City, N.Y.: Doubleday, 1972), 379.

4. James B. Twitchell, *Carnival Culture: The Trashing of Taste in America* (New York: Columbia University Press, 1992), 7.

with those that are Buddhist, Hindu, and Confucian. The entire international chess board is being rearranged in concert with the triumph
of modernization. Modernization is the great reality with which nations
must now reckon, not so much ideology.

Second, ours is the first major civilization to be building itself
deliberately and self-consciously without religious foundations. Beneath
other civilizations there have always been religious foundations, whether
these came from Islam, Hinduism, or Christianity itself. Beneath ours
there are none, and it is no surprise to learn that 67 percent of Americans do not believe in the existence of moral absolutes and that 70
percent do not believe in absolute truth — truths that should be
believed by all people in all places and all times. We are building a
world of the most marvelous ingenuity and intricacy but it is arising
over a spiritual vacuum. This means that the only legitimacy that much
of life has is pleasure, and the relentless pursuit of pleasure in a world
without moral norms leads rapidly into the kind of chaos that is now
appearing. It also means, as I shall argue, that we are now having to
depend upon litigation to do what self-restraint, moral principle, religious belief, the family, and the church once accomplished.

Third, our experience of modernity is intense to an unparalleled
extent. The world intrudes upon us as it never has before. One of the
surest indications of this is that the levels of anxiety have never been
higher. And why are we more anxious? There are no doubt many
reasons, including a heightened tempo in the workplace, greater
economic insecurity, too many choices, and perhaps family breakdown.
What is more, the extraordinary rapidity of change in our society
powerfully fixes our attention upon the future, for we need to antici-
pate events that are in the making in order to avoid what will be
harmful and to capitalize on what will be beneficial. Anxiety, however,
is nothing more than living out the future before it arrives, and
modernity obliges us to do this many times over. The future is thereby
greatly intensified for us.

Television also intensifies the present; it enables the viewer to
wander the world by escaping the boundaries of place. And if it can
make Oprah more real and more personable than one's next door
neighbor, it can do something comparable with the tragedies and des-
olations of life as well. Television takes the experience of the world and
filters it into our living room in digestible, commercially convenient
chunks, asking only that we look. However, while it can distract and
soothe, the omnipresence it bestows sits uneasily with our frail psyches
if they are loaded up day after day with its images. The repose, the

sense of disengagement from life that was once there, has now gone. Life follows us home by telephone, fax, e-mail, and television, contributing its share to the shaping of what psychologist Kenneth Gergen calls the "saturated self."

Finally, as a result of these factors that are unique to our time, we are seeing, on an unprecedented scale, a mass experimentation with new values. The avant-garde has always been with us, usually in the form of pockets of artists, philosophers, or novelists seeking to break free from the reigning conventions. In the last century, in particular, they were struggling to unhitch their vision of life from Christian and sometimes theistic assumptions, to develop new ways of thinking that would owe nothing to biblical revelation or Church teaching. However, those who make up the avant-garde are usually a minority, those who are seen to be different precisely because they have become unconventional. Today, the tables have been turned. Our whole society has become avant-garde as what is morally conventional has been overthrown. Those who are conventional across a wide array of issues are now a minority. Our society, then, is caught up in an orgy of experimentation that is without parallel.

In these four ways, at least, our society is unique. And in its uniqueness, it becomes distinguished from the past. The question that naturally arises is this: what is going to happen when the current of Reformation faith flows into this modern channel churning with change and experimentation? When Reformation faith comes into contact with this modern culture, what is going to happen to it? Will it flow on blithely as if it were still in the sixteenth century, or will it have to make adjustments to the modern context? And, if the latter, what kind of adjustments?

These questions have been asked repeatedly in the modern period across the entire front of Christian expression. For the modern world is so different from what once obtained that some have wondered if the kind of faith that was at home in the medieval or Reformation periods can survive in the modern. Yet, for all the changes in the modern world outlined above, I am struck by the similarities between Luther's day and our own.

Older Similarities

If the modern world is so different in some ways from Luther's, where might we also see similarities between that world and ours? These similarities are rooted in the fact that God does not change in his character or purposes. His sovereign providence in our world is what sustains it and is guiding it to its ordained end, and this providence cannot be diverted. The significance of God's saving acts in our world cannot change, and neither does his revelation in the biblical Word. Our experience of the world changes, as does our knowledge, but human nature made in the image of God does not change, and neither does the nature of sin. These things being so, what is striking when we compare Luther's world with our own, are not only the massive differences but also the similarities, similarities rooted in the purposes of God and in the nature of human life. These are evident, for example, when we think about the Church then and the Church now. Consider just three of these similarities.

First, in Luther's day as in ours, there was no confidence in the Word of God. There was no confidence that it could, without the teaching authority of the Catholic Church, deliver its cargo of meaning. Without tradition and without the magisterium, the Word of God could not be rightly understood and so, in the Church, it was impotent to do its work.

Luther's reply to this was that the Holy Ghost speaks plainly and is not in need of either the tradition of the Church or its teaching authority to make clear what he has inspired in Scripture. Tradition and the magisterium had become gags over the mouth of God, standing in the way of the Church hearing his speech through the Word. In this way, Luther and the other Reformers insisted that the Word of God had been taken into captivity.

The situation today in the evangelical Church is not exactly parallel to this situation, but it is close. While the inspiration of Scripture is cheerfully endorsed, there is not a lot of confidence that this Word of God can accomplish its purposes. It is almost as if it is assumed that the God who first inspired this Word unfortunately did not foresee the massive changes that have come to late twentieth-century America. The Scripture that we have is, by itself, inadequate to address the pains and upheavals that erupt so frequently in our souls. It is insufficient for the nurture, management, and growth of the Church. To make it effective, we do not resort to tradition or a formal magisterium, as do Catholics, but to business know-how and psychology. When the Word of God is hitched up to these modern enterprises, then we think that mighty things can happen. And what we do not understand, and often will not countenance, is the suggestion that the reason Catholics resorted to tradition and the magisterium and we to business know-how and psychology is that in both cases *unbelief* is at work. Modern we may be, but we share the same struggle that Christians in every age have known: can we or can we not believe that the biblical Word is God's means for accomplishing the impossible, that self-serving sinners can be turned into God-fearing and Christ-honoring people?

Second, in Luther's day people did not understand the seriousness of sin. Especially in his debate with the humanist scholar, Erasmus, Luther pounded out his belief, in opposition to what was widely believed, that sin has crippled the ability of every person to make his or her way back to God. Not only so, but human beings must understand this utter inability, this spiritual death, and own it before they can receive Christ's reconciliation through belief in the Gospel. This inner bankruptcy, however, is not easily confessed and is frequently concealed by self-righteousness. According to Luther, unless this self-righteousness is plucked up and destroyed, unless the real nature of sin is understood, the Gospel cannot be received. The greatness of God's grace will never be grasped unless it is preceded by an understanding of the greatness of sin.

Today, our society is as much in the dark on this matter as was Luther's. If sin is defined, as it is in the Bible, as missing the mark, abandoning the path, and defying authority, the mark missed, the path abandoned, and the authority defied are from first to last God's. Sin is defying God, disobeying his law, rejecting his Word, and refusing his Christ. Yet in America today only 17 percent of people understand sin in relation to God. What in the Bible makes sin to be sin has disappeared for the great majority of Americans, and the consequence is a massive trivialization of our moral life. This happens because moral offenses against God are reduced simply into bad feelings about ourselves.

Third, then as now the unique sufficiency of Christ's death on the Cross had been lost. Luther saw, as we should today, that the moral law was not given by God for human beings to become self-satisfied with their moral attainments. On the contrary, the purpose of the law is to induce self-knowledge and self-despair, which come from seeing that the best human effort always results in failure before God. Such an understanding is the precondition for receiving Christ.

Christ, therefore, has done in his work on the Cross what we cannot do for ourselves. He has taken our sin upon himself that we might receive his righteousness for ourselves. His work is the unique and only provision that God has made for sin.

Luther's generation, nurtured as it was in the piety of the Middle Ages, thought that while the work of Christ was excellent and necessary, human piety was also needed to make it fully effective and so to complete the work of justification.

The similarities today are not exact, but they are close. We do not live under the same religious canopy as they did then, and the need for salvation that was so acutely felt then is a stranger to our souls now. However, what seems unmistakably similar is that in our modern culture the contention that Christ is uniquely God's provision is offensive. And even in the evangelical Church, there is a growing acceptance that there are multiple paths to God. Furthermore, as the understanding of sin is eroded — and it is being eroded in the Church — the various self-help therapies seem more and more innocent and necessary. Medieval piety reached for moral attainment to complete the work of Christ. We reach for psychological technique and knowledge to do the same thing.

And yet, although in the sixteenth century the Word of God had been taken captive by the Catholic Church, the meaning of sin had been lost, and the death of Christ had been diluted, the Reformation still happened. The Gospel was recovered, the Church was renewed, Christian life was invigorated, and Europe was changed in deep and profound ways. If the Church then, which had been all but lost despite its outward wealth and pomp, could be recovered, so can the Church today. And if Europe could be changed as drastically as it was, so might our world today. Then as now, however, the prerequisite is a Christian life that is biblically faithful and a Church that is doctrinally shaped, morally tough, intellectually vibrant, and buoyant with a faith that can lay hold of the promises of God in the face of circumstantial disconfirmation and see God's great power at work. Is this the kind of Christian life we find in evangelical churches? The answer is that what I have described here is becoming rare and is being replaced by a kind of spirituality that, because it is walking in lockstep with the culture so often, is better able to mimic that culture than to change it.

Spirituality

The argument that I am going to develop in this book, then, is that the modern world tends to produce its own kind of Christian spirituality. This spirituality is not simply of one kind. It is rather more like a family with many members but among whose members there are also resemblances. In order to simplify this, I am going to contrast Reformation or classic spirituality with what I am going to call a postmodern spirituality. This spirituality comes in charismatic as well as noncharismatic forms and is found in seeker-sensitive churches as well as those that are more traditional.

I might have called these two streams "evangelical" and "mystical," as does theologian Donald Bloesch,[5] except that both consider themselves evangelical. Besides, these words do not get at the heart of the differences on which this book will focus. Instead, I am differentiating them as "classical" and "postmodern." By "postmodern," however, I do not mean simply that which is contemporary or very up-to-date. "Postmodern" refers to the kind of spirituality that is forged in the interactions between biblical truth and that set of instincts and intuitions which are the hallmark of our modern world. These instincts are formed by the constant pounding to which we are subjected in the modern world. This pounding is made up of the pressures, demands, and expectations of our modern culture that combine to deliver the message that we must belong to it, not simply in the sense that we must live in it, but rather that we must live by it. And what we are to live by now is a set of perceptions at the center of which is the death of both truth and morality. It is at this juncture of biblical truth and modernity that there emerge forms of evangelical spirituality that owe something to both Scripture and culture. I shall argue that what is now distinctive about these forms, despite their expressed biblical interest, is that they have largely divested themselves of what is moral, however unintentionally.

Some people, of course, have put the emergence of this post-modern spirituality in a more positive light. What I have called a postmodern spirituality, sociologist Donald Miller sees embodied in what he calls the "new paradigm churches." He accepts the thesis of Roger Finke and Rodney Stark that in America religion is subject to "market forces" that produce winners and losers just as they do in the economic world. We are living at a time when these forces are rewriting the religious landscape. The great losers have been the mainline denominations. The winners, Miller believes, are these emerging new paradigm churches, and they are winning because they are doing a better job of "responding to the needs of their clientele."[6]

This conclusion arose from his study of three examples in particular, each of which started in Southern California in the 1960's but went on to become national and international in scope: Calvary Chapel,

5. Donald G. Bloesch, *The Crisis of Piety: Essays Toward a Theology of the Christian Life* (Colorado Springs: Helmers and Howard, 1988), 81-108.

6. Donald E. Miller, *Reinventing American Protestantism: Christianity in the New Millennium* (Berkeley: University of California Press, 1997), 3.

Vineyard Christian Fellowship, and Hope Chapel. These three movements, Miller believes, are simply the "lead story" for something much
bigger that is happening in society and that is producing an understanding of Christian faith that is very different from what has been
traditional.

The key to understanding the success of this enterprise, Miller
thinks, is to see that while these churches are conservative in their faith,
they are avant-garde in their attitude toward culture. At one level, this
means that they have adopted the music of the Baby Boomers and
Generation X; they have no place for tradition, and so the places where
they meet do not look like churches, and few if any Christian symbols
are evident; worship is contemporary in style; worshippers are casually
dressed; seminary education is optional for clergy (indeed, the seminaries are often treated with contempt); diversity of personal style is
tolerated; and there is much personal affirmation going on in both the
public worship and in small group meetings during the week. These
are safe places for the wounded, those who bear the pains and disillu-
sionments that are so often the costs that the modern world exacts from
those who want its bounty. These are places where no one stands on
ceremony and where the inner recesses can be safely bared to God.

Being avant-garde culturally also means something else which, in
the long run, is going to be rather more significant than the use of
drums, guitars, and the medium of praise songs. These new paradigm
churches, Miller notes, have also responded to three themes of what he
calls the counterculture: the therapeutic, the individualistic, and the
mood of antiestablishment.[7] These themes are defining how these
churches are fashioning themselves, what they are offering, and why
they are succeeding in meeting the needs of their clientele.

Perhaps it is the case that these three themes were once the
province of the counterculture. Today, however, these are the dominant
motifs of the cultural mainstream. In the following chapter, I develop
this with respect to our individualism, and in chapter four, "The Bonfire
of the Self," I explore the significance of the therapeutic in our culture.
Both of these streams are the source, in their slightly different ways, of
the air of antiestablishment. The new paradigm churches, then, appear
to be succeeding, not because they are offering an alternative to our
modern culture, but because they are speaking with its voice, mimicking
its moves. That is why the topography of the postmodern spirituality
of these churches is different from what it was in classical spirituality

7. Ibid., 21.

and why what is moral had much more weight in the latter than it does in the former. It is time now to look more carefully at these two streams of Christian spirituality.

Classical

By "classical spirituality," I have in mind the general understanding of the Christian life — its doctrinal basis, its devotional habits, its moral character, and its responsibilities in Church and society — that was formulated by the Reformers, was passed on in deepened pastoral form by the Puritans, and has come down through history and into the present through people like Martyn Lloyd-Jones, J. I. Packer, John Stott, Francis Schaeffer, and Carl Henry. There were, of course, variations in how the Christian life was conceived within the various traditions that arose at the time of the Reformation and subsequently. It may therefore appear to be misleading to speak of this simply as one tradition. Behind the variations, however, I believe it is possible to see the simple outline of one kind of spirituality, the one that Bloesch calls "evangelical" and that I am here calling "classical."

It is true, of course, that this stream of classical spirituality has also had its dalliances with culture, for when all is said and done, no part of the Church is immune to its own fallenness, to the seductions of the worldliness surrounding it, or to the habits that any culture naturally inculcates. Classical spirituality has sprouted its own flaws and failures. It has also mimicked culture in ways that are less than full-blown moral flaws but that still are not wise.

Is it not striking, for example, how much of the theology written in this tradition over the last century has conceived of its work within the framework of science? Thus we have the Princetonian, Charles Hodge, likening the theologian to the scientist because both have "facts" to discover and explain. Theology, he said, is the "science of the facts of divine revelation so far as those facts concern the nature of God and our relation to him."[8] On the dispensational side of the equation, Lewis Sperry Chafer said much the same thing, defining theology as the "collecting, scientifically arranging, comparing, exhibiting, and defending of all facts from any and every source concerning God and his works."[9]

8. Charles Hodge, *Systematic Theology* (3 vols.; New York: Scribners, 1871-72), 1:21.
9. Lewis Sperry Chafer, *Systematic Theology* (8 vols.; Dallas: Dallas Seminary Press, 1947), 1:5.

E. H. Bancroft, writing within the Wesleyan tradition, called theology "the science of God and of the relations between God and the universe."[10] And from an Arminian perspective, H. Orton Wiley described biblical revelation as "the source of the facts out of which systematic theology is constructed."[11] The analogy between science and theology might be helpful in some ways, but coming as it did in the time when science was not only flourishing and filling our world with a tidal wave of new products, new technologies, and new techniques but was also providing the dominant model by which we understand reality, theology done in this key does look a little suspicious. Would theologians have thought this way if they had lived within a culture in which science was not important? Are there Christian misconceptions that might follow upon such cultural mimicry?

In contrasting these two kinds of spirituality, then, my argument is not that one is always culturally influenced and the other is not, but rather that they are different kinds of spirituality even though they ostensibly stand on the same doctrinal ground. Both lay claim to the common inheritance of belief — the Trinity, the divinity of Christ, his death and resurrection, the inspiration of Scripture, and other core doctrines — but the way in which these beliefs are played out internally is very different. And the simplest way to state this difference is to say that in classical spirituality what is moral is central, and in postmodern spirituality it is not. It is not that what is moral is denied in the one spirituality as that it lacks the weight which it has in the other. The buildings look alike from the outside, but they are significantly different in their internal architecture. And, as I shall later argue, the consequence of this is that doctrine in postmodern spirituality not only loses its importance but often also its shape.

To be more precise, I shall develop the argument that this difference has produced a shift in the way that the moral is experienced. It is a shift from *guilt* in the classical stream to *shame* in the postmodern. However, it is shame in a uniquely contemporary way. It is not the shame of being exposed before others because our individualism gives us permission to do whatever we like and whatever gratifies us provided that it does not cross the boundaries of what is legal. There is, as a result, very little of which people are ashamed should they get caught

10. E. H. Bancroft, *Christian Theology: Systematic and Biblical,* ed. Ronald B. Meyers (Grand Rapids: Zondervan, 1925), 13.
11. H. Orton Wiley, *Christian Theology* (3 vols.; Kansas City: Beacon Hill Press, 1940), 1:16.

or be exposed. It is, rather, the shame of being naked within one's self. It is shame experienced as inner emptiness, deprivation, loss, and disorientation. It is shame that is far more psychological in nature than moral.

It is, then, in their internal configurations that the differences are found, not in the doctrines. It is the shape given to classical spirituality by the importance of God as Other, as transcendent, as over against us, not only in the greatness of his being, but in the purity of his character. It is this that places at the center of this spirituality Christ's Cross and that defines sin, not only as what is morally wrong, but as what is an affront to God himself. It is the holiness of God that shapes the meaning of the Christian life in sanctification and service, that demands self-sacrifice and self-forgetfulness and thinks of sin as self-centeredness and self-absorption. In consequence, worship in classical spirituality is God-centered and Cross-focused, and it is God-centered because it is Christ-focused.

The most obvious aspect in the configuration of classical spirituality, then, is the role which the Holy has. It is this that gives weight and shape to the understanding of God. Whatever else needs to be said about this spirituality, God's holiness is at its center.[12] He is in himself utterly pure,

12. Nineteenth-century theology, especially in Britain and Europe, explored the tensions, as they were perceived, between God's holiness and his love. Protestant liberalism favored love over holiness to the point of eliminating the idea of God's wrath. This penchant continues in works like Daniel Day Williams, *The Spirit and the Forms of Love*. More recently, other theologians, like Karl Barth, have placed love and holiness in dialectical tension to one another. What this long discussion reveals is that both need to be affirmed — neither can be compromised — and that classical orthodoxy was correct to think that if holiness is God's moral perfection, and if love is a part of that perfection, then love is a part of holiness and can never be in tension with it. This was also forcefully argued earlier this century by P. T. Forsyth, a transformed liberal who spoke of God's "holy-love." See especially *The Cruciality of the Cross* (London: Hodder and Stoughton, 1909), *The Holy Father and the Living Christ* (London: Hodder and Stoughton, 1897), and *The Work of Christ* (London: Independent Press, 1938). In some of his works, Emil Brunner's existential leanings led to some unhelpful outcomes, but few people have surpassed the brilliance and depth of his exploration of holiness and love in the death of Christ. See his *The Mediator: A Study in the Central Doctrine of the Christian Faith*, trans. Olive Wyon (New York: Macmillan, 1934).

I have spoken here of God's holiness in terms that classical Protestantism also used, and this should not be construed in the light of the later debate in which people were inclined, in practice, to choose between love and holiness. On the understanding of love in Scripture, see B. B. Warfield, "The Terminology of Love in the New Testament," *Princeton Theological Review* 16, no. 1 (January 1918), 1-45; Leon Morris, *The Testaments of Love: A Study of Love in the Bible* (Grand Rapids: Eerdmans, 1981).

and in his purity he asserts himself against all that is fallen and corrupted in our world. This expresses itself in the biblical terms for his wrath, anger, and judgment, terms that have long since vanished from most of Protestantism and that live a peripheral existence within much of evangelicalism. This moral reality is, however, at the center of our universe and of God's dealing with it. In the end, it is upon Christ's death and God's wrath that our hope rests, for he is the last line of resistance to the triumph of what is evil and fallen. It is because of his judgment, because of the day when he will put truth forever on the throne and evil forever on the scaffold, that hope can be sustained in the midst of a world in which there is not only much corruption but in which what is corrupt is so often rewarded and so often triumphant. God, who is at the moral center of the world and who sustains the moral order, is also the one who has provided in Christ the answer to the profound moral dilemma that his moral presence evokes.

What I have been describing, however, Krister Stendahl, who served as the Dean of Harvard Divinity School, contended in a famous essay is a way of reading Paul through the eyes of later history. First in Augustine, then in Martin Luther, this "introspective conscience of the West" was given shape. To be converted came to mean passing through deep crises, knowing something of the despair of Augustine and Luther, of their awe and trembling before the face of God, and the sweetness of the Gospel's message of redemption. The crushing weight of God's moral presence was lifted at the Cross and in its place comes faith's vision of newness. Unfortunately, says Stendahl, this is not what Paul was talking about.

One finds no stricken conscience in him. Quite the reverse. Of his Jewish experience he writes: "as to righteousness under the law blameless" (Phil. 3:6). He believed in sin, but it is impossible to tell whether it weighed consciously on Paul or not, Stendahl asserts. He did not come to his view of the law "by testing and pondering its effects upon his conscience."[13] In Romans 2 and 3, Paul does argue

---

13. Krister Stendahl, "The Apostle Paul and the Introspective Conscience of the West," *Harvard Theological Review* 56, no. 3 (1956), 204. Stendahl's essay provoked a sharp response from Ernst Käsemann. The issues raised in this debate are helpfully reviewed by C. K. Barrett, "Paul and the Introspective Conscience," in *The Bible, the Reformation and the Church: Essays in Honour of James Atkinson,* ed. W. P. Stephens (Sheffield: Sheffield Academic Press, 1995), 36-48. On the discussion of these themes following the work of E. P. Sanders, see I. Howard Marshall, "Salvation, Grace and Works in the Later Writings in the Pauline Corpus," *New Testament Studies* 42, no. 3 (July 1996), 339-58.

the case against the Jews. Despite their privileges, they are as guilty as the Gentiles, but that does not mean that they were expected by Paul to suffer Luther-like pangs of conscience. What of Paul's conversion? Do we not see in this event the storm of self-discovery, Paul dumbfounded in the presence of Christ over what he has been doing? That event on the Damascus road, Stendahl argues, was simply his call to apostleship, not his conversion. And this same pattern of believing in sin, but showing no signs of personal introspection about it, carried over into Paul's view of the Christian life, too. He had very little sense of a burdened conscience. That is why he uses the language of forgiveness so infrequently.

If Stendahl had been right in his essay, the rug would have been pulled from under all of the subsequent expressions of classical spirituality that, in the most express terms, have always grounded themselves in what Paul taught. What can be said for Stendahl's argument is that Paul's epistles reveal little of the emotion of sin, nothing of the psychology of his or anyone else's conversion, and little about the way in which moral consciousness expressed itself within. Paul's purpose was always theological and only incidentally psychological. It is unwarranted to conclude from this, however, that there was no inward sense of dismay in Paul or the others who came to faith. After all, what does it mean that on Pentecost Peter's audience was "cut to the heart" (Acts 2:37), that "fear came upon every soul" (Acts 2:43)? Why, if the Philippian jailer had not known something of inward desolation did he, after his confession of faith, rejoice "with all his household that he had believed in God" (Acts 16:34)?

There are three accounts of Paul's conversion (Acts 9:1-9; 22:3-21; 26:4-20) and three significant elaborations of its meaning in the epistles (1 Cor. 15:8-10; Gal. 1:13-17; Phil. 3:4-14). It is in the third of these passages from his epistles that Paul develops what turning to Christ meant to him. The righteousness which, as a Pharisee, he had gained was just self-righteousness and worthless before Christ (Phil. 3:7). Had Paul been as untroubled about his moral standing as Stendahl imagines, he would have had no incentive to look for a righteousness "which is through faith in Christ, the righteousness from God that depends on faith" (Phil. 3:9) in place of his former righteousness. That, in fact, was the moment not only when he was confronted by the risen Christ, and at the same time confronted by his own unrighteousness, but also when God revealed his Son "in" Paul (Gal. 1:16), an inward experience matching the outer revelation.

The Damascus road event, it is true, is also understood in the New

Testament in terms of Paul's calling as an apostle, but the Philippians passage is an important exception. Here his experience is used to explicate the meaning of Christian conversion in all ages. And the reason that Paul offers no other biography, no other account of his inward travails, it would seem, is that what is normative for all time are the truths regarding the necessity and nature of conversion, not its psychology. Yet even in the absence of any further account, it requires little imagination to see that behind the sparse narrative of his own inward condition there is a Copernican revolution. He could, in his life as a Pharisee, suppose that before the law he was "blameless," but that is not all that he said. Without the law, he also says, he would not have known what it was to covet. But once he heard the law, his own sinful nature rose up in opposition to what he had heard (Rom. 7:7). As a consequence, "sin revived and I died" (Rom. 7:9). It was the death, in the end, of all for which he had striven and upon which he rested his hope. Paul tells us little more about how this inward calamity registered upon him, but what he does tell us is quite sufficient for us to conclude that his conversion was a shattering event, so shattering that this may account for the three years of solitude he needed to put back together his mental and spiritual world afterwards (Gal. 1:18).

It is the biblical truth about the need and nature of conversion that is normative, not the emotional experience accompanying it, and yet it is hard to escape the prospect that if God's indictment of sin is heard, if the Cross is understood, the sinner will have at least some sense of being overcome, of being stricken, in the presence of God. This may not produce the deep foreboding of Luther, the terror of Bunyan, the lostness of Augustine, but in some fashion the doom from which the Gospel is the delivery must have registered.

Luther's experience is not normative, but the Gospel he came to understand through his painful sojourn is. We may be astonished today at his profound, inward quaking when he offered his first Mass. Afterwards he wrote that he was "utterly stupefied and terror-stricken," overcome that he was in the very presence of God before whom all should tremble. And scattered through his works are many other somber reflections on how Christ, in whom the judgment of God is met, impinged on his inner life before his conversion. He said that he knew Christ only as "a stern judge" from whom he only wished to flee, that before Christ he used to tremble and "turn pale." Luther was terrified by the moral presence of God.

What becomes clear in expressions such as these is that the Holy stood over against Luther, that in its presence he was utterly dismayed, and that he was helpless to respond. Luther knew himself to be morally and spiritually dead in the sight of God, the weight of judgment about to crush him. The Gospel of God's justifying work in Christ, which brought life from death for Luther, was thus celebrated as a mighty act of deliverance, as though he had, as he put it, entered "the open gates into paradise itself." And it is this knowledge of himself in relation to Christ's saving work, reflected as it was in the depths of Luther's passions, that expressed a spirituality that was grounded in Paul and that is here called classic.

Luther's experience was never exactly duplicated in its emotional texture in those who followed, but the passage of the Gospel left behind many of the same distinctive marks. Because we are often so far removed from these today, not only in time, but even in understanding, it is worth considering a few of those in whom we see such marks.

One cannot miss them in the seventeenth-century English Puritan John Owen. His exposition of Psalm 130 gives powerful exposition to what I have called classic spirituality. The psalm is brief in length, but Owen expands its eight verses into 429 pages of reflective commentary!

His paraphrase of the opening verse lays the foundation for the entire explanation that follows: "O Lord, through my manifold sins and provocations I have brought myself into great distresses."[14] It would be easy to read Owen's exposition as a piece of postmodern spirituality, because he begins by elaborating on the ways in which life causes profound inward distress. These "depths" in which we sometimes find ourselves, however, come upon us not by misfortune but by God's providential hand in order that we might learn to know ourselves as we are before him and to seek his grace and forgiveness. They are felt inwardly and sometimes devastatingly, but in this God has a purpose. "Trouble, danger, disquietude invariably lead us to seek relief," Owen comments.[15] There are many false leads which we might follow in seeking relief, and at this point it becomes abundantly clear that though Owen has started with life and its perplexities, and with how these pain and disorient us, for him these experiences are morally framed. They are understood in direct relation to the character of God. In our state of inner disillusionment and bafflement, we seek divine help. But how does this come? We do not take one step toward finding God's relief until we can learn to see our lives in a moral perspective. What we so

14. John Owen, *The Forgiveness of Sin: A Practical Exposition of Psalm 130* (Grand Rapids: Baker Book House, 1977), 9.
    15. Ibid., 37.

often lack, and what God must give us, is a sense of sin. It is a "practical apprehension" that is given us, "of sin and its evils, in reference to the law and love of God, the cross and the blood of Christ, the communion and consolation of the Spirit, and all the fruits of love, mercy and grace that it has been made partaker of, or on Gospel-grounds has hoped for."[16] It is, of course, entirely possible to have such a sense of sin and for that sense "to lie burning as a fire shut up in the bones," to the continual "disquietude" of the unrepentant because they refuse to come to a "free, soul-opening acknowledgment."[17] This acknowledgment is to see sin as "rebellion against his sovereignty, opposition to his holiness, a provocation to his justice, a rejection of his yoke, a casting off of the creature's dependence on its Creator."[18] Owen then writes eloquently, and powerfully, of the nature of God's forgiveness, of its necessity, and of its greatness, without which there is no answer to the inward perplexities that life provokes because life stirs up our sin. And among the benefits of receiving such forgiveness, among the evidences of its having been received, is that "they should admire, adore, glorify and praise him, worship, believe in and trust him in all things, and seek the enjoyment of him as an eternal reward."[19] Thus Owen has set up the coordinates of a classical spirituality: the holiness of God, sin, and forgiveness. This spirituality, now entered through Christ, is not only explicated in the Gospel but must be expressed in worship. The purpose of worship is clearly to express the greatness of God and not simply to find inward release or, still less, amusement. Worship is theological rather than psychological.

In America, David Brainerd, the eighteenth-century missionary to the Indians, experienced much of what Luther had and exhibited much of what Owen had described. In his youth, he knew little about sin, though he was earnest and devoted religiously. However, when he was twenty, he tells us, the doctrines he had believed came alive with terrifying power:

> It pleased God . . . to give me on a sudden such a sense of my danger, and the wrath of God, that I stood amazed, and my former good frames which I had pleased myself with all presently vanished; and, from the view I had of my sin and vileness, I was much distressed all day, fearing the vengeance of God would soon overtake me. I was

16. Ibid., 58.
17. Ibid., 62.
18. Ibid., 89.
19. Ibid., 191.

much dejected, and kept much alone, and sometimes begrudged the birds and beasts their happiness, because they were not exposed to eternal misery, as I evidently saw I was. And thus I lived day to day, being frequently in distress.[20]

This day marked the beginning of a deep and painful struggle in which, step by step, God "discovered" or revealed Brainerd's heart to him. This did not issue in quick repentance at all but in a tumultuous struggle within. This, he says, "put me into a most horrible frame of contesting with the Almighty, with an inward vehemence and virulence, finding fault with His ways of dealing with mankind."[21] When these inward passions subsided a little, he gave himself with renewed zeal to win God's approval. He attended preaching more often and paid closer attention. He worked harder at disciplining himself and he aimed at greater moral improvement. But one morning, as he was walking in "a solitary place," he saw the futility of all that he was doing. "I was brought quite to a stand as finding myself totally *lost*."[22] Shortly thereafter, in the very same place, "unspeakable glory seemed to open to the view and apprehension of my soul."[23] He came to understand who God was, the "way of salvation was opened" to him, and he came to feel "sweetly composed" in his mind.

Postmodern

This language of being stricken in the presence of God has largely disappeared in postmodern spirituality. Today, these are not common experiences and these are not our most bedrock convictions. They are not what we sing about in church, unless we are cast back upon the older hymns. We have other habits and convictions, and our songs are often about other matters. Today, Luther's experience, or Owen's, or Brainerd's, is simply incomprehensible to many in the evangelical world. This older angst is foreign. Our literature dwells on other issues. We expect nothing like this to happen. We have become so grateful for a convert, any convert, that we do not inquire closely as to whether it

20. David Brainerd, *The Diary and Journal of David Brainerd* (2 vols.; London: Andrew Melrose, 1902), 1:6-7. An appreciative biography of Brainerd can be found in Jonathan Edwards, *The Life of David Brainerd,* ed. Norman Pettit (New Haven: Yale University Press, 1985).

21. Brainerd, *Diary and Journal,* 1:11.

22. Ibid., 1:19.

23. Ibid., 1:22.

is the Gospel that has been believed. It is enough that more people
come into the church than leave it or that a decision has been made.[24]

Wherein, then, lies the difference between a classical and a postmodern spirituality? The latter begins, not so much with sin as morally
framed, but with sin as psychologically experienced, not so much with
sin in relation to God, but with sin in relation to ourselves. It begins
with our anxiety, pain, and disillusionment, with the world in its disorder, the family or marriage in its brokenness, or the workplace in its
brutality and insecurity. God, in consequence, is valued to the extent
that he is able to bathe these wounds, assuage these insecurities, calm
these fears, restore some sense of internal order, and bring some sense
of wholeness. As one praise song puts it:

> He heard my cry and came to heal me,
> He took my pain and He relieved me,
> He filled my life and comforted me,
> And His name will shine, shine eternally.[25]

24. At few places is our distance from classical spirituality plainer than at the
point of conversion. It is, of course, impossible to know how typical the following
"Convert's First Prayer" is, or what a typical convert's prayer might be today, but it
seems indisputable that Puritanism shaped the Gospel doctrinally, biblically, and
with a degree of profundity that eludes the Church today. The prayer goes: "MY
FATHER, I could never have sought my happiness in thy love, unless thou had'st
first loved me. Thy Spirit has encouraged me by grace to seek thee, has made known
to me the reconciliation in Jesus, has taught me to believe it, has helped me to take
thee for my God and portion. May he grant me to grow in the knowledge and
experience of thy love, and walk in it all the way to glory. Blessed for ever be thy
fatherly affection, which chose me to be one of thy children by faith in Jesus: I thank
thee for giving me the desire to live as such. In Jesus, my brother, I have my new
birth, every restraining power, every renewing grace. It is by the Spirit I call thee
Father, believe in thee, love thee; Strengthen me inwardly for every purpose of my
Christian life; Let the Spirit continually reveal to me my interest in Christ, and open
to me the riches of thy love in him; May he abide in me that I may know my union
with Jesus, and enter into constant fellowship with him; By the Spirit may I daily
live to thee, rejoice in thy love, find it the same to me as to thy Son, and become
rooted and grounded in it as a house on rock; I know but little — increase my
knowledge of thy love in Jesus, keep me pressing forward for clearer discoveries of
it, so that I may find its essential fullness; Magnify thy love to me according to its
greatness, and not according to my deserts or prayers, and whatever increase thou
givest, let it draw out greater love to thee." Arthur Bennett, ed., *The Valley of Vision*
(Edinburgh: The Banner of Truth Trust, 1975), 53. This convert imagined that he
knew little, but by today's standards he would stand among the theological giants.

25. Jan Groth and Tore W. Aas, "His Name Will Shine," in *Maranatha! Music
Praise Chorus Book* (3rd ed.; Laguna Hills: The Corinthian Group, 1993), 192. The
same kind of sentiment is found in the song, "Hallowed Be Thy Name," with the
words, "You're the answer to all my problems and You solve them" (ibid., 17). In

This psychologizing of sin and salvation has an immediacy about it that is appealing in this troubled age, this age of broken beliefs and broken lives. The cost, however, is that it so subverts the process of moral understanding that sin loses its sinfulness, at least before God. And whereas in classical spirituality it was assumed that sinners would struggle with their sin, and feel its sting, and experience dismay over it, in postmodern spirituality, this struggle is considered abnormal and something for which divine relief is immediately available. That is why the experience of Luther, Brainerd, and Owen is so remote from what passes as normal in the evangelical world today.

Another difference is that the one spirituality is built around *truth*, but the other is defined by its search for *power*. In a charismatic setting this search takes the form of powerful encounters, dramatic experiences of the supernatural, healings of both physical and emotional kinds, and the exercise of the other gifts. But outside charismatic circles, the search for power is most often construed in therapeutic ways: the power to conquer anxiety, to find enthusiasm for a new week, to repair the broken connections within the self, and to piece back together ruptured relations. It is the power to restore one's daily functioning. It is power for survival.

There is yet another difference. In classical spirituality, access to God's presence is gained through believing his Word and trusting in the work of the Christ of that Word. While these beliefs are not denied in postmodern spirituality, they are not the key that opens the lock. Access in postmodern spirituality, Miller notes, comes much more through the emotions and through bodily actions. The raising of hands, palms upward, the swaying to music, the arms outstretched to heaven, the release of inward emotion, this is what opens the door to the divine reality.

While everyone even remotely within a biblical frame of reference affirms both God's love and his holiness, this postmodern spirituality greatly enlarges his love. It is because he is loving that we can hope for some sense of inward calm and order as his gift to his children. And while his transcendence and immanence are alike affirmed, it is his immanence, his relatedness, that is preeminent.

"He Is Able," we find the words, "He is able, more able to handle anything that comes my way" (ibid., 55). In "Let Your Living Water Flow," the prayer is offered: "Let Your Holy Spirit come and take control of ev'ry situation that has troubled my mind" (ibid., 168). Dennis Polen's "Everything's Gonna Be Alright" expresses the hope, "When you need a hand to hold, everything's gonna be alright in Christ" (ibid., 30). Finally, in "Cares Chorus" we find the words: "And any time that I don't know what to do, I will cast all my cares upon You" (ibid., 48).

What is so striking about the hymnody — if that is what it is — of this postmodern spirituality, however, is its parasitic nature. It lives off the truth of classical spirituality but frequently leaves that truth unstated as something to be assumed, whereas in the hymnody of classical spirituality the truth itself is celebrated. The one rejoices in what the other hides. That seems to be the most obvious conclusion to be drawn from the fact that the large majority of praise songs I analyzed, 58.9 percent, offer no doctrinal grounding or explanation for the praise; in the classical hymnody examined it was hard to find hymns that were not predicated upon and did not develop some aspect of doctrine. But that is not all. Not only is the praise in this postmodern spirituality often shorn of theological scaffolding, but what it facilitates is deeply privatized worship. One indication of this is that the Church, the collective people of God, features in only 1.2 percent of the songs; what dominates overwhelmingly is the private, individualized, and interior sense of God. By contrast, 21.6 percent of the classical hymns were explicitly about the Church.[26] The texture of the songs in the postmodern spirituality, furthermore, is more therapeutic than moral. The song presented at the beginning of this chapter may serve as an illustration:

26. The analysis for the songs often expressing a postmodern spirituality was based on the 406 songs contained in the *Worship Songs of the Vineyard* (3rd vol.; Anaheim, Calif.: Vineyard Ministries International, 1991) and *Maranatha! Music Praise Chorus Book;* the 662 hymns of *The Covenant Hymnal* (Chicago: Covenant Press, 1973) were used to test the theology and motifs of a classical spirituality. It has been rather difficult, however, to make the comparisons I have offered. This is especially true with respect to the major conclusion regarding the loss of theological character in the worship songs. The rule I used was that in any of the songs in these two books, the simple repetition of a word that could have doctrinal content would not be counted unless some small elaboration of that word occurred in the context. For example, the song "Jesus, You are Lord" contains the following words: "Jesus, You are Lord, (Jesus, You Are Lord,) Jesus, You are Holy, (Jesus, You are Holy,) Jesus, You are Lord, (Jesus, You are Lord,) Jesus, You are Holy, And I praise your name, And I praise Your name! For You are Lord, You are Lord!" Although the lordship and holiness of Christ are biblical and doctrinal themes, they were not developed doctrinally in the song, and this song was therefore not counted among those with theological content. By contrast, Graham Kendrick's "Meekness and Majesty" was counted. It develops the idea of the incarnation in the opening stanza: "Meekness and majesty, manhood and Deity, in perfect harmony, the Man who is God. Lord of eternity, dwells in humanity; kneels in humility and washes our feet." There is an obvious and successful attempt at crystallizing biblical teaching on what it means to say that the second person of the godhead took on our flesh and was incarnate. These percentages, then, should be read more as tendencies than as precise measures.

I need you to hold me
Like my daddy never could,
And I need you to show me
How resting in your arms can be so good.

I need you to walk with me
Hand in hand we'll run and play
I need you to talk to me
Tell me again you'll stay.[27]

The themes of sin, penitence, the longing for holiness appear in only 3.6 percent. And, as one might expect, while the holiness of God appears in 4.3 percent, his love, coupled with romantic imagery about loving him, ran through 10.4 percent of the songs, in comparison to about 1 percent in the classical hymnody. The thought of loving God, and occasionally of being in love with God, that characterizes postmodern hymnody has replaced the emphasis on consecration and commitment that was so characteristic of classic hymnody.[28]

At this point the essentially mystical nature of postmodern piety becomes obvious, even though it is a mysticism that is filtered through modern, psychological assumptions. This is evident, first, in the way that this kind of spirituality believes in direct access to reality. The experiencing self is admitted, as it were, into the innermost places of God directly, without any wait. The result of this assumption is that personal intuition about the purposes of God, how his will is being

27. *Worship Songs of the Vineyard*, 70-73.
28. Those in Scripture who were brought near to the holy presence of God found shame and guilt burning in their hearts, not the celebration that some of these songs go on to express. Perhaps what explains this is an unbalanced stress upon God's immanence. In one song, for example, the words of John 5:19, 30 are used as if those singing the song were Christ himself. They sing: "I have come to do my Father's will. . . . And I will drink the cup he gives . . . the hour has come, may his will be done . . . I can hear my Father speaking to me. . . . I will speak the words my Father teaches me" (ibid., 104-5). In liberal Protestantism, as well as Catholic modernism, the immanence of God, his presence beneath all human consciousness, was affirmed, and the consciousness of this presence was understood in christological terms. Each believer therefore became a "Christ" to others. This extreme stress on divine immanence is impossible without a corresponding loss of the biblical doctrine of sin.

The theme of God's holiness was present in 4.3 percent of the songs; the effect of this, though, is to remember God's moral purity but not necessarily to remind sinners of their sin. The song "Above All Others," for example, says: "I see a picture of your holiness, Oh Lord, I look into your eyes and feel a fire burn in my heart."

realized in one's personal life, tends to blur into divine revelation[29] and become indistinguishable from it. Second, the God so approached is often beyond rational categories. Third, grace in this form of Christian life is often understood as a power that brings psychological wholeness rather than as God's favor by which we are constituted as his in Christ. And worship is less about ascribing praise to God for who he is than it is celebrating what we know of him from within our own experience.[30]

If this all sounds a little different from what Luther, Owen, and Brainerd talked about, then we need to ask how the adaptations were made to modernity. What was the mechanism? One of the clearest illustrations of how easily we move from a classical kind of spirituality to a postmodern one can be found in a recent study on how the parable of the prodigal son (Luke 15:11-32) has been presented in sermons. What is interesting about this study is that it not only compares sermons on the same parable, but also shows how unconsciously the adaptations are made.

Embarrassed by Modernity

This parable of the prodigal son, of course, has always caught at the human spirit like gorse brushing sheer nylons. The depths of parental anguish, of sibling self-righteousness, and of youthful folly and regret in this story are poignant. Parents across the ages have found connections with it, as have the wayward of all times. The father may stand gazing across the fields of the first century awaiting the return of his rebel son, as he does in this parable, or he may be listening in the late twentieth century for the one telephone call that really matters. The younger son may party recklessly, yet within the constraints of Eastern decorum, or he may be smoking pot, watching porno movies, and running up credit card debts. Somehow, these differences seem not to matter. We have known too many kids, like the younger son in the parable, who have separated themselves from their parents, thrown off the traces, and heard in the lure of the "far country" — be it the beach culture of California or the street culture of New York — the promise of adventure and boundless pleasure. And for so many this has turned

29. See, for example, John Wimber, "Signs, Wonders, Cancer," *Christianity Today* 40, no. 11 (October 7, 1996), 49-50.
30. See Bloesch, *The Crisis of Piety*, 83-99.

to ashes. The grand and reckless fling ends in shabby dependence, and it matters not whether we are thinking of the muck of the pig pen then or the crazy emptiness of a drugged-out life now. We have seen the once carefree spirits sooner or later impale themselves helplessly on their own stupidity.

Some of these kids, against all odds, have come to their senses and have begun to see their own world from within, rather than the way they once pretended it was. Until this moment, being "real" is something that has eluded them. They have seen no further than the next moment, and in their self-abandonment they have tried not to know themselves. But then small snippets of reality keep intruding like those invisible drafts of icy air in the winter that somehow manage to triumph, easing their way in through cracks, floorboards, and beneath doors, despite the most determined resistance. Some of these kids may even have come to see the gaunt figure of death waiting patiently, like a vulture who knows that time is on its side. And in that moment they also see their father's face. They stumble out, cross the street weakly and unevenly, find one of the few coins that remain, and dial home.

We have known the older brother, too, the one who is dutiful and upright. There is no resentment against parental authority, but there is smoldering resentment against his wayward sibling. There is smug self-righteousness in having played life by the rules, the kind of self-righteousness that finds grace incomprehensible because forgiveness, for him, seems so unnecessary. Here, too, it matters little whether we are thinking of the Pharisees of Christ's day or of upright churchgoers today whose virtue has also become their undoing.

This story, whose figures we know so well, nevertheless has a snag. The truth is that it is not, most importantly, about fathers and sons. It is not, in the end, a story about stormy, reckless rebellion, suffering parental patience, and an older brother who sets out to earn his father's love and cannot understand how that love could simply be given. These are but the props which serve a much bigger story, and a rather different story, the one about sin and redemption, and this we read with more difficulty because we are moderns.

When the son "came to himself" he began to rehearse how he would approach his abandoned father. It would not be with words of recrimination. There would be none of the ploys of our contemporary moment, the relish with which the parent would be cast in the role of the wrongdoer and the son in that of the wounded victim. No, he would be truthful. He would say to his father: "Father, I have sinned against heaven and before you, and I am no longer worthy to be called your son; treat me as one of your hired servants" (Luke 15:18-19). That is how he rehearsed his return, and that is what he said on seeing his father. This is the fulcrum around which the whole story turns. Not only is the rebellion identified, accountability owned, and forgiveness extended — a forgiveness grasped by the younger son and rejected by the older brother (15:28-32) — but now we see unmistakably that this troubled home is actually a picture of our human condition.

The snag, of course, is that its particular kind of moral pathos and accountability before God, the thought about the unmerited nature of God's grace, is really quite alien, even incomprehensible, in our modern world. We talk easily about the kid who was last seen heading for the fun and sun in Florida and shake our heads at the breakdown of the home today, but we can only stammer when it comes time to think of ourselves in the shoes of either of these brothers and to name our own sin before God. These ideas are embarrassed in the presence of modernity. So, how are we going to preach this story?

It was the sermonic treatment of this parable that sociologist Marsha Witten used to examine how far and in what ways the experience of the modern world has intruded upon the way in which Christian faith is presented.[31] For preachers are caught between the secular assumption, now everywhere present in the churches, that the self can be crafted, developed, actualized, and the biblical notion that the self is corrupted, fragmented, and incapable of healing itself. Moreover, in a secularized world, God has vanished beyond the periphery of what is meaningful, while in the biblical world he stands at its center. Nothing therefore offends modern sensibilities quite so much as the biblical notion of sin and the consequences of not believing. How, then, did these preachers negotiate the treacherous waters between the rocks of unchanging biblical truth and the swirling currents of relativizing modernity?

31. Marsha G. Witten, *All Is Forgiven: The Secular Message in American Protestantism* (Princeton: Princeton University Press, 1993). This study is a piece of qualitative research (structured discourse analysis) that utilized sermons from only two denominations, the Southern Baptists and the Presbyterian Church, USA. Forty-seven sermons were analyzed, all preached between 1986 and 1988. Given the absence of quantitative data and the fact that the sermons were not denominationally representative, it is not possible to generalize on how widespread the tendencies she has identified are. The study is useful, however, in illustrating the *mechanism* by which the transformation of doctrinal themes occurs. The gist of her findings can be found in Marsha G. Witten, "Preaching About Sin in Contemporary Protestantism," *Theology Today* 50, no. 2 (July 1993), 243-53.

Most sermons navigated these waters only with great difficulty, and most took on so much water that by the end the sermon was no longer seaworthy. A few, on one end of the spectrum, were compelled to state the biblical truth about sin in defiance of our cultural norms; a few, on the other end, succumbed to secular, cultural norms with apparently few struggles. But the great majority were found somewhere between these choices. It was in this middle area that great ingenuity was used in declaring the biblical truth about sin but in doing so in such a delicate and civil way, in such a modern way, that even those who were distant from the realm of biblical truth would experience little of that distance in hearing the parable preached. And the most disconcerting thing about this is the unselfconscious way in which it was accomplished, and hence the bargain of having biblical truth on modern terms was held out with utter sincerity.

First, there is the declaration to be made that all are sinners. But what does such a declaration mean? The sermons revealed many intriguing strategies for softening the impact of the statement on the hearers. These typically aimed at depersonalizing the statement so that, while the belief in the sinfulness of all was declared, this was not often heard as a personal indictment: "Not only has everyone else sinned but *you* stand guilty before God." Sometimes this doctrine was mitigated by the suggestion that the major burden of this truth has to be borne by someone else. Most commonly, it was children who provided in these sermons the best illustrations of what it meant to be a sinner. In a few cases, the truth of our sinning had to be carried principally by the Jews or our seemingly worst offenders: assorted criminals, prostitutes, addicts, homosexuals, those who are different, and even the ugly,[32] leaving those who are more mainstream and ordinary somewhat unscathed.

Others, who asked the congregation to see themselves in one of the two brothers, nevertheless went on to minimize the sin with which the congregation was identifying. And a common ploy here was to resort to therapeutic language. The brothers received detached, value-free evaluation, almost as if their cases were being written up clinically, and then the identification was made, not so much with the ethical quality of their characters, as with the wounds and hurts that they must have felt in their different ways. "In so doing," Witten writes, "the sermons position the listeners . . . as vicarious clients in a mass session of Rogerian therapy, as the talk displays a style of therapeutic warmth, ac-

32. Witten, *All Is Forgiven*, 92.

ceptance, and tolerance."[33] After all, the older brother may seem un-
lovable at first sight, but the picture changes dramatically when we come
to understand, as it was suggested, that he suffered from what we know
today as a narcissistic personality disorder. That is, he was preoccupied
with his own grand achievements, which he exaggerated in his own
mind, and he became enraged when what he had done went unrecog-
nized. He was driven by a sense of entitlement and, unfortunately, was
devoid of any sense of empathy. These are what we should see in this
text, and these are the marks of this disorder. When we dress this brother
in these clothes, his smug self-righteousness suddenly melts into a
malady about which he is quite unconscious and with which most in the
congregation are unwilling to identify. They can, however, pity him, and
in that compassion they find their own distance from the reality of sin
of which the parable is actually speaking. Pity, in a therapeutic world,
takes the place which judgment does in a moral world. And whereas
the parable started out speaking about the human condition, it has now
ended up as simply an interesting tale about human foibles. We can
hear it from a distance and in a way that asks that we make few or no
judgments about ourselves.

At the heart of this new reading of the parable is a rather different
understanding of the self from what prevails in classical, Protestant
spirituality. There, the self is not to be treated as innocent, nor is it to
be indulged. Indeed, sin is defined in terms of self-love, self-centeredness, self-delusion. But here, in this stream of modern spirituality, the
self is understood in terms of psychology. The self is unhappy, not so
much because of sin, as a lack of realization, or an inability to adjust to
the social environment. So conversion in these sermons was presented
as incorporating God into the self so that the self could have more
meaningful relations with others.[34] "God is the clue to one's true self,"
declared one preacher.[35] And underlying this is the same belief about
the necessity of the self's openness that characterizes contemporary
psychology. That is, we all have the capacities for deep, meaningful
relations with others, but in order to realize these relations we must give
expression to our feelings even as we must listen respectfully to others
who bare their feelings. "Self-knowledge and self-disclosure," Witten
says, "are essential for an intimate relationship, these sermons suggest,
even though self-disclosure places people at risk of embarrassment and

33. Ibid., 98.
34. Ibid., 107.
35. Ibid., 110.

attributions of weakness."[36] However, this self-revelation is so expressive of what we are innately as human beings that it carries with it a blueprint of what we were originally in the Garden of Eden. The feelings therefore become a kind of inner voice that tells us who we are. That we are often not "in touch" with our feelings provides the most pervasive understanding of sin in these sermons. As the title to Witten's book suggests, this is, indeed, the "secular message in American Protestantism," even as it is also a new, modern mysticism.

The biblical teaching about sin is thus domesticated to accommodate secular notions about the self. These are widespread in the Church today, mediated through safe Christian channels such as the booming book and video market, as well as being absorbed from the workplace, movies, and television. This teaching is domesticated to meet the cultural needs for tolerance. In most cases, this seems to happen intuitively and apparently with very few intentions of bypassing what Scripture actually says. The world in which the cultural demand of tolerance is heard is one in which all values are privatized. People can believe what they want and, within the law, do what they want, but it becomes intolerable if they imagine that what they believe includes standards of belief and morality that are applicable to others. Today, that is the unforgivable sin. It is the blasphemy against the (secular) spirit.

What we think of the self and what we think about God are closely related. And what the study of these sermons showed is what we see everywhere else. As the moral nature of the self is lost, the understanding of God's holiness as part of his transcendence is also lost. So it was in these sermons. As God's moral nature faded from human view, so the truth of his relatedness grew in size, transcendence vanished, and immanence loomed large. The result is that in 82 percent of the sermons "God is portrayed exclusively or predominantly in terms of the positive functions he serves for men and women."[37] Principally these are that he relieves negative feelings like anxiety and doubt. That is the point in believing, and this is principally what God is thought to offer believers. Because this work of calming our jangled nerves can only be explained by his exceptional generosity and caring, many of these sermons came to focus on God's feelings. His feelings as a father and a sufferer were at the core of the sermonic treatments, rather than his moral character. The majestic vision of God that we see in Calvin and Luther, Witten concludes, has been softened for modern purposes in

36. Ibid., 112.
37. Ibid., 35.

American Protestantism. God is now so much more mellow than he used to be, and the focus of our interest in him centers in the relief he can provide for our frayed private lives by placing us in a stable family (the Church), relieving our decisions of some of their uncertainties, and offsetting our guilt and self-doubt by his reassurances.

This is, of course, enormously appealing to modern congregations, because they are overwhelmingly preoccupied with their own internal worlds. What fills our minds today are not the matters with which Augustine, Luther, Owen, and Brainerd were so engaged. In a therapeutic world such as ours, what has our attention, and often our money, is how to cope with our wayward personalities, with anxiety, self-doubt, uncertainty, negotiating the stages of life, as well as its calamities like job losses, infidelities, broken marriages, and college tuition. These are the things around which our psychological energies are focused, because these are intensely real to us. To the people who lived in a morally understood world before the onslaught of modernity, our preoccupations would have been remote, even as theirs are to us. For them, what was intensely real was what was true and right; for so many today, what is intensely real is what offers inner relief.

If the mechanism of accommodating Christian faith to modernity is what Witten has described, then it takes no great ingenuity to see that Christian faith of this kind is going to succeed and fail at the same time, and quite quickly. It will succeed for a while in the churches that have been able to adapt to their modern clientele. It will begin to fail, however, in these same churches because it has stripped itself of answers to modern life by reducing itself to being an echo of that modern life. It will be too late for the Pied Pipers of these "new paradigm" churches and their followers when reality comes crashing in, as it surely will. The modern world is so painful, so costly, so brutal to life that mimicking its rhythms, rather than providing an alternative to them, will soon be seen to be the hollow charade, the empty mirage, that it is. The happy campers in modernity's playground are blithely unaware that this is a dangerous neighborhood. It is this theme that I must now begin to explore in the following chapters.

CHAPTER II

The Playground of Desire

Virtue is a gift of the gods. Unfortunately, there are no gods.

H. L. Hix

Rebels and Restrainers

What is striking about our culture today is that its corruption is not simply at the edges. It is not simply found among the cultured elite, the New Class standing at the gates of our national institutions to bar entry, if possible, to those whose views are not left of center. It is not simply found among postmodern academics who are bent upon overturning all meaning and moral principle, or among vicious street gangs, or among rappers who spew forth obscenities and violence, or among the venders of pornography, or in venal politicians, or in the acrimonious and fractious way in which we have sometimes conducted our public business. What is striking is that this corruption is ubiquitous. It is not located in this or that pocket of depravity but is spread like a dense fog throughout society. It is even spread by those who are safe, ordinary, dull, and dim-witted, and not only by the incendiary and bellicose, the subversive and antisocial. Supreme Court nominee Robert Bork, who at times seems exasperated with contemporary society, is nevertheless correct when he says that "the traditional virtues of this culture are being lost, its vices multiplied, its values degraded — in short, the culture itself is unraveling."[1] The overwhelm-

---

1. Robert H. Bork, "The Hard Truth About America," *The Christian Activist* 7

ing majority of Americans believe that our society is slipping ever deeper into a "moral decline." This is no longer a case that has to be argued. It is the place from which our conversation starts.

Many people have the sense that the moral eclipse we are experiencing is somewhat new. The "good old days," they recognize, may become idealized with the passage of time, but they nevertheless think that, from a moral angle, the past must have been better. They have the sense that we are slipping away from a world that was more wholesome than ours is. What probably accounts for this is not a particularly detailed knowledge of the past, which would make such a comparison possible, but the eerie sense, within our own memory, of a significant disintegration of the moral fabric of life as we have known it. Knowing this, we infer that periods of the past must have been much more elevated than our own.

This, of course, is a questionable conclusion. What does seem to be the case, however, is that often, as periods succeed each other, some of what takes place is driven by reaction. The Apollonian impulse is often followed by the Dionysian. An age in which the moral boundaries are moved ever outwards is eventually overtaken by an age in which the boundaries are duly contracted in an effort to restore life. In broad and rather general terms, this seems to have happened as the eighteenth century, an age of significant boundary expansion, was followed by the nineteenth, in which the attempt was made to draw the boundaries much tighter, and this has been followed by the twentieth, in which the boundaries are now again expanding. Our sense of this movement fuels the belief, for many, that we are living in a time of dangerous moral decline, though for others, like Camille Paglia, this signals the happy conquest of the West by the pagan spirit. It is worth pondering this sequence of the centuries briefly.

The picture that may come to mind of the eighteenth century, with women in frills curtsying and men in their sartorial finery bowing, actually conceals the harsh and crude realities of that time, as historian James Collier has noted.[2] Hygiene was, to say the least, rudimentary.

(October 1995), 1. Bork's *Slouching Towards Gomorrah: Modern Liberalism and American Decline* (New York: HarperCollins, 1996) develops this theme more extensively and makes many acute observations about American life. Whether the decline Bork laments is simply the consequence of liberalism remains questionable. Bork has accurately perceived the symptoms of cultural decline, but for a cause sufficient to explain this he needs to be able to see that the liberalism he blames is simply one small strand in the environment that modernity has spawned.

2. James Lincoln Collier, *The Rise of Selfishness in America* (New York: Oxford University Press, 1991), 3-7.

Bathing was infrequent. The same clothes were worn week after week. Houses were frequently surrounded by decomposing litter and piles of manure whose stench was considerable. Human waste was often discarded carelessly in the streets without regard for pedestrians. Churches were unheated, and it was not unknown for dogs, cats, chickens, and pigs to wander through the sanctuary during worship and for bats to flit through the rafters.

This was the Age of Enlightenment. Timothy Dwight, who became president of Yale in 1805, became much alarmed by what had taken place. The "infidelity" that had overtaken the land, one whose spirit combined religious hostility and moral laxity, was driven by three motives, he claimed: "opposition to Christianity; devotion to sin and lust; and a pompous profession of love and Liberty"[3] and elsewhere he said that this outlook posed "as much evil to mankind as any doctrines which can be proposed."[4] The Church had cause to be alarmed. By the end of the eighteenth century, 90 percent of Americans had never darkened the door of a church. The Church as a whole was in profound decline. The Puritan impulse had been lost, only to be recovered somewhat in the Great Awakening in the early part of the century, and then it was to be lost in the latter part of that century. It was not until 1792, in fact, that the Second Great Awakening began in the Connecticut river valley. These new revivals, one person wrote later, "blessed not only New England, but the whole of our country as it then was."[5] And early in the nineteenth century, Nathaniel William Taylor, the Yale theologian, in an address to the Connecticut Legislature, said of these revivals that in their "power and extent, there is nothing to be compared, in any other portion of Christendom."[6] That judgment might have involved a little hyperbole, but the revival was, nevertheless, significant.

The eighteenth century saw a decline not only in church going and religious understanding, but also in the family. Lyman Beecher, the Connecticut churchman, observed that the root cause of the problem was the Enlightenment's belief, as he put it, that "human nature is too

3. Timothy Dwight, *A Discourse on Some Events of the Last Century, Delivered in the Brick Church in New Haven, on Wednesday, January 7, 1801* (New Haven: Ezra Read, 1801), 21.

4. Timothy Dwight, *Sermons* (2 vols.; New Haven: Hezekiah Howe, 1828), 1:334.

5. Edward Packard, *Sermons and Addresses, Commemorative of the Seventy-Fifth Anniversary of the Second Congregational Church, Dorchester* (Boston: F. Wood, 1883), 24.

6. Nathaniel William Taylor, *A Sermon Addressed to the Legislature of the State of Connecticut at the Annual Election in Hartford, May 7, 1823* (Hartford: A. H. Maltby, 1823), 22.

good to be made better by discipline,"[7] and the result was that children were "insubordinate and are not being instructed."[8] These were, of course, the sentiments of many in the Church who lamented the hostile intellectual climate and the growing debauchery in society which had taken such a toll on the family.

Along with the Enlightenment came many of the societal ills by which we are again surrounded today. At the beginning of the eighteenth century, for example, premarital pregnancy was at 10 percent, but by the end of the century it had risen to 30 percent. There was significant drunkenness during this time, too. The crusades in the nineteenth century against alcohol, which were to triumph in Prohibition in our own century, may seem heavy-handed in retrospect, but it is worth noting that the average person in the eighteenth century consumed almost exactly twice as much alcohol as does his or her counterpart today. The truth is, that along with the "enlightenment" of life in the eighteenth century there also went a considerable coarsening of life. And when the Revolution opened the doors of political freedom, the way was also opened for every other kind of freedom as well, including that of being emancipated from all moral principle.

During the second half of last century, the associations with British Victorianism were considerable. In our own time it has become fashionable to deride this period. The moral dissolution that the Enlightenment had produced, however, had been reined in a little by the end of last century. Both in Britain and in America a new resolve became evident that life should become more ordered and disciplined, that moral conventions needed to be honored, and that the family needed to be respected. Manners and morals changed, and respectability became a desirable thing. This expressed itself in many ways, such as a concern for maintaining a good reputation, honoring conventions of speech and behavior that embodied the new cultural ideal of upright living, and dressing more modestly. These changes, of course, also gave Victorianism a bad name, because the underlying realities were often at odds with the public performance of rectitude. Victorians fell short of their ideals, and hypocrisy might have been their besetting sin. What needs to be judged, however, is whether it is worse to fall short of moral ideals than to have none that can be violated. If that age was cursed

7. Lyman Beecher, *A Reformation of Morals, Practical and Indispensable: A Sermon Delivered at New Haven on the Evening of October 27, 1812* (Andover: Flagg and Gould, 1814), 15.

8. Ibid., 2.

with the scourge of acting with bad faith, this might still be judged preferable to our situation today, in which hypocrisy is no longer necessary given the unassailable triumph, and overwhelming acceptance, of vulgarity in our culture and of the "right" to one's personal "lifestyle."

The reversal in manners and morals of that period cut across life in its entirety. Despite the massive influx of immigrants in the last century, the wrenching social changes as industrialization took root, and the gathering momentum of urbanization, crime rates (as seen in cities and regions) actually appear to have declined very significantly as we move from one end of the century to the other. Family life, though under siege because of these changes,[9] was nevertheless treated more solicitously. Premarital sex was frowned upon. As a result, by 1920 illegitimacy had fallen to 3 percent and even in 1960, at the inauguration of the so-called sexual revolution, it only stood at 5 percent.[10] Despite the most ambitious provision of sex education programs in our history — and maybe because of them — and in spite of unfettered access to contraceptives, illegitimacy has increased 400 percent since 1960.[11] In 1990, in the worst pocket of illegitimacy in our society, 65.2 percent of Black children were born to unmarried mothers. Once the illegitimacy rate rises above 26 percent, Charles Murray estimates, poverty becomes endemic and virtually irreversible. This is exactly the point at which White America has now arrived, and the specter of hopelessness, violence, and decay which so many of our inner cities present may portend much wider decay in the society as a whole. Furthermore, between 1960 and 1993, the divorce rate increased 200 percent with the consequence that less than 60 percent of children live with both of their biological parents.[12] And since *Roe v. Wade* legalized abortion in 1973, an estimated 28 million unborn children have lost their lives, something which was virtually unknown in the last century or its predecessor.

9. These tensions are skillfully explored in Christopher Lasch, *Haven in a Heartless World: The Family Besieged* (New York: Basic Books, 1979). Stephanie Coontz, however, is correct in arguing that the "crisis of the family," which became so evident a century later, and which "became the key to explaining the paradox of poverty amid plenty, alienation in the midst of abundance" is not the only explanation of our current social disintegration. Indeed, it is as much a reflection of that disintegration as a cause. See her *The Way We Never Were: American Families and the Nostalgia Trip* (New York: Basic Books, 1992), 256.

10. Gertrude Himmelfarb, *The De-moralization of Society: From Victorian Virtues to Modern Values* (New York: Alfred A. Knopf, 1995), 223.

11. William J. Bennett, *The Index of Leading Cultural Indicators* (Washington: The Heritage Foundation, 1993), 10.

12. Ibid., 23.

National statistics on crime were calculated for the first time only in 1960 in America, and they show the astonishing breakdown in the social order that has taken place since then. Between 1960 and 1993, the population increased by 41 percent, but violent crime rose by 560 percent.[13] The U.S. Department of Justice in 1987 projected that eight out of ten people will be the victims of violent crime at least once in their lives. The most active incubator for this violence is in the 10 to 17 age group, where the rate of the perpetration of violent crime has soared 400 percent since 1960. Although crime rates enjoyed an unexpected reversal in 1996 and 1997, the overall picture does not bode well for our future. Since 1960, the rate of teen suicide has risen more than 200 percent, making it the third leading cause of death among our young people.[14]

Crime rates have been rising during this time throughout the industrialized West. This is not simply an American phenomenon. The figures just cited are not evidence that Americans are uniquely bad but, rather, that Americans are typically modern. What modernization has done has been to spawn moral relativism, to break down the cultural restraints that had provided some resistance to lawless behavior, and to enlarge greatly the powers for doing mischief. Modern technology, social scientist James Wilson has noted, has enabled people "to commit crimes over a much wider territory, to reach more victims, and to take more lethal actions than once was the case."[15]

The story these statistics tell, however, concerns only what is most graphic. Just as telling, and perhaps of more interest, are those that measure more private matters, such as our moral intentions, matters which may not always be matters of law at all.

Americans today, say researchers James Patterson and Peter Kim, "stand alone in a way unknown to any previous generation."[16] They are alone, not least, because they are without any objective moral compass. "The religious figures and Scriptures that gave us rules for so many centuries, the political system which gave us laws, all have lost their

13. Ibid., 3.

14. Ibid., 13. On the connections between crime and modernization see James Q. Wilson, "Incivility and Crime: The Role of Moral Habituation," in *The Content of America's Character: Recovering Civic Virtue*, ed. Don E. Eberly (New York: Madison Books, 1995), 63-78.

15. James Q. Wilson, *The Moral Sense* (New York: Free Press, 1993), 10-11.

16. James Patterson and Peter Kim, *The Day America Told the Truth: What People Really Believe about Everything That Matters* (New York: Prentice Hall, 1991), 27.

meaning in our moral imagination."[17] While the great majority of Americans believe that they actually keep the Ten Commandments, only 13 percent think that each of these commandments has moral validity. It is no surprise to learn that 74 percent say that they will steal without compunction; 64 percent say that they will lie if there is an advantage to be had in doing so; 53 percent say that, given a chance, they will commit adultery; 41 percent say that they intend to use recreational drugs; and 30 percent say that they will cheat on their taxes. What may be the clearest indicator of the disappearance of a moral texture to society is the loss of guilt and embarrassment over moral lapses. While 86 percent admit to lying regularly to their parents, 75 percent to a friend, 73 percent to a sibling, and 73 percent to a lover, only 11 percent cited lying as having produced a serious level of guilt or embarrassment. While 74 percent will steal without compunction, only 9 percent register any moral disquiet. While pornography has blossomed into a 4 billion dollar industry that accounts for a quarter of all the videos rented in shops, seen in the thriving hotel business or on cable, only 2 percent experience guilt about watching.[18] And, not surprisingly, at the center of this slide into license and moral relativism is the disappearance of God. Only 17 percent define sin as a violation of God's will.

The moral terrain that was once dominated by a set of beliefs and virtues to which wide public assent was given is now breaking up. The television programs of the 1950s and 1960s, such as *Ozzie and Harriet, Leave It to Beaver,* or *Father Knows Best,* were successful in part because in their very moralizing they were keying in on a widely shared moral consensus. This consensus, admittedly, was not entirely benign. It was often discriminatory against women and minorities, and it had an authoritarian air about it. Few people would have questioned their "doctor's orders" or sought a second opinion. And fathers expected to be obeyed, not least because they "knew best." In the 1960s all of this was swept aside, the good along with the bad. The "waning of traditional values," sociologist Amitai Etzioni says, "was not followed by a solid affirmation of new values; often nothing filled the empty spaces that were left when we razed existing institutions." The result, he adds somewhat ruefully, is that today we have "rampant moral confusion and social anarchy."[19] The causes of this sea change are, however, quite complex.

17. Ibid.

18. Ibid., 48, 57.

19. Amitai Etzioni, *The Spirit of Community: The Reinvention of American Society* (New York: Simon and Schuster, 1993), 24.

There is no question that we are now a more diverse people than we once were. In 1990, the census discovered in America 300 races, 600 Indian tribes, and 70 different Hispanic groups. As our social diversity has expanded, our national unity has been strained,[20] but the waves of immigration this century are hardly at the center of this problem.

The problem is our secularization. This has decimated any moral consensus that once was present. Today, not only is the public square stripped of divine meaning but so, too, is human consciousness. Amidst all of the abundance and the technological marvels of our time, what is true and what is right have lost their hold upon our society. They have lost their saliency, their capacity to shape life. Today, our moral center is gone. It is not merely that secularization has marginalized God, relegating him to the outer edges of our public life from whence he becomes entirely irrelevant, but we have also lost our understanding of ourselves as moral beings. In our *private* universe, as in that which is public, there is no center.

At the most obvious level this is suggested by the fact that 67 percent of Americans do not believe in moral absolutes — that is, in moral norms that are enduring and applicable to all people in all places and all times — and 70 percent do not believe in truth that is similarly absolute.[21] That is, they do not believe in absolutes that are enduring because they reflect unchanging, ultimate reality. However, the ethic of tolerance that is substituted can sometimes function as absolutely as what it is replacing. Tolerance can be highly intolerant of those who do not embrace its relativism, even as liberal culture can be exceedingly illiberal in regard to conservative views.

The inability or refusal, on the part of a majority of Americans, to allow any transcendent reality to prescribe moral norms for life means, then, that running through our society is a San Andreas fault line. It may be reflected at the level of conflicting values, but it also

---

20. The relationship between America's central core values and its more recent diversity is explored in Arthur A. Schlesinger's *The Disuniting of America: Reflections on a Multicultural Society* (New York: W. W. Norton, 1993).

21. This double rejection of absolute morality and absolute truth is not without significance, since the Bible also links these two matters. Truth is both the opposite of what is intellectually false and of what is morally defiled; intellectually, light is truth in contrast to error; morally, light is what is pure in contrast to what is evil. This yoking of belief and behavior, what is true and what is right, in the biblical understanding of truth is perhaps nowhere more succinctly stated than in John's words: "If we claim to have fellowship with him [God] yet walk in [moral] darkness we lie and do not live by the truth" (1 John 1:6). See also John 1:4, 5, 9; 3:19-21; 7:18; 8:12; 12:35, 36, 40; Eph. 4:25; 1 John 2:8-11, 27.

involves competing worldviews.[22] And since the great majority of Americans do not believe in absolutes, Jerry Falwell was guilty of considerable chutzpah in calling his movement the Moral Majority. Traditional Christians of all kinds are a cognitive minority in modern America, and they appear to be such in the Church as well.

As we look back over our own century, what we see is not only the reaction against the moral culture of the past but such profound ignorance of, and disregard for, moral life that we seem bent on exceeding the debauchery of the eighteenth century. However, this quest for emancipation, which may seem unarguable and may be irresistible, is also unsustainable by our society.

Culture — the significance that we attach to the events of everyday life — functions in our world like grammar does in a language. We are usually unaware of the rules that govern our language. This is true, of course, of those who never learned the rules very well in the first place, but it is also true of those for whom they are now second nature. In the same way, much of our behavior in the past, much of the way in which we made our judgments about life, was framed and explained by cultural rules, even though they may have been registering on us subconsciously. These same rules were also operating widely in the society. In fact, it was this sense of culture — this sense of the presence of self-evident rules about how life should be conducted — that made much of our behavior almost automatic, because these cultural rules provided markers against what is illicit and lent plausibility to what is right. Culture is not a means of special revelation but a vehicle of general revelation, and if this revelation is not suppressed it does sound both the Yes and No to our behavior, for it can serve as our collective conscience.

Today, however, traditional, consensual culture is dying. Whether one looks at speech, at sexual mores, at what is taken to be "normal" for late twentieth-century people, the former rules have been dismantled. As the inherited meanings die, each situation becomes one for which there is no precedent and for which there are no external norms. We become completely autonomous. Then, as life is recast in psychological form, the only reality remaining is the self, which is then

---

22. Perhaps the principal contribution of James Davison Hunter's *Culture Wars: The Struggle to Define America* (New York: Basic Books, 1990) is that he demonstrated that two competing worldviews are at stake in contemporary ethical debates. In one worldview, inhabited by conservative Jews, Catholics, and Protestants, there are absolute values. In the other, inhabited by liberal Jews, Catholics, Protestants, and secularists, there are not.

pitted against society in a damaging dynamic that will be explored shortly.

The pertinent question to ask, then, is how, in the years between 1910 and 1970, the United States could, as Collier puts it, "turn from a social code in which self-restraint was a cardinal virtue to one in which self-gratification is a central idea."[23] Our sense that self-gratification is a right stands at the heart of this moral change. The internal ethic of the self — what is right for *me* — has become the means by which all external standards, external controls, and external expectations are remitted.[24]

It is not possible to follow out this story historically, showing step by step how we have replaced the moral world in which self-restraint was a virtue by one in which the new virtue is self-gratification. What I do need to do, though, is to try to illumine the dialectic now at work that places the breakdown in our culture in an uneasy relationship to our social structures.

Obeying the Unenforceable

The cultural accord that has shaped our past was actually a matter of tough and deliberate virtue. This virtue lay in our simple insistence

23. Collier, *The Rise of Selfishness in America*, 4.

24. At an academic level, this produces what Alisdair MacIntyre has called the ethic of "emotivism." This ethic is part of a cultural ethos in which there is no rational way to secure agreement on ethical matters. Emotivism enlarges on this failure by claiming that "every attempt, whether past or present, to provide a rational justification for an objective morality has in fact failed" (MacIntyre, *After Virtue*, 19). The bygone conceptual framework is considered fraudulent, and without the existence of any other warrant for what is held to be ethical, what one feels must suffice. In the end, public life and private life each come to operate by a different "moral calculus." Thus in many university contexts, issues are decided not by reason but by passion. The principal critiques of MacIntyre's *After Virtue*, and even more his *Whose Justice? Which Rationality?* have not disputed his description of the loss of moral language but whether secular nihilism can, in fact, be reversed by appealing to Aristotle. For a theological reflection on MacIntyre's philosophy, see John Milbank, *Theology and Social Theory: Beyond Secular Reason* (Oxford: Blackwell, 1990), 326-79. This same case for saying that ethical discourse has collapsed has also been made with uncommon precision by G. E. M. Anscombe. She argues that the field of moral philosophy should be abandoned because it is no longer possible to argue for what is morally right and wrong and therefore the whole discussion of differences in ethical positions from the past is now irrelevant. See "Modern Moral Philosophy," in *Ethics*, ed. Judith J. Thomson and Gerald Dworkin (Cambridge: Massachusetts Institute of Technology Press, 1968), 186-210.

among ourselves that we had to preserve three domains in society. Lying between law on the one side, and freedom on the other, would be a middle territory for the cultivation of character and the affirmation of truth, one which would be as vital to the preservation of our society as law and freedom are. This accord, to be sure, now seems quite quaint following the postmodern assault on all virtue and meaning, but the truth is that unless it can be recovered our society will stand in greater and greater jeopardy.

Today we are experiencing the competition between law and freedom to occupy this middle territory, which has been vacated. The result is that the fires of license are stoked constantly by our growing moral relativism and by our individualism, but at the same time they have to be constantly doused lest they engulf our society. We therefore have to resort to law and governmental regulation to contain what we have unleashed. We live precariously on the knife-edge between chaos and control. What was once an open space between law and freedom, one governed by character and truth, is now deserted, so law must now do what character has abandoned. That seems to be the best way to understand many of the cultural strains, the turmoil and disarray, that mark our time.

Of course every society needs laws and the weight of the judicial system to enforce those laws. In every society there are flagrant violators who rob, swindle, beat, and massacre, and society acts by a rather simple calculus. It acts against the violator to issue just deserts, to protect itself from being ravaged further, and perhaps to attempt reforming the wrong-doer.

Along with establishing the right of law, the Constitution also secures a large role for freedom in our society. It secures for its citizenry freedom from unwarranted intrusion by the state into both private and public life. The Constitution is less clear about what we are free *for* than what we are free *from*, but that itself may be part of its genius. It is because we are free from state tyranny that originality and creativity and, indeed, Christian believing have all been able to flourish in America.

Lying between law and freedom, however, has always been this third domain. It is the domain of character, the practice of private virtue, such as honesty, decency, the telling of truth, and all the other kinds of moral obligation. It is the domain of public virtue, such as civic duty, social responsibility, philanthropy, the articulation of great ideals and good policies, all of those things which might be encompassed in Paul's statement that the Gentiles, "who have not the law do by nature what the law requires" (Rom. 2:14). This third domain is what must

regulate life in the absence of legal coercion and governmental regulation. It is where law and restraint are *self*-imposed. The demands come
from within, not from without. In this area we find what John Silber,
the former president of Boston University, has called "obedience to the
unenforceable." This was the language of an English jurist earlier in
this century, John Fletcher Moulton, who went on to say that the "real
greatness of a nation, its true civilization, is measured by the extent of
this land of obedience to the unenforceable. It measures the extent to
which the nation trusts its citizens, and its area testifies to the way they
behave in response to that trust."[25]

Today, this middle territory is shrinking daily just when our understanding of ourselves as moral beings collapses, and it is being
co-opted by the two domains that lie on each side of it. Law must now
do what church, family, character, belief, and even cultural expectations
once did by way of instructing and restraining human nature. What is
going to happen, then, if we keep stoking the fires of our rampant,
amoral individualism and have to keep dousing those fires with greater
and greater recourse to litigation and regulation? Our society is going
to become a platform on which more and more collisions occur. It is
going to be host to more and more thwarted, frustrated, and impeded
desires. The stage is being set for endless conflicts. How will all of this
be resolved? Should we expect greater chaos or greater control in the
future? The answer, of course, depends on how our freedom, now
channeled through our individualism, and how our legal system, established by the Constitution, choreograph their ballet. But we can say
with certainty that this is not the way things were meant to be. In the
end, the whole of our society will pay the cost for this indulgence.
Indeed, it is already paying that cost.

We are caught, then, in the crossfire of two impulses, each of which
threatens to dominate all of life. From the one side arises the impulse
to eliminate moral boundaries at any point where they might conflict
with our desires for self-gratification or self-realization; from the other
side, there arises the counter impulse to restrain this license if only for
the safety of society. Thus it is that the clash between freedom, as we
now understand this, and law also becomes the clash between the
individual and society. It is a contest in which the self stands in one

---

25. John Silber, "Obedience to the Unenforceable" (unpublished address,
Boston University, 1995), 2. Silber's brief discussion of the three domains is, for my
purposes here, more helpful than the typical threefold division of private, public,
and voluntary associations.

corner, glowering across the ring, and society stands in the other corner, looking no less determined. We must now look, then, a little more closely at these forces in contention.

Bowling Alone

As they reflect on the results of their survey of American attitudes in the 1990s, Patterson and Kim conclude that we "are the law unto ourselves." We have made "ourselves the authority over church and God," and we have made "ourselves the authority over laws and the police."[26] This set of attitudes is nicely summed up by the Washington lawyer who said: "To be perfectly honest, some laws seem to apply to me, some I disregard. Some tenets of the Catholic Church add up, some are absurd, or even insulting. I don't need the Pope, the press, or some lowly cop to tell me how to live my life."[27] This statement reflects how the internal ethic of the self becomes the means by which the control of all external authorities, from God to the state, is remitted.

The enthronement of the self is the calling card that modernity has left everywhere, not simply in America. It was discovered in Europe by the network of social scientists, cultural analysts, theologians, and philosophers who teamed up to produce *The European Values Study* in 1990.[28] What they discovered was that with the single exception of Norway, people in all European countries, including those who are formally Catholic, have substantially abandoned a traditional moral structure and replaced it by one centered on "autonomy" and "self-expression." They, too, have adopted the ethic of the self. This transformation is apparently the look of the future and is especially pronounced among those under 35 who, these researchers say, inhabit a different "cultural universe" from those over 50. Only 55 percent of Europeans, as a result, say that they believe in sin understood as the

26. Patterson and Kim, *The Day America Told the Truth*, 27.
27. Ibid.
28. In this 1990 study, 29 countries were surveyed with a representative sampling of at least 1000 people in the major countries. The tool used contained 444 questions, and each respondent was also interviewed for about one hour. The purpose of this study was to discover whether Europeans share common values, to what extent those beliefs are still Christian, whether an alternative to Christianity is emerging, and what the implications might be for European unity. For a further analysis of these themes as they relate to Britain, see Digby Anderson, ed., *The Loss of Virtue: Moral Confusion and Social Disorder in Britain and America* (London: Social Affairs Unit, 1992).

violation of an objective moral norm. What is true in Europe is true wherever modernity has taken root. Everywhere, it remakes life in such a way that the past is stripped away, place loses its significance, community loses its hold, objective moral norms vanish, and what remains is simply the self. It is in the self that substitute moral meaning has to be reconstructed. In America, however, this current of modernity also coalesces with the deep undercurrents of individualism that have always been here.

Individualism, however, has been present in different ways in America's past. Sociologist Robert Bellah and his colleagues speak of four different strains: biblical, civic, utilitarian, and expressive.[29] What they have in common is, first, the belief in the dignity and worth of the individual and, second, the belief that the individual is more important than society. That being so, anything "that would violate our right to think for ourselves, judge for ourselves, make our own decisions, live our lives as we see fit, is not only morally wrong," they say, but "sacrilegious."[30] These forms of individualism differ from each other because they differ in how they work out these central ideas. It is with expressive individualism, however, that Bellah's book is much concerned, for, as the authors see it, this is now the dominant form of individualism in America, and they are alarmed about the social consequences.

Expressive individualism, which grew out of the Romanticism of the late eighteenth century and today has an especial affinity with our therapeutic culture, assumes that all people have a unique core of intuitions and feelings within them that is then coupled with the understanding that they have the inherent right to pursue and express these intuitions and feelings. This often expresses itself as a desire for refuge from the harsh competition produced by capitalism. Where this happens, expressive individualists seek to be free from all constraints and, in consumption and leisure, find solace for the wounds the soul absorbed at the workplace. These are the psychological compensations for the brutalities of the work week and, as I shall argue in the next chapter, when we know who the healers are we know what the sickness is from which deliverance is being sought. Our healers today, who live

29. Robert Bellah et al., *Habits of the Heart: Individualism and Commitment in American Life* (New York: Harper and Row, 1985), 142. Bellah himself traverses some of this territory in briefer scope in his "The Quest for the Self: Individualism, Morality, Politics, in *Interpretive Social Science: A Second Look* (Berkeley: University of California Press, 1987), 365-83.

30. Bellah et al., *Habits of the Heart,* 142.

on the conquest of our society by this type of individualism, are our psychotherapists and our advertisers. Together, they are offering a secular version of regeneration for those in pursuit of the renewal of the self.

Expressive individualism, then, is driven by a deep sense of entitlement to being left alone, to live in a way that is emancipated from the demands and expectations of others, to being able to fashion its own life in the way it wants to, to being able to develop its own values and beliefs in its own way, to resist all authority. To be free in these ways, many have come to think, is indispensable to being a true individual. And much has happened to this ideal from the time last century when Tocqueville, the French observer who visited America, first described it.[31]

Last century's individualism was one in which personal responsibility played a large role. It was the kind in which people thought for themselves, provided for themselves, owed nothing, and usually worked out their independence within a community, loosely defined though some of these were. This produced the kind of person who, in the language of the Harvard scholar, David Riesman, was "inner-directed." That is, this person was guided by an internal gyroscope of character and belief and, as a result, saw it as a virtue to have clear goals, to work hard, to live by ethical principle. This person probably admired those who had taken lonely stands and triumphed over adversity by inner fortitude, because he or she thought that this was what life was really about. This, says Riesman, is the kind of person who would rather be right than be president.

Today's individualist, by contrast, would rather be president than be right. It is not character that defines the way that expressive individualism functions today, but emancipation from values, from community, and from the past in order to be oneself, to seek one's own gain. This attitude is, in consequence, unprincipled in a traditional sense, for its central and only principle is the self. "The freedom of our day," declared a Harvard valedictorian, "is the freedom to devote ourselves to any values we please, on the mere condition that we do not believe them to be true."[32]

31. Alexis de Tocqueville, *Democracy in America*, ed. J. P. Mayer, trans. George Lawrence (Garden City, N.Y.: Doubleday, 1969).

32. Robert Bellah, *The Good Society* (New York: Alfred A. Knopf, 1991), 44. Today, it is not ideology that poses the greatest danger to America but what former National Security Adviser Zbigniew Brzezinski calls "permissive cornucopia." His argument is that following the spectacular failure of totalitarianism in the twentieth

It is this attitude, many believe, that is eating away at civic virtue, about which there is a lively debate today.[33] Robert Putman, the Harvard professor of government, has given new visibility to the discussion with a small and seemingly inconsequential essay.[34] In his studies in Italy,[35] he has seen how vital civic virtue is to a nation's prosperity, a point more recently argued by Francis Fukuyama under the language of "trust."[36] Business, Fukuyama argues, operates at less cost when there is plenty of "spontaneous sociability" in the workplace, because this helps to forge links between people in the interest of the enterprise. It becomes a form of capital, and those businesses that are without it suffer. The discussion on civic virtue goes far beyond this, however.

---

century, and the rise of democracy worldwide, the United States is now the world's leader, but whether it will be able to discharge its responsibilities has become doubtful because of its rotting fabric. He sees a society "in which the progressive decline in the centrality of moral criteria is matched by heightened preoccupation with material and sensual gratification" (Zbigniew Brzezinski, *Out of Control: Global Turmoil on the Eve of the Twenty-First Century* [New York: Charles Scribner's Sons, 1993], 65). Along a slightly different line, Tom Englehardt explores the disillusionment that has come upon America as it struggles to find meaning in the world now that the old "story" — the contest between the good West and the evil Marxist world — has faded away. See his *The End of Victory Culture: Cold War America and the Disillusioning of a Generation* (New York: Basic Books, 1995).

The inherent lawlessness of American society, however, has given our advertisers a field day. The theme of transgressing boundaries has become a staple. John Leo points out that the early pioneers were Nike's slogan, "Just Do It!" (in other words, don't think about it and don't let anything stand in the way of your doing it) and Burger King's "Sometimes, you gotta break the rules." The imitators have been numerous. Bacardi Black Rum, which advertises itself as "the taste of the night," goes on to say, "Some people embrace the night because rules of the day do not apply." Easy Spirit shoes even latched onto this theme, promising a shoe that "conforms to your foot so you don't have to conform to anything." Ralph Lauren's Safari celebrates "living without boundaries." Even staid and reliable Merrill Lynch declares that "Your world should know no boundaries." And Nieman Marcus encourages its customers to relax because there are "No rules here." John Leo, "Decadence, The Corporate Way," *U.S. News and World Report* (August 28–September 4, 1995), 31.

33. On the European parallels to this discussion, see Jean L. Cohen and Andrew Arato, *Civil Society and Political Theory* (Cambridge: Massachusetts Institute of Technology Press, 1995), 29-82.

34. Robert D. Putnam, "Bowling Alone: America's Declining Social Capital," *Journal of Democracy* 6 (January 1995), 65-78.

35. Robert D. Putnam, *Democracy and the Civic Community: Tradition and Change in an Italian Experiment* (Princeton: Princeton University Press, 1992); and *Making Democracy Work: Civic Traditions in Modern Italy* (Princeton: Princeton University Press, 1994).

36. Francis Fukuyama, *Trust: The Social Virtues and the Creation of Prosperity* (New York: Free Press, 1995).

Civic virtue is the ability to make working alliances in small groups for the common good. There are large areas in our public life where this virtue, not motivated by profit and self-interest, is indispensable. What Putnam has argued, somewhat mistakenly, is that we are now living in a time when voluntary associations, from church to the Boy Scouts, to the League of Women Voters, are in decline.[37] Some of his figures and assertions have been contested, but there can be no question that he has put his finger on a vital aspect in any healthy society and one that, in some ways, is in decline in America. He speculates that television, by privatizing leisure, has had much to do with the disappearance of the public forum for virtue. Undoubtedly this is part of the explanation, but we cannot overlook the way in which our expressive individualism melts the bonds between people, erodes the sense of responsibility for society, and makes us a law unto ourselves. Television may be a villain, but it is far from being alone in the villainy evident today.

This kind of individualism also inadvertently achieves something else: it reduces life to what is petty and paltry. In its presence great causes die, as do heroes. The reason for this, philosopher John Taylor has argued, is that the freedoms we cherish — choosing the life we want and doing what we want — are all pursued in a secularized world, "a flattened world, where the horizons of meaning become fainter."[38] Gone is the medieval Great Chain of Being, or even an understanding of creation in which there is something larger and more pressing than our private desires. What remains, the materials out of which we must now fashion meaning, are simply the acts of choosing. "This sets up a vicious circle that heads us towards a point where our major remaining value is choice itself."[39] Thus our preoccupations, in the absence of any overarching structures of meaning, concern the small, the petty, the trivial, and not the great, the eternal, and the enduring. In his own way, Søren Kierkegaard saw this coming. He mourned the loss of passion in believing in the Church, but even he could not have foreseen the extent to which this has transformed both Church and society today.

The autonomy to devise our own values in a "value-free" world is, of course, precisely why contemporary individualists do not find connections into that world. It is why our social capital is flowing away,

37. For an illuminating discussion of Putnam's essay, see Robert Wuthnow, *Christianity and Civil Society: The Contemporary Debate* (Valley Forge, Penn.: Trinity Press International, 1996), 14-26.

38. John Taylor, *The Ethics of Authenticity* (Cambridge: Harvard University Press, 1991), 69.

39. Ibid.

why there is not always sufficient "spontaneous sociability," and why, in so many ways, we are bowling alone. These individualists are, Riesman says, "ignoring those issues of relatedness to others and commitment to keep intact the precarious structure of civilization."[40] This is true, but we should also say that all of this is not the result simply of a small oversight, a mental slip. This is the world that our new therapeutic individualism has spun, a world where relatedness is in short supply and commitment to the precarious structure of civilization is vanishing. And this is partly why therapists have come to assume such a large cultural role today. They try to enable the self to make the adjustments necessary to finding meaning in and connections to life. However, this is often done under the language of enhancing the self, of enabling it to transcend itself, rather than that of limiting itself through moral obligation, service, self-sacrifice, and commitment to others. Self technique thus becomes the new moral nurturing. More than that, the manipulation of the self has itself become the new (secular) religious order, but this order constitutes our problem in society, not its solution.

The language in which this self-interest expresses itself often has a kind of triumphant inevitability about it. After centuries of captivity, waves of oppression, horrible afflictions by the religious, the self is now finally being freed. This language is, however, deceptive, for what accompanies it — what historian Christopher Lasch describes as "selective apathy, emotional disengagement from others, renunciation of the past and the future, a determination to live one day at a time"[41] — bespeaks a self not in recovery but in disintegration. These techniques for self-management are no more than strategies for psychological survival. The brave and heady talk grows louder, in direct proportion to which the soul grows thinner and emptier.

This moral space between law and freedom shrinks daily, for what cannot be enforced, it is now assumed, should not be a matter of obedience. We are free to do, or say, or think, or be anything that we

40. David Riesman, "On Autonomy," in *The Self in Social Interaction*, ed. Chad Gordon and Kenneth Gergen (New York: John Wiley and Sons, 1968), 446. I have also attempted to sketch out how our individualism has developed, and why it is now so problematic, in my *No Place for Truth*, 149-86. From a different angle, Carol Gilligan has sought to find ways for women to recover some sense of connectedness in a society driven by the obsessive insistence on autonomy. See her *In a Different Voice: Psychological Theory and Women's Development* (Cambridge: Harvard University Press, 1993).

41. Christopher Lasch, *The Minimal Self: Psychic Survival in Troubled Times* (New York: W. W. Norton, 1984), 57.

want, short of crossing the line of illegality. Everything that is not illegal is therefore morally permissible. This attitude, in itself, is a recipe for profound social disorder, because there are many forms of dishonesty, of antisocial behavior, that are not illegal at all. But its most pernicious outcome, the one with the deepest effects, is hardly noticed at all: we have lost our ability to talk about Good and Evil.

This deficiency has long been in the making, but its size and importance have been much enlarged in recent decades. Literary scholar Andrew Delbanco places the beginnings of the problem well back into the last century. He notes the dismemberment of the self that occurred as industrialization reshaped the country. We lost our sense of "we" in community, and this was replaced by the lonely "I." Lone bowlers are obviously not an instant creation of our time. The older kind of world, in which God ruled sovereignly and presided over its moral order, has been fracturing for a long time. To soldiers involved in the Civil War, for example, and to the nation as it watched, it was a matter of blind chance who survived and who did not. To pray for grace increasingly became more embarrassing than to hope for luck. Sin, by the end of the last century, was rapidly fading as a belief, and how could it have been otherwise, he asks? "Sin, after all, means transgression against God. But God had been replaced by fortune, and fortune makes no moral judgments. . . . In what amounted to a new paganism, the concept of evil devolved into bad luck, and 'good luck' became the new benediction."[42]

The loss of moral centeredness, a loss occasioned by the disappearance of God, by the supplanting of providence by chance, and of moral purpose by self-interest, changed everything. It changed the meaning of death, since there was no one to whom the dying were going. And it changed the meaning of life, since what had given life meaning had now gone. Writing as early as 1929, Walter Lippmann described the "modern man" as having:

> moments of blank misgiving in which he finds that the civilization of which he is a part leaves a dusty taste in his mouth. He may be very busy with many things, but he discovers one day that he is no longer sure they are worth doing. He has been much preoccupied; but he is no longer sure he knows why. He has become involved in an elaborate routine of pleasures; and they do not seem to amuse him

42. Andrew Delbanco, *The Death of Satan: How Americans Have Lost the Sense of Evil* (New York: Farrar, Straus and Giroux, 1995), 153.

very much. He finds it hard to believe that doing any one thing is
better than doing any other thing, or, in fact, that it is better than
doing nothing at all.[43]

Americans had been slow to see that as the old moral map faded,
they would be left, not with an alternative, but with no map at all. It is
true that the neo-orthodox theologians, like Reinhold Niebuhr, tried
to staunch the flow in moral understanding and to preserve the understanding of human nature as sinful before God. They did have a few
moments of success, but these turned out to be quite fleeting. The real
story of our time was being told through the relentless march of secular
rationality as it destroyed all before it. Today, Delbanco says, it has left
moderns with only one conclusion: "to acknowledge that no story about
the intrinsic meaning of the world has universal validity."[44]

This loss of a moral framework to our everyday life is evident in
so many ways. Some years ago, psychologist Helen Lynd noted that
teachers and "sophisticated" parents were abandoning the moral framework in which guilt had played a part in training children. No longer
were children being told that they were "good" or "bad," or even that
a certain action had been "good" or "bad." Now, she said, "the words
good and bad have been replaced by mature and immature, productive

43. Ibid., 188.
44. Ibid., 221. John Diggins has recognized the consequences of this in our
political life and has sought to retrieve from the Founding Fathers and subsequent
thinkers those values and beliefs which, if reaffirmed, might restore to our political
order some authority. See his *The Lost Soul of American Politics: Virtue, Self-Interest,
and the Foundations of Liberalism* (New York: Basic Books, 1984). Others have moved
in a different and more religious direction. Robert Wuthnow has suggested that civil
religion now has two forms, one that articulates the goals of the political left, the
other, those of the political right. "On the conservative side, America's legitimacy
seems to depend heavily on a distinct 'myth of origin' that relates the nation's
founding to divine purposes." This is what gives America a special place in the
world and a certain divine approval to its foreign policy initiatives. The liberal view
of America does not root its interest in America's founding under God; it argues
that America has a role to play in the world, not because it is some kind of chosen
people, but because of the ethical responsibility that follows upon its position of
power and its wealth in the world today. "Rather than drawing specific attention to
the distinctiveness of the Judeo-Christian tradition, liberal civil religion is much
more likely to include arguments about basic human rights and common human
problems." Robert Wuthnow, *The Restructuring of American Religion: Society and Faith
Since World War II* (Princeton: Princeton University Press, 1988), 244, 250. Both
forms of civil religion, however, miscarry; they are unable adequately and convincingly to shore up the fallen middle between law and freedom. See also Robert
Wuthnow, *The Struggle for America's Soul: Evangelicals, Liberals, and Secularism* (Grand
Rapids: Eerdmans, 1989), 97-114.

and unproductive, socially adjusted and maladjusted."[45] These new words described the same actions as the old, and they carried the same weight, but they had become morally neutralized. If it was once good to work hard, that was now transformed into simply being mature. Sexual harassment that had been bad became a symptom merely of being maladjusted. This was the argot of the 1950s and 1960s. It was to be overtaken in the following decades by a far more radical outcome, as we shall see, in which right and wrong contracted wholly into the self and were absorbed into the terms of self-interest.

In the meantime, our language has continued to betray the fact that our moral vision has faded. We no longer have failures, only underachievers. We no longer do things that are wrong but simply those that are inappropriate. We no longer talk about a person's character but evade the difficulty of making moral judgments by speaking of his or her lifestyle. We cannot face squarely the awful afflictions that leave people handicapped; we circumvent the reality and say blandly that are differently abled. We no longer have druggies but substance abusers. The very expression "substance abuse" implies that there is a proper use for these illegal drugs and that the addict simply overused what might quite properly have been used at a lower dosage or with less frequency. By speaking of substance abuse, we largely excuse ourselves from making a moral judgment, even over something illegal. In these and many other ways, moral language is in full retreat before our disposition not to think in moral categories.

In 1992 and 1993, the public followed the custody battles being fought between Woody Allen and Mia Farrow. At issue was Allen's fitness as a parent, given his secret affair begun with Farrow's nineteen-year-old daughter, who was also the stepsister to the other children in the family. William Doherty, a family therapist, has noted that none of the counselors or therapists who testified were willing to say that what Allen had done was "wrong." Allen, one said, "may have made an error in judgment," and the problem was that this is a "postmodern family." The judge was exasperated by the morally neutered language of "bad judgment" and "lack of judgment," and he went on to deplore the fact that "sleeping with our children's sister" has supposedly come to mean nothing at all in our "postmodern" families.[46]

45. Helen Merrell Lynd, *On Shame and the Search for Identity* (London: Routledge and Kegan Paul, 1958), 16.

46. William J. Doherty, *Soul Searching: Why Psychotherapy Must Promote Moral Responsibility* (New York: Basic Books, 1995), 4.

This loss of moral categories, the loss of a transcendent sense of Good and Evil, does not, however, rid the world of those who are evil; it simply blinds us to the real nature of their actions. For now, evil becomes ordinary, routine, a part of life as natural and inevitable as cats killing mice.

It was this loss that so struck Hannah Arendt, who attended the trial in Jerusalem of Adolf Eichmann, the Nazi bureaucrat who became such an important cog in the Nazi killing machine.[47] Her account of the trial takes the reader through the thicket of legal complexities with a sure touch, but it focuses upon the strange contradiction that became so clear during the trial. The prosecution struggled to depict Eichmann as a monster, the epitome of vicious, callous brutality. In actual fact, Eichmann appeared as nothing of the kind. Psychiatrists who examined him found no mental illness, and throughout the trial he conducted himself with dignity and restraint. One of the only moments when his outward calm became a little ruffled, another observer noted, was when, at the very end, he was asked to stand and hear the verdict that he had been found guilty. The "only signs of his inner terror," this observer wrote, "were a sucking of the lips and the clasping and unclasping of the hands."[48] This aside, he was in full control of himself, and he seemed so ordinary. He was not a monster, but a gray, conscientious bureaucrat who was just going about his work as he was expected to do. He gave no evidence that he had had to endure any self-reproach for his actions in working to ensure that millions would go to their deaths. It was the very matter-of-factness of his account of himself, that it had been emptied of moral considerations, which made his evil seem rather banal, mundane, and routine.

The truth is that we are alone, and so our evil becomes commonplace and ordinary. There is no One outside of ourselves against whom its enormity can be measured. If the world outside of us recedes — the world of God's sovereign order, of moral norms and social obligations — the world inside must become enlarged to compensate for the loss. If the natural advances as the supernatural retreats, the subjective becomes enlarged to fill the void left by the disappearance of the objective. Today, nothing is as real to us as the intuitions, the feelings, the fears and pleasures of the self; the world that Luther, Brainerd, and

47. Hannah Arendt, *Eichmann in Jerusalem: A Report on the Banality of Evil* (New York: Viking Press, 1963).

48. Moshe Pearlman, *The Capture and Trial of Adolf Eichmann* (New York: Simon and Schuster, 1963), 562.

Owen inhabited is barely even comprehensible to moderns. Modernity has launched us in the pursuit of our own inward reality. This is the ball to which it has invited us, and it is here that we dance in merriment around the self.

Control

If we are daily stoking the fires of our moral license, commissioned as it is by the search for self-fulfillment, we must also douse those fires daily by recourse to the law. Litigation and regulation must now do what civility, self-restraint, honesty, and charitable concern once did.

Since the 1960s, legal scholar Gregory Sisk says, "a vision of the federal judiciary as the moral tutor appointed for a recalcitrant society has become dominant in the American legal academy and increasingly in the courts themselves."[49] The courts have taken it upon themselves to elevate certain values and to discount others. In *Roe v. Wade,* for example, the Supreme Court not only discovered a legal right to abortion in the Constitution but, by doing so, tacitly extended moral permission to people to act on that right. And later on, in the 1992 case, *Planned Parenthood v. Casey,* three of its justices went on to suggest that the acceptance of this moral principle was required as a matter of good citizenship. The Constitution intended that the courts would provide a small part of social morality, but in the dwindling world of the "obedience to the unenforceable," the courts now threaten to provide the only morality, and some of it, at least, has become a bit questionable.

The courts, in fact, have engaged our society across the entire spectrum of its life, from the most weighty to the most insignificant. In February, 1996, for example, Antonina Pevnev, the mother of a three-year-old girl, received a restraining order from Judge Charles Spurlock of the Suffolk Superior Court in Boston against the three-year-old son of Margaret Inge. Apparently these two toddlers had a spat in the sandbox, and the Court had to issue its injunction in order to preserve the peace at Charles River Park playground.[50]

Is it entirely out of place to speculate how this dispute might have been resolved in an earlier time? An inkling of parental sense about

49. Gregory C. Sisk, "The Moral Incompetence of the Judiciary," *First Things* 57 (November 1995), 34.
50. Roderick MacLeish, "Is Litigation Becoming an American Pastime?" *The Boston Globe* (March 8, 1996), 23, 27.

what is and what is not acceptable behavior in public for a three-year-old would have placed a lid on this dispute even before it started.[51] But if the mothers lacked that, and lacked the moral sense that such a situation called for, would the fathers not have intervened? And if they could not see how this sandbox storm could be quieted and a few good lessons about life learned, would they not have sought advice from other family members, from neighbors, or friends? If the conflict was still raging, would they not have sought the counsel of their minister? In the past, there have been many intermediate agencies — families, neighbor-hoods, churches, cultural expectations, and moral principles — that would have come into play in conflicts such as this. Today, there are often none, and the only recourse is the final recourse, the Court.

It was no small irony, then, that the Supreme Court greatly pro-voked the Christian Coalition in 1997 by striking down the Communica-tions Decency act. This act had been passed to ban children's access to pornographic material on the Internet. The justices were, of course, mainly concerned with preserving the first-amendment right to free speech, offensive as its exercise is in this case. There was, however, a grain of common sense in their ruling, too. Given our technological abilities today, parents can block this material from their homes. Is it not better for them to exercise moral leadership than to depend on the law to do it for them? It would have been much worse had the Court ruled that children had a right to view such material. This is not quite as far-fetched as it may sound. Instead, the court asked parents, schools, and libraries to do for themselves what Congress had asked the law to do.

The law's control over society has been greatly enlarged in our time through the discovery of, and appeal to, rights. America nourishes 70 percent of the world's lawyers. It is, therefore, inevitable that there should be endless pressure on the court system to convert as many desires as possible into rights. At the same time, the matter of personal rights follows naturally upon our constitutional freedoms to live our lives as we want, within the bounds of law, even if that means that we hold views and live in ways that are repugnant to others. Rights once belonged only to the privileged and powerful, but today they belong

51. On this theme, see Richard Lynn, "Self-Control: The Family as the Source of 'Conscience,'" in *The Loss of Virtue: Moral Confusion and Social Disorder in Britain and America*, ed. Digby Anderson (London: Social Affairs Unit, 1992), 121-33. Lynn, a British psychologist, explores the role of parents in socializing their children, especially by developing in them the mechanism of self-control.

to the poorest and least powerful. Thus in a society where rights are entrenched, the most ordinary have to be respected. This is a kind of enforced morality, observed oftentimes only because of the fear of litigation, but because of this, philosopher Charles Taylor says, "the moral world of moderns is significantly different from that of previous civilizations."[52]

The courts have not been bashful about encouraging this quest for rights. They have widened constitutional guarantees to free speech, to freedom from unwarranted search and seizure, to reproductive freedom, and, somewhat more sporadically, to equal education and equal opportunity. The great benefit of a right is that, once established in law, it cannot be overturned. A right lodged in the Constitution is a right that government is pledged to defend, regardless of the financial and social cost and without respect for the size of the opposition to the possession of that right. Rights are therefore eminently desirable things to have. They are especially desirable in a culture that is spinning into license and lawlessness, for they provide a social defense that character once, without the law's coercion, extended to others as a matter of duty or conscience.

There are, however, less official expressions of the "law" in society that nevertheless still seek to control and restrain what is judged to be wrong. And much of this surrogate assertion of "law" has gone hand in hand with issues of gender, ethnicity, and sexual orientation. Multiculturalism in the 1960s, for example, was initially an expression of the civil rights movement. It sought to allow visibility to women and ethnic minorities who had been excluded from positions of power and influence in society. It sought to welcome cultural differences and to see in these differences what would enrich, rather than impoverish, the country. It was an argument that some advanced from Christian premises and others on the Enlightenment principles of liberty, equality, and justice for all. Multiculturalism today, however, has largely lost its ideals, given our postmodern context, and has rapidly degenerated into a search for group power. Todd Gitlin, the cultural critic, has traced out the path of this disintegration by showing that as commonalities became exhausted, differences had to be enlarged.[53] What followed this breakdown was often not the embrace of other cultures but an ugly cen-

52. Charles Taylor, *Sources of the Self: The Making of Modern Identity* (Cambridge: Harvard University Press, 1989), 11.

53. Todd Gitlin, *The Twilight of Common Dreams: Why America Is Wracked by Culture Wars* (New York: Metropolitan Books, 1995).

soriousness toward other groups and viewpoints. Ironically, multiculturalism today is not about culture at all but about politics and power and
about what Richard Bernstein calls the "dictatorship of virtue."[54]

In 1995, the University of Massachusetts, following a number of
other universities,[55] proposed a policy on harassment that went well
beyond the constitutional safeguards of citizenship. This policy was
designed to disallow certain kinds of speech with respect to women,
ethnic minorities, students who were pregnant, those who had the HIV
virus, and those who were gay. No one could make derogatory comments about a student's cultural practices, the language he or she
spoke, or his or her political affiliation. The law, however, is a blunt
instrument in a case like this, for while it may prevent some ostracism
it might also prevent some legitimate and necessary conversation.
Should our universities not be places where ideas are aired and tested
without fear of retribution? Surely it is only in Marxist countries that
the thought police have been allowed a presence on campuses. In this
case, would a student fall foul of the new law for expressing judgments
about the morality of homosexuality? Would political liberalism be
protected from all critiques?

This proposed law was apparently made necessary because of
growing intolerance on campus. The middle domain of character and
truth telling had been invaded by our amoral individualism, which often
speaks with an uncivil tongue. The solution proposed, though, was not
to recover what had been lost but to control the consequences of that
loss. When moral principle breaks down, we are left with no other
recourse than that of law. Placing all our hope in legal constraint,
however, is going to produce problems worse than those whose remedy
is being sought through the restraint.

But what is the alternative? The alternative to this kind of exercise
of "law," unfortunately, is usually the evasion of moral responsibility.
For on the underside of our culture is the cultivation of victimhood.
This is at the confluence of the deep currents of individualism, the
therapeutic framework in which we think, and the loss of the moral
fabric to life. "The ethos of victimization," writes Charles Sykes, "has
an endless capacity not only for exculpating one's self from blame,
washing away responsibility in a torrent of explanation — racism, sex-

---

54. Richard Bernstein, *Dictatorship of Virtue: Multiculturalism and the Battle for
America's Future* (New York: Alfred A. Knopf, 1994).
55. See Dinesh D'Souza, *Illiberal Education: The Politics of Race and Sex on
Campus* (New York: Free Press, 1991).

ism, rotten parents, addiction, and illness — but also for projecting guilt onto others."[56] This "depersonalization of blame" is a sure symptom of the decay in our character and the loss of our older moral vision.

Today, we stand at the turbulent meeting place of these two swirling, swollen currents. From one side, the loss of moral vision threatens to undo culture along its entire front; from the other side comes the escalating recourse to law in order to contain a society that is splitting its own seams. This contest between license and law is one that, in the absence of recovered moral fiber, can only become more shrill, more frustrating, more culturally destabilizing, more damaging, and more dangerous.

It is this cultural dilemma that now drives the debate between Democrats and Republicans, the one wanting more law and the other more freedom. Would it be inappropriate to suggest that both parties are partly wrong and partly right? Republicans, I believe, are right that government regulation is burdensome and sometimes ineffective, but they are slow to see the consequences of having less law in a culture whose moral character is worn, where "obedience to the unenforceable" is tepid. Democrats are right to fear what will happen in such a society where the heavy hand of the law is lifted, but they rarely see that the law cannot restore what we have lost, which is our sense of "obedience to the unenforceable." The law is no substitute for what we have lost. We can, for example, pass laws against murder, but not against hatred; against adultery, but not against lust; against fraud, but not against lying; against violence, but not against the emotional neglect of children. We can condemn abuse, but we cannot command kindness. We can condemn bigotry, but we cannot require civility. Republicans ask for more freedom, Democrats for more law, but freedom in the absence of public virtue is as disastrous as more law because of the absence of public virtue.[57]

56. Charles J. Sykes, *A Nation of Victims: The Decay of the American Character* (New York: St. Martin's Press, 1992), 11.

57. This dilemma is significantly illumined in Michael J. Sandel's *Democracy's Discontent: America in Search of a Public Philosophy* (Cambridge: Harvard University Press, 1996). He points out that in the early 1990s, conservatives like William J. Bennett were arguing that public policies should reflect the nation's deepest values and that what had once been outside the scope of politics, such as family and social issues of a moral kind, had now become its driving force. Many liberals (like Donna Shalala), who were abandoned by Clinton in his 1996 presidential bid when he occupied ground conservatives had had to themselves, continued to reflect the older attitude that morality should be disengaged from policy making. However, it is one thing to see the place of morality and the importance of civic virtue for the health of society, and another to find it in a nation much given to its expressive individualism.

Today, a door of unprecedented opportunity is opening before the Church. In order to walk through this door, however, the Church must come to terms with life as it really is and engage that life from an uncompromisingly biblical standpoint. This is easier said than done, because the cultural context in which we live favors those forms of spirituality, Christian and otherwise, that are marching to the tune of 1990s culture, rather than those that are seeking to be faithful to the God of biblical revelation. What so many of these new spiritualities have in common is that they are offering benefits for the self and asking for little or no spiritual accountability. Designer religion of the 1990s allows itself to be tailored to each personality. It gives but never takes; it satisfies inner needs but never asks for repentance; it offers mystery and asks for no service. It provides a sense of Something Other in life but never requires that we stand before that Other. And what I have called post-modern evangelical spirituality is increasingly a part of this picture because it has failed to understand the way modernity has shaped the self. It is to that subject that we must now turn.

CHAPTER III

On Saving Ourselves

Modern man . . . is not the man who goes off to discover himself,
his secrets and his hidden truth; he is the man who tries to invent
himself. This modernity does not 'liberate man in his own being'; it
compels him to face the task of producing himself.

Michel Foucault

Surviving and Assembling Ourselves

Beneath the surface of our life, with its daily routines and schedules, profound currents of change are flowing. A century ago, for example, the great impediment to relationships was distance. Most relationships took place within the small circumference one could walk. That meant that most relationships took place within stable communities, among family members, townsfolk, and the church, all of which were rooted in a place.[1] The horse and carriage extended that range but, of course, at the cost of time.

---

1. See Joshua Meyrowitz, *No Sense of Place* (New York: Oxford University Press, 1985). John McKnight has suggested that modern society has replaced the loss of community — community that was always rooted in place — by new kinds of "communities" that clearly cannot fill the role the older communities had. These include the professions in general, the medical community, the therapeutic community, the welfare state, and the criminal justice system, which has become necessary because we have become overwhelmed by what we have created in modern society. He argues that today "our society is the site of the struggle between community and institution for the capacities and loyalties of our people" (John McKnight, *The Careless Society:*

This pattern has now mostly disappeared, because what once curtailed relationships — distance — has been annihilated. First with the train, then more potently with the automobile, then with air travel, distances were shrunk and the circumference within which relationships were possible was enlarged. That was not all. With telegraph and telephone and now with e-mail, our prospects for personal contact have become global. Indeed, as MIT scientist Michael Dertouzos says, our new technology is making of us "Urban Villagers," still traveling down to the local supermarket for provisions but during work hours interacting with people in cosmopolitan centers far from home and even on the other side of the world.[2]

Then, beginning with radio, but more importantly with movies and television, we were able to relate to those whom we had never even met, to see their facial expressions, enter into their sorrows, enjoy their triumphs, and live, however fleetingly, through their images. We have undergone a staggering enlargement of our personal circumference, which now contains within it many whom we "know" without actually ever having met. What does this do to us? How does this transformation change the way we see our world, other people, and even ourselves? To begin answering these questions we need to think about the residue left behind by our numerous, accelerated encounters with the modernized world.[3]

Community and Its Counterfeits [New York: Basic Books, 1995], 168). The struggle, however, has long since ceased. Community has more or less vanished, and institutions are dominant. McKnight is correct, though, that they cannot actually take the place of community.

2. Michael Dertouzos, *What Will Be: How the New World of Information Will Change Our Lives* (New York: HarperCollins, 1997), 280-81.

3. I am here summarizing the argument in Kenneth J. Gergen, *The Saturated Self: Dilemmas of Identity in Contemporary Life* (New York: Basic Books, 1991), 48-80. Elsewhere, Gergen has argued that the new technologies that produced the automobile, air travel, radio, television, and computers "operate as a group to undermine the conditions of homogeneity" on which personal relations must depend. See his "Technology and the Self: From the Essential to the Sublime," in *Constructing the Self in a Mediated World*, ed. Debra Grodin and Thomas R. Lindlof (Thousand Oaks, Calif.: SAGE Publications, 1996), 131. I have also attempted to describe these same transformations in life by reconstructing the changes that have come about in the small town of Wenham, Massachusetts over the last century and a half in my book, *No Place for Truth; or, Whatever Happened to Evangelical Theology?* (Grand Rapids: Eerdmans, 1993), 17-52. For Gergen's further reflections on the postmodern self, see his *The Concept of Self* (New York: Holt, Rinehart, 1971) and in response, see R. L. Russell and M. D. Gaubatz, "Contested Affinities: Reaction to Gergen's (1994) and Smith's (1994) Postmodernisms," *American Psychologist* 50, no. 5 (May 1995), 389-90.

Social Ghosts

Let us begin by reflecting on what could be a normal day. At the beginning of this day there are fifteen voice mail messages that have accumulated in one's absence; the advantage belongs to those wanting to communicate over those receiving the communication, for the absence of one conversation partner is no longer an impediment. There are also e-mail messages. At the click of a mouse, cyberspace is opened up, and, if one so desires, one can begin the day in solitary worship (perhaps with hundreds or thousands of others who remain entirely unknown) at the First Church of Cyberspace, selecting the music and the sermon one would like to hear. Prayer requests can be sent in, though the destination to which they are then shuttled off is not entirely clear, and there are still impediments to downloading the elements of Communion.[4] During the day there will be telephone calls, some from across the country and perhaps even internationally, including many from people whom one has never met. Perhaps there will be a conference call that will link people across thousands of miles. There will be a flight to catch for a quick airport meeting, and there one will run into two acquaintances, one of whom has been living in South America and the other in Asia, neither of whom one has seen in years. When one returns home, weary from the journey, the first stop will be the mailbox. It will be stuffed with catalogs slickly soliciting interest in thousands upon thousands of items, many of which one could never even have imagined. This is simply a small part of an incessant barrage, day after day. There will be letters, bills, and Ed McMahon wanting to divest himself of ten million dollars. No sooner does one enter the house than the telephone rings. The alumni association is just keeping in touch. Then, for the third time in two weeks, one is alerted to a new product for septic tanks; but it is useless to protest, because on the other end of the line a tape recorder is mindlessly doing its business. "Once we lived with silence," French sociologist Alain Touraine remarks, "we now live with noise. Once, we were isolated,

---

4. "If cyberspace is a digital ocean," writes Jeff Zaleski, "then Christianity online is its tidal wave. As of early 1997, Christian Web sites made up 80 percent of the Web sites of the world's five major (i.e. most influential) religions. Yet the four other major world religions — Judaism, Islam, Buddhism, and Hinduism — together claim about 2 billion adherents, the same number that Christianity claims." Jeff Zaleski, *The Soul of Cyberspace: How Technology Is Changing Our Spiritual Lives* (New York: HarperCollins, 1997), 99.

and now we are lost in the crowd. Once, we received too few messages, and we are now bombarded with them."[5]

More people pass through our lives today, more quickly, than ever before. We are exposed to an almost endless number of new people, new situations, new products, new organizations, new businesses, and new opportunities. With some of our technologies, the encounters are superficial and we are engaged little. Others, however, intensify these relations. This is true of television, some of whose characters become more real to us than the people next door, for our contact with the person whose image we see is far more sustained, and perhaps far more pleasant, than the real people around the corner. This can certainly be the case in cyberspace. There are now numerous cases of people who have never met, never seen each other, who have fallen in love; some have even abandoned marriages to pursue their new fantasy. And it is true of many a teenager's identification with a rock band, known only through their music and videos, but which becomes more intense than many other personal relationships, even within the family.

These encounters clearly do not leave us unaffected. They leave behind their remnants within us, from which we weave an internal dialog of admiration, emulation, or consternation. They are the "guests" who do not leave, the "social ghosts" who remain. This is a kind of psychological over-populating, Kenneth Gergen argues, which is having profound effects as it "saturates" the self. For one thing, it leads to our investment in a multiplicity of projects — commercial, personal, informational — that become increasingly difficult to sustain because each is separate from the other, each is in its own unique universe, and in each the demands made upon us exceed our abilities to respond. Many contemporary people are soon suffused by a seeping sense of self-doubt, a sense of inadequacy, because the lines of these relationships are spread so far and wide that coping becomes impossible. They may also find that life easily settles into a pattern of superficial contacts with people that involve few, if any, enduring commitments. This pattern has also come to plague the Church, where we often have proximity with little real community.

Furthermore, this massive intrusion, this invasion from the outside world, slowly picks apart the sense people have of themselves as unique beings. According to art historian Katherine Hoffman, the ways in which people relate to one another, their gestures and speech patterns, "are so thoroughly impregnated with a rhetoric absorbed through the air-

5. Alain Touraine, *Critique of Modernity* (Oxford: Blackwell, 1995), 91.

waves that we can have no certain claim to the originality of our actions." She goes on to say that "every cigarette, every love affair echoes down a never ending passageway of reference — to advertisements, to television shows, to movies, to the point where we no longer know if we mimic or are mimicked."[6]

Everything is now cast in the image of television. The lines that once divided political conventions and sports events, hard news from TV dramas, the real world from a make-believe world, have become quite thin. Reality making, in fact, is now big business. "In the contemporary world," Stuart Ewen, an astute writer on modern culture, says, "where the mass media serve as increasingly powerful arbiters of *reality*, the primacy of style over substance has become the normative consciousness."[7] More than that, television's reach has also meant "the globalization of show business," James Twitchell charges, and with the dominance of the marketplace in all aspects of our life there has also come the "trashing of taste" and "the triumph of vulgarity."[8]

The modern experience of living in a world of heightened uncertainty and of increasing options of all kinds, from products, to careers, to relationships, means that internal biography is pressured into becoming increasingly flexible, multifaceted, and malleable enough to adapt to the many new situations. "The more tradition loses its hold," writes sociologist Anthony Giddens, "and the more daily life is reconstructed in terms of the dialectical interplay of the local and the global, the more individuals are forced to negotiate lifestyle choices among a diversity of options."[9] This means that internal consciousness is

6. Katherine Hoffman, *Concepts of Identity: Historical and Contemporary Images and Portraits of Self and Family* (New York: Icon Editions, 1996), 201.

7. Stuart Ewen, *All Consuming Images: The Politics of Style in Contemporary Culture* (New York: Basic Books, 1988), 2. See also Philip J. Rossi, "Moral Imagination and the Media: Whose 'World' Do We See, Whose 'World' Shall It Be?" in *Mass Media and the Moral Imagination*, ed. Philip J. Rossi and Paul A. Soukup (Kansas City: Sheed and Ward, 1994), 264-72.

8. James B. Twitchell, *Carnival Culture: The Trashing of Taste in America* (New York: Columbia University Press, 1992), 261-74.

9. Anthony Giddens, *Modernity and Self-Identity: Self and Society in the Late Modern Age* (Stanford: Stanford University Press, 1991), 5. Over long periods of time, the discoveries, artifacts, and tastes of other cultures tend to become universal possessions; see Ralph Linton, *The Study of Man* (London: Appleton-Century-Crofts, 1936), 326-27, as cited in George M. Foster, *Traditional Societies and Technological Change* (New York: Harper and Row, 1973), 16-18. What has changed today, of course, is the speed of interpenetration of cultural tastes and achievements across national boundaries. Most notable is the Americanization of the rest of the world through movies, rock music, business products and services, and technology.

changed. Like it or not, we are engaged in what Walter Anderson calls "eternal shopping in the bazaar of culture and subculture."[10] We are making decisions, Giddens says, "not only about how to act but who to be," and these decisions go to "the very core of self-identity, its making and remaking."[11] What is remarkable about this is our far-reaching ignorance of the transformation of our very selves. We are sleepwalking into the twenty-first century, oblivious to the fact that our experience of the modern world is changing how we think about ourselves and our world. To pursue this theme further, we need to think about one of the chief devices in effecting this change: choice.

Pro-choice

The notion of choice is, of course, one of the hallmarks of our time. In traditional societies, there are few decisions to make; in modern societies we become overwhelmed by the number of choices or options that we have. As Peter Berger, Boston University sociologist, notes, the role that fate or tradition once played has been replaced by that of choice. In traditional societies, great swaths of life were not open to choice at all; these included one's social standing, the kind of work one did, the person to whom one was married, the clothes one wore. And it was fate or fortune that assigned what life held in store for one, including its calamities. Today, however, all of this has changed. Social standing, for example, can often be acquired, for it is largely a matter of *perception*. It is, therefore, something that can be created or purchased. Vocation is chosen from among many alternatives. Parents have little or no role in their children's marriage choices. When and if we decide to have children is now a matter of choice, and we think that by prudent anticipation some calamities can be avoided — a belief that sustains the entire industry of predicting the future.

Modernization accelerates our social pluralization. Where there

10. Walter Truett Anderson, *Reality Is Not What It Used to Be: Theatrical Politics, Ready-to-Wear Religion, Global Myths, Primitive Chic, and Other Wonders of the Postmodern World* (San Francisco: HarperCollins, 1993), 7.

11. Giddens, *Modernity and Self-Identity*, 81. Our identities, Madan Sarup writes, are the constructs woven out of "what we consume, what we wear, the commodities we buy, what we see and read, how we conceive our sexuality, what we think of society and the changes we believe it is undergoing." Our identities are affected by "what we think of ourselves"; "advertising, fashion, popular culture and the mass media are also powerful institutions to be considered." Madan Sarup, *Identity, Culture and the Postmodern World* (Athens: University of Georgia Press, 1996), 105.

was one institution, now we have thousands; where there was once one sexual partner, we may now have many; where there once was one product, we now have dozens competing for the same consumer. (Revlon makes 177 shades of lipstick to ensure that just the right shade is available for its discriminating customers.) Where there once was one style, we now have multiple options.[12] What is new about our situation is both the intensity of the barrage of choices — the many things among which we must choose — and the fact that we now think that who we are can also be a matter of choice.

An immediate and disquieting consequence follows from this. If the circumstances of life are indeed determined by choice rather than by fate, then there is always the possibility that one chose unwisely. This is what lies behind some of our unease; we sometimes imagine what would have resulted if we had chosen a different career path, or a different spouse, or a different place to live. Things could have been different from what they are. The very reality of choice robs us of contentment over the paths we have taken.

The same reality of choice drives the quest for liberation. Things could be different from what they are; this is the dominant assumption of modernity, and it has spurred much technological innovation, driven the search for new products, and contributed to many of the medical breakthroughs. However, this assumption is also thought to apply to the person, which is a rather different matter. What gender now means could be different, so could our values, so could the way we present ourselves to others. Indeed, things could be different within the self, too; if people did not think so, the entire self-help industry would collapse overnight. This is the thread that Wendy Kaminer, who has written perceptively on many aspects of our culture, traces through the codependency groups, the testimonies on television talk shows, the latter-day advocates of positive thinking, the twelve-step programs, the various recovery groups, the New Age phenomenon, and some popular evangelical authors.[13]

Empty Selves

The reality of change, even of change in our own *personae,* has greatly fueled hope that the self can be freshly reassembled and refurbished.

12. See Peter L. Berger, *The Heretical Imperative: Contemporary Possibilities of Religious Affirmation* (New York: Anchor Press, 1979), 1-31.
13. Wendy Kaminer, *I'm Dysfunctional, You're Dysfunctional: The Recovery Movement and Other Self-Help Fashions* (Reading, Penn.: Addison-Wesley, 1991).

Across a broad front we gather materials for the construction of ourselves. We build a public self in what we buy and what we voluntarily choose to do. This front runs from cuisine (Thai, French, or Mexican tonight?), to fashion (Ferragamo shoes or faux furs?), to particular products (antiques or Swedish contemporary?), to music (Bach or the Grateful Dead?), to sexual lifestyles (monogamous or casual, heterosexual or gay?), to beliefs (Christian, New Age, or postmodern doubt?). Beneath it all is the same compulsion to be in a state of constant inward evaluation, taking an inventory of needs and wishes, and then reaching out for a "product" to satisfy the felt emptiness and to project who we are. The "product" may, indeed, be a product like a new car, but it also may be a new face, a new diet, or a new hormonal therapy to hold off the approach of old age, or a new projection of the kind of person whom we would like to be. This takes channel surfing to a high art as we slide from product to product, from relationship to relationship, from style to style, seldom lingering long before the shape of our internal inventory tugs us in another direction in search of different fulfillment. Not only have the advertisers had a field day with the disappearance of brand loyalty, but so too have parts of the evangelical world that have been quick to appreciate that the religious market is also now consumer-oriented. Seeker-sensitive churches are following a simple instinct that corporations spend millions to hone. There is a buyer's market in religion, too, and the matter of projecting a church's "style" successfully can be a matter of big business.[14] It is the key, many think, to success.

Malls

Nowhere are these changes in our social landscape better epitomized than in our malls. If Gothic cathedrals symbolized feudal society with its sense of being, of hierarchy, and most importantly of all, of God's transcendence, malls symbolize for us the consumer culture in a secularized world. Malls are *our* cathedrals. They are a unique blend of high commercialism and undaunted fantasy. They blend the experience of walking down the street of a small town and gazing in the windows with what cultural analyst Lauren Langman calls "indoor worlds" with accouterments like "atriums of plants and trees from far away climes, marble fountains with multicolored light shows with lasers, holograms

14. See Steven Waldman, "The Tyranny of Choice," *The New Republic* (January 27, 1992), 23.

and strobes with backdrops of chrome water."[15] Much as Disney World set out to create the happiest place on earth where the tawdry and the corrupt have been banished[16] — indeed, where spent gum and cigarette ends are scooped out of sight quickly and routinely — so malls have become "utopia of consumption" where "carnivals and spectacles of consumption gratify desires and sustain images of self."[17] They are not just places to which we come to buy articles; through careful control of lighting, temperature, and visual displays, they create an alternative reality, a kind of earthly heaven in which the pleasures are endless and the gratification promises to be enduring. Here we find ourselves and construct our identities. The British rock group, the Clash, addresses this in its song, "Lost in the Supermarket":

> Lost in the Supermarket
> can no longer shop happily,
> I came in here for a special offer
> 'Guaranteed Personality'.[18]

Our malls are the predictable and inevitable answer to the problem of our fragmenting self. Lauren Langman speaks of this modern problem as that of "a decentered selfhood" or "an enfeebled self," Christopher Lasch of "the minimal self," Philip Cushman of "the empty self," and Donald Capps of "the depleted self." They all appear to have the same thing in mind. Given our highly mobile society — we are not rooted in place, community, or family — and given the way that our exposure to modern life slowly empties us out, a continual sense of self has vanished for many of us. That is what makes the construction of identity necessary, whether by means of style or lifestyle. The result is a series of badges for recognition that we wear for short or longer periods, but none becomes a permanent part of our *personae*.

In our periodic visits to malls, then, what comes into play is the sense of our emptiness and the hope of its being filled, which Langman

15. Lauren Langman, "Neon Cages: Shopping for Subjectivity," in *Lifestyle Shopping: The Subject of Consumption,* ed. Rob Shields (London: Routledge, 1992), 49.

16. See the penetrating critique of modernity, using Disneyland as a metaphor, by Stephen J. Fjellman, *Vinyl Leaves: Walt Disney World and America* (Boulder, Colo.: Westview, 1992).

17. Langman, "Neon Cages," 48.

18. Cited in Rob Shields, "Spaces for the Subject of Consumption," in *Lifestyle Shopping*, ed. Shields, 12.

calls the "dialectic of enfeeblement and empowerment."[19] Not only articles but also meaning comes in the transaction, for the popular culture mediated by television that reverberates through the malls is offering balms for the lonely, excitement for those who are bored, and fulfillment for those who are inwardly deprived and empty. All desire, be it for people or things, springs from a sense of emptiness or deprivation, and in malls this emptiness is both aroused and, at the same time, soothed. The many products we purchase in these malls, places that are quite unlike life, build up our self-image and leave a trail of pleasurable emotional experience. They are the sacraments that are passed out in these, our secular cathedrals, sacraments that both point to and also mediate the salvation for which the empty have come.

Hard Bodies

In this transformation of ourselves, there is perhaps no part of the social landscape where these postmodern assumptions about the construction of our own identity are worked out more painfully than in the belief that what it means to be a man, or a woman, can also be changed. It is true, of course, that manhood and womanhood are partly cultural creations. They are matters of cultural nurture. What much of our current belief assumes, however, is that they are *only* matters of nurture, not of nature at all, and that our most fundamental identities as men and women are matters of choice and of construction.

In many ways, the ideal of manhood — to take only one side of the gender divide — that has come into our own century had its origins in the classical period of Greek civilization, though it also owed much to Christian understanding. The Greeks believed that manly beauty was both a physical and a moral matter. They thought that a man's body and comportment, historian George Mosse notes, should "exemplify power and virility" but also "proportion and self-control."[20] The assumption always was, however, that in the ideal man, bodily strength would go hand in hand with moral health and mental agility. This belief issued in many of those virtues that have so often been thought to make up the essence of manliness: heroism, courage, the strength to take a lonely stand, endurance, leadership, and moderation. The ideal assumed the union of body and soul, and for this

19. Langman, "Neon Cages," 43.
20. George L. Mosse, *The Image of Man: The Creation of Modern Masculinity* (New York: Oxford University Press, 1996), 13.

reason it has fallen on hard times in the modern era as souls have melted away and been replaced by selves. Being a man is not something given to one by nature but is something that can, and perhaps must, be constructed.

Until relatively recently, sport was one of the important arenas in which the ancient ideal was exhibited, for games were contests not only of strength and physical skill but of manly virtue as well — courage, good conduct, learning how to win and to lose well, and cooperation. Professional athletics in America, now driven by an endless torrent of cash and doing its business in a culture in which the social virtues have eroded, has abandoned the ethical ideals of sport almost entirely and greatly elevated the aggressive dimension: power, domination, the control of the opponent, and intimidation. Most football games are rituals of male bonding for the fans, but they are also replete with instances of "unsportsmanlike conduct" from one end of the game to the other. Yet only the most egregious and violent ever get flagged by the referees. This tilting of the scales away from the ethical and toward the animal may well account for the fact that the attitudinal differences experienced by men and women over sport are deeper than many of the other differences that distinguish them, such as cultural background, ethnicity, and social class.[21] And the stripped-down version of what it means to be a man that professional sport magnifies — physical power, domination, and a sculpted body — has generated a kind of emasculated masculine ethic: what is "hard" is good and what is "soft" is bad.[22]

One of the most interesting developments in the unfolding of this ideal was the way in which it became refocused during the Reagan presidency. Reagan believed that his major contributions were his restoration of a vigorous economy, lifting the nation's morale, and withstanding the Soviet empire, but there was also another accomplishment. He refurbished the masculine ideal. He not only mastered the regal dimension of the presidency but was seen riding his horse with a straight back, chopping wood, and remaining cheerful in the face of adversity, such as the assassination attempt. The political dimension of his withstanding Marxism was also a masculine thing, for

21. Some of the same developments evident in men's sport are also present among women, too. See Madelein Blais, *In These Girls, Hope is a Muscle* (New York: Atlantic Monthly Press, 1995).

22. Don Sabo, "Doing Time, Doing Masculinity: Sports and Prison," in *Sex, Violence and Power in Sports: Rethinking Masculinity*, ed. Michael A. Messner and Donald F. Sabo (Freedom, Calif.: Crossing Press, 1995), 165.

it showed his steely resolve. Although he spoke his mind in an affable way, there was a side to him that was gallant, strong, and silent. All of these angles on the Reagan image have also been considered manly things.

Both Nixon and Reagan derided the Carter presidency as having been "soft," and by implication their own presidencies had the masculine virtue of being "hard." In the 1996 presidential contest between Dole and Clinton, however, this was to cost the Republicans, for while a majority of men supported Dole, even more women supported Clinton. Republicans were thus left to ponder exactly what the political ramifications of the gender divide now meant.

In the 1980s some of these glimpses of what masculinity had come to mean — or at least how it was being thought about — made their way into the movies. In the POW films in particular — *Rambo: First Blood, Part 2; Missing in Action;* and *Uncommon Valor* — a new kind of male hero emerged. The heroes of the 1970s, like Dirty Harry, were often social recluses; these new heroes were more populist. They were taking the cause of the people in an offensive against a government that was bungling in its workings and uncaring in its outlook. Susan Jeffords, an English professor at the University of Washington, notes that the "heroes of hard body films are not heroic in defiance of their society but in defiance of their governments and institutional bureaucracies."[23] They are more like contemporary Robin Hoods, rescuing the innocent from the clutches of the evil and uncaring. And in this they foreshadowed one of the more troubling excrescences of masculinity in the 1990s: the militias.

However, by the 1990s other expressions were in the making. If the triumph of the marketplace had marked the Reagan years, a decade later family values began to replace financial accomplishment as most befitting for a man. The strength of the man now began to be channeled inward. In *Kindergarten Cop*, for example, Arnold Schwarzenegger, the quintessential hard body and law enforcer, had become the devoted family man.[24] These heroes began to turn away from economic rewards to the rewards of the families they had often neglected in the past, a point the Dole campaign tried to exploit in 1996

23. Susan Jeffords, *Hard Bodies: Hollywood Masculinity in the Reagan Era* (New Brunswick, N.J.: Rutgers University Press, 1994), 19. For an extensive and incisive account of the role of entertainment in American culture, see William D. Romanowski, *Pop Culture Wars: Religion and the Role of Entertainment in American Life* (Downers Grove, Ill.: InterVarsity Press, 1996).

24. Ibid., 141.

and which the Christian organization, Promise Keepers, has articulated with some success.[25]

Whether these glimpses of what real manhood has come to mean simply reflect parts of a stereotype might, of course, be argued. In a postmodern environment, ideals are simply constructions, and one always has to ask who is doing the constructing. This is especially the case where movies are used to search the culture's soul, for moviemakers are a cultural elite quite unrepresentative of most in society. Show business and big business have also been known to share the same bed, and money has corrupted both art and morals. Furthermore, ideals may also be psychological adjustments to perceived deficiencies, and these images of what real manhood should be about may therefore say less about what manhood is than about what it is not. Nevertheless, it was also clear in the 1980s that this was ground in urgent need of some fresh plowing. The men's movement sought to do just that.

In his best-selling book, *Iron John,* the storyteller and poet Robert Bly proposed in 1990 that being a man had been seriously misconstrued. The model that he felt needed to be constructed lay somewhere between what was taken as normative in the 1950s and what had become normative in the 1970s. The 1950s man was boyish, optimistic, hard-working, and supportive of his wife, but he understood little about the female psyche. He appreciated their bodies but not their souls. Reagan represented a "mummified" version of this ideal. By the 1970s, however, men had become "soft." While they had lost their hard, aggressive edges and would ideally neither harm the earth nor start wars, they also had little vitality. Somewhere between these models, Bly believed, the 1990s man should emerge, and the way to do so was by discovering the Wild Man within.

25. On some of the new responses to the crisis in masculinity, see Evelyn A. Kirkley, "Is it Manly to be Christian? The Debate in Victorian and Modern America," in *Redeeming Man: Religion and Masculinities,* ed. Stephen B. Boyd, W. Merle Longwood, and Mark W. Muesse (Louisville, Ky.: Westminster/John Knox Press, 1996), 80-88. Robert Vorlicky has looked at the portrayal of men in contemporary American drama in his *Act Like a Man: Challenging Masculinities in American Drama* (Ann Arbor: University of Michigan Press, 1995). He succeeds in locating "in dramatic art those cultural phenomena that incorporate, if not outrightly interrogate, men's gender issues: the women's liberation movement, the Civil Rights and Black Power movements, gay liberation, and the multiple incarnations of a men's movement" (p. 253). Elsie B. Washington has pursued some of the same themes in regard to relations between Black men and women. She notes that the extreme tensions between many Black men and women has been echoed in rap music and explored in movies like *Waiting to Exhale.* Her book contains the transcripts of interviews with Black men and women. See her *Uncivil War: The Struggle between Black Men and Women* (Chicago: Noble Press, 1996).

The source of wholeness was not to be found in the feminine side of a man's nature — passivity, empathy, sensitivity — but in taking back what had been lost: real masculinity in which what is primitive is reintegrated with what is civilized. This is a process that only men can teach men.

As it turned out, this Wild Man, this hidden essence of masculinity, could be enticed out into the open only by some homespun psycho-therapy, which included the beating of drums, sweat lodges, and the transformation of men into primitive savages who went loping through the bushes with spears in their hands. If all of this seems a little strange, it had company on the other side of the gender divide. The pagan goddess worship formally embraced by the Unitarians also found drums and comparable incantations helpful in rousing the spirits. And at a more mundane level, other feminists have been busy rediscovering the feminine self. Morwenna Griffiths, British professor and feminist, has spoken with disdain of the kind of abstract thinking that has dominated Western philosophy because it has been so entirely dominated by males. Women must now turn away from this and turn toward their own autobiographies as the source of truth. Critical autobiography uses personal experience to reflect upon and to reconstruct the meaning of life. The objective is for women to extricate themselves from the social, cultural web and to remake themselves. Indeed, the second part of her book bears the title, "Constructing Ourselves," and she argues that "each individual creates her own identity, although she is constrained by circumstance in doing so."[26] From this assumption — that we can become cocreators of our own reality — Anderson speaks of the women's movement as "the world's largest course in constructivist ther-apy" that has "been underway for some decades now and shows no signs of nearing termination."[27] On both sides of the divide, then, men and women, by means that may differ a little — Bly borrows heavily from Jung and Freud, Griffiths from social theorists — believe that being male or female is a matter of construction. Culture may get in

26. Morwenna Griffiths, *Feminisms and the Self: The Web of Identity* (London: Routledge, 1995), 93. Marya Schechtman, writing from a philosophical point of view, argues that "a person creates his identity by forming an autobiographical narrative — a story of his life." She suggests that there is a distinction between a person as a human being and the person as a person. A person comes to be a person by organizing "the content of her self-narrative, and the traits, actions, and expe-riences included in it." This is what lies behind the current feminist interest in everyone "telling her story." See her *The Constitution of Selves* (Ithaca, N.Y.: Cornell University Press, 1996), 93-94.

27. Anderson, *Reality Is Not What It Used to Be,* 141.

the way, as might one's own personal history and relationship to one's mother or father, but the building blocks are there to be found and a new person is there ready to emerge.

What, then, is the common thread running through our shift from fate to choice, the discovery of the emptiness of the contemporary self, the more accented role that style plays, the emergence of malls as our new temples to consumption, and the belief that the meaning of maleness and femaleness are matters for self-construction? It is a new understanding of the self. This is not a thread we will easily find unless we realize that modernity is a "movement from one constellation of background understandings to another which repositions the self in relation to others and the good."[28] Self and society cannot be understood apart from each other. A "certain kind of 'self' calls for a certain kind of society," argues historian Wilfred McClay,[29] but it is also the case that a certain kind of society calls for a certain kind of self. A society like ours — consumer driven, suffused with change, large and anonymous in its workings — produces a sense of self that is alien. It calls for a self that can adjust and transform its public presentation as circumstance requires. And it excites the thought that even the self could be different from what it has been. The self can be liberated.

A liberated self, it turns out, is no longer tethered to what used to be thought a virtue: consistency. Consistency, in this new, postmodern framework, becomes the hobgoblin of foolish minds. If consistency was once the hallmark of firm, rooted character, it is now the major impediment to the successful construction of the self. A flexible biography, a self that can adapt as needed to different environments, that can remake itself, refurbish itself, reinvent itself, reimagine itself and even remake its body, is the obvious psychological counterpart to our market-driven economy with its plethora of choices and required adaptations. The core of unchanging moral conviction is thus swept aside in the current of modern, psychological adaptation. "The systematic hunting down of all settled convictions," says Philip Rieff, "represents the anti-cultural predicate upon which modern personality is being organized,"[30] and it

28. Charles Taylor, "Two Theories of Modernity," *Hastings Center Report* 25, no. 2 (March–April 1995), 24.

29. Wilfred McClay, *The Masterless: Self and Society in Modern America* (Chapel Hill: University of North Carolina Press, 1994), 5. This is a historical study from the Civil War to the present showing the interconnections between social events and the literature of the period.

30. Philip Rieff, *The Triumph of the Therapeutic: Uses of Faith after Freud* (New York: Harper & Row, 1968), 13.

threatens to destroy the culture, because no culture can survive such an assault on its moral structure.

We must now focus more attention on how this changed perception has come about. If the reason for its construction is the contemporary sense of the self's emptiness and unreality, if one of the means of its reconstruction is consumption, why has life taken this particular turn? What lies beneath it?

This liberation of the self involves a conceptual shift with two closely related aspects: first, the replacement of character by personality as the fundamental category for thinking about the person; second, the replacement of human nature by self-consciousness. The most important outcome of this shift is the devastation that it has wrought on the moral life.

From Character to Personality

Today, we cultivate *personality* (a word almost unknown before the twentieth century) far more than we do *character,* and this is simply the concomitant to the way in which values have come to replace the older sense of virtue. One of the small, telltale signs, among many others, of such a shift is the way letters of reference have changed. In the last century, these letters were not confidential as they are now but were carried by the person. They were character references and spoke of the person's virtue and social habits. They would often be read by the person as a matter of satisfaction and produced when necessary. Today, a discussion of personal character and social habits might well be considered rather inconsequential and, perhaps, inappropriately intrusive in a letter of reference. Instead, matters of competence and personality are regarded as important.

The change came exactly at the turn of the century. The warning of an impending shift in the national mood came in the form of a growing sense of nervousness that Americans began to exhibit and that William James thought was the result of too much work. He counseled more relaxation. But there were many other responses. Some rushed to aid the ailing American psyche with a fresh rash of utopian writings; others leaned on new scientific analyses to learn about what was happening. More social and cultural analyses were offered, and, of course, psychology and psychotherapy began to emerge as important conceptual frameworks for understanding the person. Much more was going on than met the eye. For while life was becoming more abundant, it was also becoming thinner, its purpose more obscure. Increasingly people began to express their sense that life was losing its reality.[31] What now seems clear is that they were beginning to pay the price of being modern, for this sense of unreality, this emotional dread of being adrift, of having lost connections to the outside world, is the calling card that our highly urbanized, technologically driven world always leaves behind. The tremor that first registered at the turn of the century has only intensified as the decades have passed. In order to come to terms with this shaking of the internal foundations, psychologist Warren Susman has discovered, writers of advice manuals at the turn of the century abruptly changed direction.

Until this time, the self had been understood in terms of character, of virtue to be learned and practiced, of private desires to be denied.[32] The words that had most commonly been used to describe this character, Susman found, were *"citizenship, duty, democracy, work, building, golden deeds, outdoor life, conquest, honor, reputation, morals, manners, integrity,* and above all, *manhood."*[33] These virtues were all sustained by a belief in a higher moral law, a belief that rapidly began to sag and disintegrate. Around 1890, the focus abruptly shifted from character to personality. The adjectives most commonly used to describe personality became *"fascinating, stunning, attractive, magnetic, glowing, masterful, creative, dominant, forceful."*[34] None of these words could easily be used to describe someone's character. Character is not stunning, fascinating, or creative. Character is good or bad, while personality is attractive, forceful, or magnetic. Attention therefore was shifting from the moral virtues, which need to be cultivated, to the image, which needs to be fashioned. It was a shift away from the invisible moral intentions toward the attempt to make ourselves appealing to others, away from what we actually are and toward refining our performance before a public that mostly judges the exterior. The self-sacrifice of the older understanding made way for the self-realization of the new. Now, it became important to find one's self, to stand out in the crowd, to be unique, to be confident, and to be able to project oneself.

31. This malaise and uncertainty of the spirit is brilliantly depicted by Jackson Lears, *No Place of Grace: Antimodernism and the Transformation of American Culture, 1880-1920* (New York: Pantheon Books, 1981).

32. Gertrude Himmelfarb, *The De-moralization of Society: From Victorian Virtues to Modern Values* (New York: Alfred A. Knopf, 1995), 53-169.

33. Warren I. Susman, *Culture As History: The Transformation of American Society in the Twentieth Century* (New York: Pantheon Books, 1984), 273-74.

34. Ibid., 277.

Certainly by the 1930s, and before Alfred Adler's discovery of inferiority complexes, the change had been completed, the earlier character ethic having been displaced by the new personality ethic. "During the first three decades of the twentieth century," historian Richard Huber writes, "the output of personality ethic success literature was abundant," though it was initially aimed mainly at salesmen.[35] They were coached, step by step, in all the techniques of personality that could be used to move potential buyers toward a sale. So effective were these techniques that the "traveling salesman" became a byword for what was slick, clever, and so skilled in persuasion that buyers needed to be cautioned. But soon the circumference of this literature began to widen until, in 1936, it captured the imagination of the nation through the most widely purchased nonfiction book of the twentieth century: Dale Carnegie's *How to Win Friends and Influence People*. It was also the first major piece in the now flourishing and diversified self-help literature. When he died in 1955, Huber says, Carnegie was "king of the personality ethic." There are now, however, many pretenders to the king's throne.

The crucial moral change that resulted from this development, cultural historian Jackson Lears has written, "was the beginning of a shift from a Protestant ethos of salvation through self-denial toward a therapeutic ethos stressing self-realization in this world," one that has produced, in our own time, an obsessive interest in both bodily fitness and psychological health.[36] Of course people have always had an interest in their health and have always desired remedies from diseases, but prior to the twentieth century these preoccupations were understood for the most part within religious and ethical frameworks. Today, these frameworks have dissipated, and the quest for health is now understood simply in terms of the self. It is this secular quest, this fretful preoccupation with a fragile and uncertain well-being, that has provided the context in which both psychologists and advertisers have sought to promote their own understanding of the regeneration of selfhood.[37]

---

35. Richard M. Huber, *The American Idea of Success* (Wainscott, N.Y.: Pushcart Press, 1987), 250.

36. T. J. Jackson Lears, "From Salvation to Self-Realization: Advertising and the Therapeutic Roots of the Consumer Culture, 1880-1930," in *The Culture of Consumption: Critical Essays in American History, 1880-1980*, ed. Richard Wightman Fox and T. J. Jackson Lears (New York: Pantheon Books, 1983), 4.

37. Personality is about being "somebody," and it is no surprise that Martin Luther King countered the marginalization of Blacks in American society with his philosophy of "somebodyness." It was an attempt to create social personality on the

This crucial change has also shaped the way we now think about happiness. Philosopher Deal Hudson argues that psychological happiness "has become an unquestioned first principle of the present age." As a result, "the cultivation of satisfaction, pleasure, and emotion now takes precedence over the nurturing of moral and institutional character."[38] This shift is not entirely new, of course, but the scope of our social experiment and the innocence of its participants do set it apart as quite distinctive. For what is unusual is that people now think that happiness has little or nothing to do with the moral life, that it can be pursued as an end in itself, that it is something which can either be bought or, at least, manufactured.

We are now faced with competing visions of the self. The older interest in character, which unwittingly owed much to biblical teaching, however indistinct that teaching had become in the wider culture during the last century, presumed that growth in the person comes about through moral limitation, through self-sacrifice and self-control,[39] and that therein lay the springs of personal satisfaction and even happiness. The pathway to selfhood went along the road of moral obligation, and this produced a solid sense of the self. The role that this higher law played has now been replaced by the demands of a higher self, and, paradoxically, this sense of the self has fragmented. The vision that sprung from personality was one of unlimited self-expression, self-gratification, and self-fulfillment. However, as the self emptied out it became a receptacle to be filled with the impressions of others. Thus the freedom to "be one's self" was soon held hostage to the views of others, the world of fashion, and the pressure of social trends. And without a clear sense of the self, the ability to deny the self began to weaken. Standards became blurry, and without a religious framework of meaning to give sense to reality, people began to experience a troubling and painful sense of dislocation.[40] They were becoming weightless. As

---

foundations of an understanding of the image of God, and the link between these was the philosophical system of Boston personalism. See Garth Baker-Fletcher, *Somebodyness* (Minneapolis: Fortress Press, 1993), 59-78.

38. Deal W. Hudson, *Happiness and the Limits of Satisfaction* (London: Rowman and Littlefield, 1996), xi.

39. See Charles E. B. Cranfield, "Self-denial," *Expository Times* 104 (Fall 1994), 143-45.

40. Alienation, boredom, and a sense of despair are not unique to modernized, twentieth-century culture. These are threads woven throughout our literature. See, for example, Reinhard Kuhn, *The Demon of Noontide: Ennui in Western Literature* (Princeton: Princeton University Press, 1976). In the postmodern context, however, these themes intensify and take on their own particular form. On this, see Michael

Charles Taylor has noted, the "existential predicament in which one fears condemnation is quite different from the one where one fears, above all, meaninglessness."[41]

Nowhere is this disengagement between personality and character more plain than in the way that celebrities have replaced heroes in our culture, and in the way that villains have disappeared. A hero was someone who embodied what people prized but did so in such a way that others wanted to emulate him or her.[42] A celebrity may also want to be emulated, but the grounds of the emulation have now changed. A celebrity usually embodies nothing and is typically known only for being known. Fame, in our world of images and manipulation, can be manufactured with little or no accomplishment behind it. In Daniel Boorstin's rather caustic comparison: "The hero was distinguished by his achievement; the celebrity by his image or trademark. The hero created himself; the celebrity is created by the media. The hero was a big man; the celebrity is a big name."[43] It is our *commercial* culture that produces the celebrity, whereas it was the *moral* culture that, more often than not, elevated the hero. As celebrities replace heroes, image replaces character, and commercial culture replaces that which is moral, we are left with a kind of individualism that festers with lawlessness.

The Protestant work ethic was foundational to nineteenth-century culture. Perhaps this ethic became part of a myth, for in America the assumption was that all of the obstacles to advancement that were related to class had been removed and been replaced by what hard work, honesty, and diligence could accomplish. We have become free to become whatever we aspire to be. Perhaps it is not quite as simple as that. Thrift, moderation, and diligence also have to be hitched up to some talent, and there is no question that class and privilege, if now more subtle, are nevertheless powerful ingredients in the mix that results in success, if not in every case, at least in many. But in our dream, we chose freedom, even if the outcome was an inequality of accomplish-

---

David Levin, *The Opening of Vision: Nihilism and the Postmodern Situation* (New York: Routledge, 1988). For a discussion of the philosophical and theological engagements with nihilism, see Karen L. Carr, *The Banalization of Nihilism: Twentieth-Century Responses to Meaninglessness* (New York: State University of New York Press, 1992).

41. Taylor, "Two Theories of Modernity," 18.

42. Dick Keyes, *True Heroism: In a World of Celebrity Counterfeits* (Colorado Springs: Navpress, 1995), 14-16; see also Joshua Gamsun, *Claims to Fame: Celebrity in Contemporary America* (Berkeley: University of California Press, 1994).

43. Daniel J. Boorstin, *The Image; or, What Happened to the American Dream* (New York: Atheneum, 1962), 61.

ment, while Marxists chose equality of accomplishment and possessions, dismal as these rapidly became, over freedom. At the same time, the Protestant work ethic, and the habits that went with it, did mean that the good often also did well. Nineteenth-century Americans looked askance at self-indulgence, they believed in patient accumulation, they considered self-discipline a virtue and self-indulgence a vice, and in combination these virtues inadvertently produced much wealth.[44] The abundance this ethic so often produced, however, was best thought of as the byproduct and not the end of work. And certainly the assumption that is now widespread, that this abundance contains within it the balm for our troubled selves, was entirely unknown in the last century.

One of the most important consequences of this changing internal terrain has been the way in which guilt has been secularized and relocated. The older "Puritan" moral conscience with its sense of inward pollution, of moral culpability before God, which we saw in Luther, Owen, and Brainerd, has been rubbed so thin in its passage through the modern world as to have become invisible. This sense of pollution has been moved outward and relocated in the body. In the Victorian period, the distress of the body, with its vapors and intestinal poisons, was thought to impose itself upon the soul. We have reversed this. We think the distress of the self can be dissolved in the body.[45] As "churches empty out," journalist Nancy Brewka Clark has perceptively noted, "health clubs flourish; as traditional fervor wanes, attention to the body waxes," the passion for aerobics becoming a secularized quest for eternal life as the intrusions of age are resisted. Thus the pain of the workout becomes the modern version of the penance of the monk's hair shirt. The work of the sole leads to the healing of the soul.[46] Much of our advertising has become religious in its form, offering regeneration and recovery to consumers by pushing products for the senses, to which our inner distress has been relocated. Thus, as we shall see, our healers have a two-pronged approach to our sense of dis-ease: advertisers speak to the body as if the healing of the self can be addressed there, and psychotherapists address the obscure depths within the self where shame is found.

44. Christopher Lasch, *The Culture of Narcissism: American Life in an Age of Diminishing Expectations* (New York: Norton, 1978), 52-53. See also his later reflection on these themes in "The Culture of Narcissism Revisited," *The World and I* (May 1990), 511-23.

45. Jackson Lears, *Fables of Abundance: A Cultural History of Advertising in America* (New York: Basic Books, 1994), 140.

46. Nancy Brewka Clark, "Faith in the Flesh: An Essay on Secular Society's Preoccupation With Life (Somewhat) Eternal," *Lynn Magazine* (October 1985), 18.

As our emphasis has shifted from producing goods by hard, dil-
igent work to selling and consuming those goods, a change has also
occurred in our self. It is a change from the moral self-improvement
that, in the last century at least, was the accepted goal for so many to
the psychological self-preservation of our own times. It has replaced
our dependence on hard work by being able to seduce others instead.
"In earlier times," Christopher Lasch writes, "the self-made man took
pride in his judgment of character and probity; today he anxiously scans
the faces of his fellows not so much to evaluate their credit but in order
to gauge their susceptibility to his own blandishments."[47] Why is this?

As these changes began to rumble through society, the whole idea
of what constituted success also began to change. Last century's acceptance of the centrality of moral virtue also provided the standards by
which success could be measured. It was not measured by the abundance
of the goods accumulated but by how the accumulation had been
accomplished. Was it done with integrity, by restraining the appetites
of indulgence, by standards of fairness and respect? In this sense, success
was something to which all could aspire, regardless of how well they
had actually prospered. With the withering of this internal virtue, the
standard by which success was measured changed from matters of
character to those of personality. Whereas the approval of others arose
out of a consideration of their accomplishments — that they had lived
a good life — now we substitute for this an alternative accomplishment,
that we have made ourselves likable instead. We wish to be admired,
rather than esteemed, Lasch says, envied rather than respected. Our
actual accomplishments are of far less significance than the fact that we
become known as those who have "made it." And whereas the older
kind of accomplishment was durable, the newer kind is ephemeral, for
those who are known as having made it may as rapidly become unknown
within the receding memory of their observers, or fall within their
estimates, which are always fickle and changing. What this means in the
corporate world, then, is that devotion to the responsibilities of the
position is but a part of upward mobility. The other part is that one
must be well thought of, and this has only a tangential relationship to
how well one has worked. It is entirely possible to create an aura of
personal success around a record of incompetence.[48] The art of the
upward move has as much to do with creating favorable impressions as
with doing good work.

47. Lasch, *Culture of Narcissism*, 53.
48. Ibid., 61.

Here, however, we come across a contradiction that continues to rattle American society today. On the one hand, our contemporary wisdom says that we are to become unique, to stand apart from everyone else, to value our feelings, to be "personalities." On the other hand, we are to be likable, to fascinate, to win others over by our magnetism. We have to present an image to the social fraternity that will be impressive while, at the same time, having to stand apart from that fraternity if we are to be "individuals." This new configuration of things requires that we walk alone and yet be connected. Not only so, but the pursuit of self-fulfillment inevitably undercuts our capacity for being liked by others. So, how do we fly in the face of conformity by becoming different, while conforming enough to be liked? How do we pursue self-interest without obliterating our web of connectedness to others? These are the conundrums to which late twentieth-century culture has no answers, and the implications of our silence are serious. How can we have an ordered society while sustaining this vision of emancipated selves?

When the self was conceived through character, a bridge was immediately established to society. The bridge was the moral order, which bound the self to others in the bond of commonly owed obligations. When the self began to be experienced and expressed within personality, there was no longer a bridge to society, for there was no longer a moral order to regulate private and public behavior. The bond of obligation between people in society snapped. This is what lies beneath our fragmenting society, examined in the previous chapter, and this is what is now placing in jeopardy our democracy.[49] This is the price we are beginning to pay for the narcissistic personality we have been cultivating.

These changes, which began at the turn of the century, and which I have only been able to sketch in the broadest way, have only intensified within our heightened consumer culture. This "shift from character to personality," Philip Cushman sums up, "reflected a profound change in the cultural terrain of the era. The self was in process of being configured into a radically different shape."[50] Not only has this meant that personality, rather than character, has become our primary category of understanding, but in concert with this the self has emerged in place of human nature.

49. See Jean Bethke Elshtain, *Democracy on Trial* (New York: Basic Books, 1995), 5-27.

50. Philip Cushman, *Constructing the Self, Constructing America: A Cultural History of Psychotherapy* (Reading, Penn.: Addison-Wesley, 1995), 65.

From Nature to Self-consciousness

For many centuries in the West, the exclusive language of self-under-standing was that of human nature. The language was not exclusively Christian, though in its Christian form it did do service for the belief that all human beings are made in the image of God. This language therefore enabled people to say that beneath all of the surface partic-ularities of gender, ethnicity, age, education, occupation, and culture there was a shape to human life that was the same in all places and times. Within Christian theology the exact nature of the image of God has been debated, but there has never been any doubting that human beings are not simply a collection of genes and electrical impulses, nor are they simply the products of their circumstances, nor can they be understood exhaustively through their gender and ethnicity, nor are they simply machines of consumption. They are spiritual beings. They share in their creation what gives them surpassing value, and this is the same in all people.

This is suggested, for example, in the comparisons which Jesus made. "Look at the birds of the air. . . . Are you not of more value than they?" (Matt. 6:26; cf. 10:31). "Of how much more value is a man than a sheep!" (Matt. 12:12). Nor are human beings simply things. "For what does it profit a man, to gain the whole world and forfeit his life? For what can a man give in return for his life?" (Mark 8:36-37). This is news, indeed. The Marxists would have sacrificed many lives to gain the whole world, and we in the West have sacrificed many unborn children to gain personal affluence and domestic tranquillity.[51] But why cannot wealth, power, and aggrandizement be compared in value to the loss of one life? The answer is that one life is worth more than these things because of one's intrinsic value as an eternal being.

In the life of the Church, the value that we have as bearers of God's image has been easy to profess but hard to implement. Every society has its own ways of assessing who is important and who is not, who has value and who does not (cf. James 2:1-12). To the extent that the Church believes the biblical testimony, to that extent it is committed to an egalitarianism that has to be defended in every culture. On the grounds of creation, the Church has to say that no human being is intrinsically less valuable than another, and on the grounds of its doc-trine of sin, it also has to declare that regardless of personal piety or

51. See Robert H. Bork, "Inconvenient Lives," *First Things* 68 (December 1996), 9-13.

moral development — or, for that matter, of how depraved a "lifestyle" someone has maintained — no person stands closer to, or further from, God than another with respect to salvation. We are equal in our value and equally ruined in our sin. That is the kind of egalitarianism to which the Gospel commits the Church.

In every age there are threads of continuity and discontinuity. What may be different from age to age is the political organization, the kind of economy that exists and how it works, the architectural style, the nature of the calamities that occur — such as war, famine, natural disasters, or social upheaval — the dominance or absence of religion, life expectancy, the scope of medical care, and any number of other factors that impinge on daily life. In these areas, life in seventeenth-century America, for example, was very different indeed from life in the twentieth. At the same time, if Christian assumptions can be accepted, life in these two times also shared some things. Human nature has remained unchanged as created and fallen, as has God in his character and purposes, as has the truth of the revelation he has given us in the Bible, as has the significance of his redemptive acts and most importantly the birth, death, and resurrection of Christ. These have not changed. They are the threads that are woven through ages that, in many other ways, have no connections with each other at all. They give continuity to life amidst its many jarring discontinuities. For this reason, there is only one Gospel applicable to all people in all places and believed in the same way in every age. If this were not so, Christian faith would mean something entirely different today from what it meant last century, and faith would mean something entirely different in America than in Asia, Europe, or Africa.

Today, however, the language of human nature has vanished. There are no doubt many reasons for this. To start with, the older discussion of human nature, in both Protestantism and Catholicism, consciously and explicitly built upon a distinction between the natural and supernatural; in our secularized age, the supernatural has either been discarded or relocated within the natural, thus altering what "human nature" might mean. The older discussion also had a tendency, now seen to be fatal, of imagining that there was deposited in every body a kind of eternal essence that was the same everywhere and that could be considered in abstraction from a person's actual life; today, the whole tide of learning from psychology to philosophy to theology to sociology is moving in the opposite direction in wanting to overcome the mind/body distinction. Today, we want to talk about people, not about souls.

Part of this transition has also come about because of our need to make internal adjustments to the emergence of the modernized world.[52] Those who lived in Luther's day thought of themselves in relation to the world around them, to their town, to the baron or duke to whom loyalty was owed, to their family. Their consciousness was defined by these relationships in a way that is no longer possible today. The outside world has grown in its immensity because of our heightened consciousness of it through information technologies, but we no longer relate to it as peasants did to their town. In this sense, Marshall McLuhan's catchy reference to our "global village" is one of the more outlandish oxymorons of our time. The truth is that the globe overwhelms the individual. It cannot offer the human interconnections, the fabric of community, that the village once did. The globe can no more be a village than wisdom is ever likely to become conventional or sense common.

As our society has changed, as the density and size of its cities has increased, its population swelled, its technology grown, its capitalism flourished, its lines of information proliferated, we have felt ourselves to be more and more alien in its world. The weight of our consciousness has therefore shifted from the external world to the internal world, and our identity is increasingly forged, not through relationships to place, community, family and church, but through the exploration of the inner world of the self. "One of the things that make the world 'modern'," writes Susman, "is the development of consciousness of self."[53]

When we were emancipated from the hard work and from many of the uncertainties of life that characterized previous ages, we also found that we had been released from many of the demands that those times imposed on the self. This preoccupation with our own consciousness, therefore, has increasingly been pursued outside the markers of moral obligation. In the last century, the culture conveyed a moral vision that many found to be inwardly compelling. Ours has no such vision. In its place stand beliefs that release us from all such constraints and that propose in their place, Philip Rieff argues, "the superiority of all that money can buy, technology can make, and science can conceive."[54] In other words, whereas therapy was once organized around a set of

---

52. See Kenneth J. Gergen, "The Social Construction of Knowledge," in *Self and Identity: Contemporary Philosophical Issues*, ed. Daniel Kolak and Raymond Martin (New York: Macmillan, 1991), 372-85.

53. Susman, *Culture As History*, 271.

54. Rieff, *The Triumph of the Therapeutic*, 253.

moral commands — "you must not" and "you must" — now therapy has replaced these by the thought that you must be your own person, do your own thing, buy what gives you pleasure, and make of yourself what you can. We pursue our own consciousness as a thing in itself. Indeed, our entire culture is being reordered around the self understood as completely autonomous from others, from the past, from moral obligation, and from civic duty.

We have also rewritten the religious question.[55] That question was always how we might be consoled in our journey through this valley of tears. Socrates found consolation in the good, the beautiful, and the true; the New Testament finds it in Christ's redemption; Marx and liberation theology found it in the journey toward a more just world. But we find it simply in ourselves. We have become both our own patients and therapists, deeply committed to the gospel of self-fulfillment.

The inevitable outcome to this is the emergence of a new kind of person, what Rieff calls "psychological man." Rieff roots this transformation in the influence of Freud, but Freud would have little influence in the wider culture if that culture did not, in its own way, provide apparent authentication for what he argued. Our culture itself gives psychologists their currency; psychologists are as powerless as anyone else to shape the culture. And what our culture suggests is that all of the greatest treasures of life are at hand, quite simply, in the self. "Religious man was born to be saved," Rieff says, but "psychological man was born to be pleased."[56] "I believe" has been replaced by "I feel." The problem is that we have not been feeling so well recently.

According to Christopher Lasch, in the 1960s therapists and psychiatrists began to see a different kind of patient.[57] Many of their patients prior to this time had been neurotics with obsessive and compulsive behavior, but they were increasingly replaced by a new kind of patient, the forerunners of whom Freud had seen and had refused to treat because he believed they were impervious to analysis. In the 1960s, these patients often had fragmentary selves, weak or vacant consciences, and they engaged in covering up their inward deficiencies, their sense of anxiety, by exaggerating their accomplishments. They were filled with a vague sense of dis-ease. Dissatisfaction, like a fog, seeped into all the nooks and crannies of their life. They often had a pervasive feeling of emptiness. Their self-esteem oscillated between a sense of

55. Ibid., 29.
56. Ibid., 24-25.
57. Lasch, *The Culture of Narcissism*, 37.

self-importance that was either greatly enlarged or greatly diminished. They were chronically bored, restless, uprooted, always seeking instantaneous gratification without emotional involvement. And often their disquieting images of themselves translated into a preoccupation with the body and with physical health. As it came to be analyzed, the symptoms of narcissism, it was agreed, were an exaggerated sense of self-importance; fantasies about the possession of unlimited power, success, or beauty; feelings of rage, shame, humiliation, or emptiness when criticized; the need to exploit others and a corresponding inability to sustain good relations with others; and a sense of entitlement to things, positions, and people. Lasch suggests that the symptoms of this disorder had actually become the traits of our culture. In a remarkable way, this constellation of traits has become a much more widely evident trademark of our passage through modernized culture, in which personality now eclipses character. If the narcissist classically has a shrunken, fragmentary self, our culture has similarly become hollowed out and lost its core. If the narcissist covers up the emptiness by exaggerated self-importance and fantasies of power, our culture is covering up its hollowness by fads and fashions, ceaseless consuming, and the constant excitement of fresh sexual conquest. This is going to lead, as I shall suggest, to an entirely new understanding of salvation.

When these new preoccupations flow into the postmodern world, rife as it is with antinomian individualism, self-consciousness becomes radically relativized. From the older stress on *human nature*, which is the same in everyone, we moved to *self-consciousness*, which is different in everyone. The vocabulary of the self, the words we use to understand its life, is quite different from that of nature. The language of the self is that of fulfillment, of choice, of autonomy, and of identity. The language of nature speaks to our relationships to God, to the creation, to others. It acknowledges that we occupy our place in creation as human beings, made in the image of God, who have commonalties with all human beings. It is, therefore, the language of the moral universe that arises from who God is. To speak of nature leads naturally into a consideration of virtue: civility, responsibility, self-control, self-denial, duty, service, generosity, fidelity, fortitude, and goodness.

By contrast, one's self-consciousness is not the same as anyone else's, for the life circumstances, personalities, and social location of others are all different. The consensus, therefore, is that the language of the self, rather than that of human nature, provides a far more productive way of thinking about ourselves, given the endless variations on what we can do, buy, and be. It is not human nature, which we all

have in common, that best describes who we are, but rather our differences of consciousness. We experience ourselves as unique individuals.
This heightened sense of the uniqueness of our own consciousness
drives many of our social conflicts, from the altercations about gender
to the argument that no one outside a particular ethnic group can enter
into its history or understand its experience.[58]

One of the most disconcerting aspects of the modernized world
is that the public and private spheres are, as Jackson Lears notes, "both
more carefully separated and more subtly meshed than they were
before."[59] The separation may be unintended and inadvertent, as when
it creates a sense of alienation felt by many, but it is deliberate when it
insists that religion cannot intrude its beliefs and interests into the
public square. On the other side of the equation, however, stands the
massive intrusion of the modern world into private life.

There is a vanishing barrier between our public discourse and
matters that were once veiled from others, a point that the French
postmodern philosopher, Michel Foucault, has illumined, arguing that
even the most intimate aspects of private life come wrapped in cultural
meaning. But the traffic moves in both directions. If cultural meanings
invade our interior life, matters of inner intimacy are now strewn across
our public life. The television talk shows have discovered an inexhaust-
ible reservoir of people willing to talk openly and without embarrassment about matters that would have made their mothers blush a generation ago. President Clinton, equally without reserve, spoke to his MTV
audience about his choice of underwear. Advertising, which is a large
part of our public world, has learned how to dip its bucket into the well
of our inner desires and fantasies; it projects those desires and images
as part of its merchandising prowess. If our secularized culture insists

---

58. To the extent that citizens begin to retribalize into ethnic or other "fixed-
identity" groups, Jean Bethke Elshtain comments, "democracy falters. Any possibility for human dialog, for democratic communication and commonalty, vanishes
as so much froth on the polluted sea of phony equality. Difference becomes more
and more exclusivist. If you are black and I am white, by definition I do not and
cannot, in principle 'get it'. There is no way we can negotiate the space between
our given differences . . . mired in the cement of our own identities, we need never
deal with one another. Not really. One of us will win and one of us will lose the
cultural war or the political struggle. That's what it's all about: power of the most
reductive, impositional sort" (Elshtain, *Democracy on Trial*, 74). See her further
discussion of this theme under the heading, "The End of Democracy: The Judicial
Usurpation of Politics," *First Things* 67 (November 1996), 18-38, and "The End of
Democracy? A Discussion Continued," *First Things* 69 (January 1997), 19-29.

59. Lears, *Fables of Abundance*, 137.

that religious belief keep its head down and stay out of the public view, it also invades our inner life, dissolves the boundary separating what is private, internal, and intimate, and insists that it come out into the open. Many people have lamented the resulting loss of shame,[60] a loss that certainly has opened the way for the current tidal wave of pornography.[61] It is true that shame — by which we usually mean the embarrassment someone might feel if some aspect of one's life, usually intimate or unethical, is exposed to the view of others — is waning. Yet I shall argue that shame as a sense of inward nakedness is deeper than ever, only without moral bearings or substance.

Perhaps the most useful way to see how modern people view their predicament is simply to ask who their healers are. In our society, as I have suggested, the two most trusted forms of healing come through the language of advertising and psychotherapy.

The New Healers

There now seems little doubt that our new healers are offering salvation on strictly secular terms, terms that may bypass moral issues entirely. In psychotherapy, though, this situation stems from a long internal development.

Probably the most momentous step along this road happened when psychotherapy drifted away from its original context in medicine. That was where Freud had placed it, and he had cherished the hope that it would one day be recognized as science. In the early days, those seeking help came to those offering it as patients to doctors. In time, this changed. Clients now came to counselors, while counselors began to experience more freedom in constructing their therapies. Ironically, the profession began to look like a substitute religion, with its "priests," dogmas, rituals, orthodoxies, and heresies;[62] what it offered sometimes looked like spirituality built on secular assumptions. And soon, rank amateurs were offering their own therapies and treating themselves.

60. See the excellent analysis of this in Rochel Gurstein, *The Repeal of Reticence: A History of America's Cultural and Legal Struggles Over Free Speech, Obscenity, Sexual Liberation, and Modern Art* (New York: Hill and Wang, 1996), 32-60, 288-309.

61. Among the best discussions of this theme is Anthony Giddens, *The Transformation of Intimacy: Sexuality, Love, and Eroticism in Modern Societies* (Stanford: Stanford University Press, 1992).

62. This theme was developed in Paul Vitz, *Psychology as Religion: The Cult of Self-Worship* (Grand Rapids: Eerdmans, 1977).

Psychotherapy is both peculiarly adapted to the late twentieth century and a telling representation of it, psychologist Lucy Bregman has argued. It has arisen out of the sense of emptiness and meaninglessness that many modern people experience, and it could not have survived in a traditional society. It belongs amidst the complex, pressure-filled modern world, with its dense cities and technological conquests. It is an expression of that world with all of its human cost, the personal dilemmas it forces, the hollowing out of life that it effects, and its narcissism.[63] It is at once both the proffered cure for and the symbol of the troubled, empty self. And, most importantly, it is a *secular* spirituality. In substantiating this point, Bregman says that even though its metaphysical framework is often obscured, psychotherapy nevertheless has such a framework. It is a means to "revision" the self; it has become a technique for "self transformation." It is, in Bregman's words, "a new framework for the ordering of interiority, for interpreting life's meanings and each person's place in the cosmos."[64] It is, however, a metaphysic in which the moral has died.

Psychotherapy's disengagement from the medical context made possible its extraordinary success in the culture, because the practice of this secular spirituality was cut loose from its superintendence by the experts. In the encounter groups of the 1960s and the self-help books of the 1970s, the practice of this spirituality was taken in new directions; by the 1990s it had become popularized and was virtually ubiquitous. The willingness to talk about one's inner fears, rages, secrets, and perversions, it was assumed, was important to one's "recovery." Whereas this talking originally took place in the context of trust established by the expert therapist, by the 1960s trust was transferred to the encounter group, and by the 1970s to almost anyone who would listen. The television talk shows have made hay while this therapeutic sun has been shining. So has the growing body of self-help literature; ever inspirational, it has nevertheless succeeded in minimizing the complexities of life and reducing its remedies to techniques. The self-help literature assumes that healing is possible because the self carries within it the means of its own healing. What is needed is simply the right technique to tap into this potential. It therefore offers a secularized form of salvation.

---

63. See Michael Beldroch, "The Therapeutic as Narcissist," in *Psychological Man*, ed. Robert Boyers (New York: Harper Colophon Books, 1975), 105-23.

64. Lucy Bregman, "Psychotherapies," in *World Spirituality: An Encyclopedic History of the Religious Quest*, vol. 22, *Spirituality and the Secular Quest*, ed. Peter H. Van Ness (New York: Crossroad, 1996), 273.

That we also have an offer of salvation in advertising, however, may not be quite so evident. All advertising falls somewhere along a continuum; on one end is the business of informing the public; on the other end, that of persuading the public to buy, not only by making compelling associations between the product and some personal status or achievement, but also by offering some psychotherapy. In this sense, products are offered as a means to fill the emptiness of the modern self. It is advertising in this category, rather than that which predominantly offers information, that is in view here.

National advertising, as Philip Cushman argues, has undoubtedly "transformed America's concept of the individual from citizen to consumer." On the surface, it has done so by promoting intensely private, satisfying experience as life's real objective, to be had "by the purchase and consumption of goods and services."[65] Therapeutically dominated advertisements offer a magical elixir for life's problems, but what they are really offering is not so much an alternative life as an alternative *lifestyle*. These advertisements inform the viewer about the goods for sale, but they also offer up a vision of life. They link words and images in stories that embody the fantasies we have about the prospects of our own social transformation, and as such they are powerful, didactic tools. Consumers buy the lifestyle, however skeptical they may imagine themselves to be, "in a vain attempt to transform their lives because their lives are unsatisfactory and — without massive social change — ultimately unfixable."[66] The "pursuit of the good life" has therefore been replaced by the pursuit of "the good *things* in life."[67] A sense of well-

---

65. Cushman, *Constructing the Self, Constructing America*, 68. Two rather different views of advertising have emerged. Some, like Daniel Boorstin, have seen advertising more as a product that is neither good nor bad in itself. Others, like Stuart Ewen, have focused on the malignant intentions of big business and view advertising as a tool for duping an unsuspecting public. See his *Captains of Consciousness: Advertising and the Social Roots of the Consumer Culture* (New York: McGraw Hill, 1976). There is some truth to Ewen's argument, but he does not focus sufficiently on the fact that advertising "works" because consumers want it to work. He leaves unanswered why contemporary Americans are so vulnerable to the allure of purchase. Ronald Berman, *Advertising and Social Change* (London, SAGE Publications, 1981), succeeded in looking at this matter in a preliminary way, but the decisive study is Jackson Lears, *Fables of Abundance: A Cultural History of Advertising in America*. On advertising as a tool, see David W. Stewart and David H. Furse, *Effective Television Advertising: A Study of 1000 Commercials* (Lexington: D. C. Heath, 1986).

66. Cushman, *Constructing the Self, Constructing America*, 81.

67. Ibid., 68. See also the chapter entitled, "The Meaning of Possessions" in Peter K. Lunt and Sonia M. Livingstone, *Mass Consumption and Personal Identity: Everyday Economic Experience* (Philadelphia: Open University Press, 1992), 59-85.

being in life, as an end in itself rather than as an accompaniment to the moral life, then becomes the overwhelming *summum bonum*. Here psychology and advertising are plying the same channel. As we have been transformed from moral actors and citizens into consumers, we also find that we must become patients, for the sense of well-being that we seek, and that we think can be bought, remains elusive. The very emptiness of the modern self sustains both our psychologists and our merchants.

In America, it is not only necessity that sells products but desire. It is what we want, not merely what we need. We desire not only the goods but what comes with the purchase, which is, preeminently, our advancement. It is visibility, standing, attraction that we are buying; it is to be chic, cool, to be among the cognoscenti. Advertising, therefore, is about fashioning a psychological world in which want is unobstructed.

None of this would be effective, however, if advertisers, using their statistical surveillance of private life, did not project "powerful images of selfhood" that carry "the promise of magical self-transformation through the ritual of purchase."[68] In other words, the premise of the industry, and the principal explanation of its success, is that it is able to tap into the emptiness of the modern self. More than that, many advertisements boldly address that self, and for more than a century have honed messages that are replete with religious motifs. It is not simply a sense of well-being that they offer but a sense of salvation. "The language of progress and spiritual and physical fulfillment," Stuart Ewen has observed, is suffused throughout advertising, and advertising is the voice of this progress and spiritual fulfillment.[69]

It is hard to miss the redemptive themes in the many dreamy scenes of sensuality that we have so often seen in perfume advertisements, scenes that waft across the viewing public with the promise of bodily regeneration, even renewed sexual attraction, if one simply purchases the product. There is a life here that can be bought, a fantasy that can be consumed. One also thinks of the outdoor buddies in the Old Milwaukee advertisements who murmur to themselves, "It doesn't get any better than this." And for no more than the cost of a few beers at that. One thinks, too, of Sustacal, a mixture of nutrients for the aging, which offers access to the fountain of youth. Its advertisements show two apparently retired couples, one chipper and vibrant, the other flat and cheerless. The difference? Sustacal. Sustacal "can't add years to

68. Lears, *Fables of Abundance,* 139.
69. Ewen, *All Consuming Images,* 5.

your life, but it might help add life to your years." The variations on these themes are virtually endless, and there can be little doubt that what is being offered is a materialistic version of the biblical doctrine of regeneration. Even the revivalistic practice of giving testimonies is aped. Prior to the purchase of this or that product, it is implied, there was only defeat, despair, embarrassment, apathy, and boredom. After the purchase, everything changed. The world looked different, problems were overcome, personal defeats gave way to a life now full of new hope and endless prospects.

Advertising is about problem solving. A visitor from outer space dropping in for an evening of television watching would be given a very interesting view of our society. What is uppermost on our minds, apparently, is not the rotting of our inner cities, the insecurities of the marketplace, the debilitating pace of life, families breaking apart, children on drugs, a dangerous crime rate, or the sense of loss and disorientation that so many people experience. No, it is none of these things. What is uppermost on our minds is our bad breath, body odor, indigestion, gas, and constipation. Advertising traffics not in what is complex but in what is fixable. It offers diet plans on the assumption that everyone can be seduced by the thought of losing weight. It sells cosmetics on the expectation that all women can be allured by the prospect of improving their appearance. It fills the air with beer commercials and links these to suggestions of sexual conquest. Advertising assumes that all people are searching for something that will improve their chances in life, make them more attractive, make life more fun, ease the gnawing sense of emptiness within, and it offers something eminently simple and buyable as a solution.

The transition to the consumer paradise that America has become would have been impossible without the inner changes described in this chapter. The transition required not simply the apparatus to produce the goods and services that we want but the *moral permission* to indulge ourselves in their purchase and use. However, it was not so much that the permission was granted as that the obstacles before it simply fell away. A clear moral sense of the self stands as an impediment to consumer indulgence; a psychological sense of the self craves consumption as a way of discovering itself and easing its pains. As the religious has given way to the psychological, any opposition to the message of secular salvation — to have is to be — simply evaporated.

Our advertisers have therefore become the priesthood of our prosperity, as devout in their devotion to the good life as priests once were to the higher life. Rarely have advertisers gone out of their way to attack traditional moral norms. They have simply surpassed those norms, replaced them, by pointing to a different kind of life, one centered in therapeutic recovery rather than moral rootedness, and one promising psychological wholeness and a new kind of regeneration. That this promise has an elusive, dreamy quality to it, that it promises much more than it actually delivers, is apparently no impediment to the capacity of advertisers, not only to sell their products, but to sell life. We are, in the most profound ways, buying what they have to sell.

Odd as it may seem, both psychotherapists and advertisers address emotional needs, indeed, very often the *same* emotional needs. Their means, however, are very different. But whether by a product or by a technique, whether through purchase or through analysis, what is being offered is an answer to the diffusion of our identity and to the ache of our self. Side by side, they tap into our belief that the end of life is self-realization. They speak to those who know themselves to be a tangle of inner contradictions, those who drift in a fog of confused intentions and goals, whose emptiness is unfilled, who long for psychological vigor. But they have become the means of remitting all moral demands in our search for self-assurance and self-satisfaction.

They are the mirror in which we now see ourselves. We have become consumer beings, believing that we are what we have, that what we lack by way of a solid sense of selfhood can be recovered in the way we dress, what we purchase, and how we remake ourselves. Our consumption, our endless search for fun, now serves the same purpose that moral passion once did but without the cost that passion once extracted, the cost of lonely lives and doctrinal seriousness. The single-minded pursuit of fun extracts no cost at all, once it has been paid for.

And so we have come to believe that we know something that no other culture has known. We believe, says Philip Rieff, "that we can live freely at last, enjoying all our senses — except the sense of the past — as unremembering, honest, and friendly barbarians all, in a technological Eden,"[70] in love with life but in the end destroying it, because with all of our brilliance and sophistication, we have built a morally indifferent culture in which virtue almost inevitably perishes. It may seem that our acquisitive spirit has betrayed us into wanting too much. That is true, but it is accompanied by a more damaging mistake: we also want too little. We imagine that the human spirit can

70. Rieff, *The Triumph of the Therapeutic,* 4.

be treated casually, stuffed with CD players, sleek new cars, and movie images, plied with psychological nostrums, and somehow not notice the difference. It is, in fact, in wanting too much that we have also come to want too little — and the human spirit has noticed.

CHAPTER IV

The Bonfire of the Self

Each person in our society has received the burdensome gift of the overgrown self.

Roy F. Baumeister

The ideology of personal growth, superficially optimistic, radiates a profound despair and resignation. It is the faith of those without faith.

Christopher Lasch

Modernity has irreversibly rearranged the calculus of life's costs and benefits, making our world both much better and, in some ways, much more difficult to live in. It has left us with a world at which we marvel but a world that is sometimes psychologically painful to endure.

The advantages of living in the modern world are evident and numerous. They range from a marketplace filled with an abundance of goods and services, to modern medicine, which has pushed back the frontiers of disease and extended the length of life remarkably. We have more choices and more products. We communicate with more people, at greater distances, than ever before. We travel further, in less time, and with greater ease than ever before. Our vision of life is not bounded by place but encompasses the whole world. We have more entertainment, more diversions, more leisure, and more money than ever before. Technology has magnified our powers and extended our reach. Utopians might well have dreamed of all this bounty — indeed, one or two came close to doing so — but, like the moon, its light is also accompanied by shadows.

To change the image, all this bounty means that we must pay a toll to enter the highway of modernity. We must pay an invisible cost, one borne inwardly, at many different points. To start with, as our economy has become globalized, competition has increased; as a result, our work week has significantly lengthened over the last two decades, imposing on us rush, wear, and tear. Levels of stress and anxiety have risen by every measure, and with each succeeding generation in the twentieth century depression has increased threefold. If we have more products and more options, we also must reckon with more standardization. Nothing symbolizes this standardization better than the modern, dehumanized apartment, box set upon box. "The apartment-box," writes Michael Jones, "not only looks the same the world over; it creates the same sort of malaise in the human soul."[1] Even the graffiti is the same. And yet this far-reaching conformity is attended by equally far-reaching confusion. The underside to our unparalleled abundance is a gnawing sense of uncertainty. To feast on the abundance also requires that we must sometimes drink from a cup of apprehension. We inhabit the whole world psychologically, but we are often uprooted from place, community, and even family, left to wander our society as perpetual migrants. Migrants of old took their extended families, animals, and possessions with them; our contemporary migrants mostly travel alone and unencumbered. If, therefore, our reach has been extended into the whole world, it is because our roots no longer anchor us to place. If more people pass through our lives each day than ever before, comparatively fewer matter to us at a personal level. Modern medicine has greatly extended the length of life, but the circumstances of its closing chapters are often much harsher, much more lonely, than they used to be when death was swifter and family closer. And these costs are also evident in more slippery, less tangible matters, such as our lost sense of identity. We may imagine that we can construct ourselves, that we can assemble ourselves into new configurations, but the cost we must pay is a lost sense of stability and continuity in our lives. It is a mangled and lost sense of identity.

Modernity is thus a two-edged sword. It gives and it takes away. It blesses and it curses. It fills and it empties. It illumines and it obscures. And nowhere is this two-sidedness more evident than in the way that

---

1. E. Michael Jones, *Living Machines: Bauhaus Architecture as Sexual Ideology* (San Francisco: Ignatius Press, 1995), 44.

those who have fed upon its largesse, who have allowed themselves to become consumer beings, have lost their capacity to think of themselves as *moral* beings. In losing their bearings in any reality beyond what is experienced in the self, they lose their understanding about who they are. If they have much, they now also have little. This is the paradox that I want to explore in this chapter, especially as it relates to how our experience of the modern world has changed the internal terrain of our moral understanding. Our constant exposure to modern life inclines us to understand some of our disconcerting experiences less in terms of guilt and more in terms of shame.[2] Why has this happened and what are the consequences?

2. One of the most notable and interesting developments in psychological, but especially psychiatric, thinking in recent times has been the attempt to differentiate shame from guilt even while recognizing that they are closely related to one another. This is the technical parallel to what is more unconsciously apparent in the wider society. One of the first American thinkers to give prominence to shame was Erik Erikson in *Childhood and Society* (New York: Norton, 1950). He saw shame as a thread that ran through each identity crisis because it is part of the mistrust, doubt, guilt, inferiority, role confusion, isolation, and depletion of creativity that we must overcome. Helen Merrell Lynd's *On Shame and the Search for Identity* (New York: Harcourt, Brace, 1958), which came out eight years later, built on Erikson's work. She saw guilt and shame as being different, but each arises from the same source of internal aggression. There have been other landmark studies along the way. Silvan S. Tomkins's two volumes on emotions, *Affect/Imagery/Consciousness: I. The Positive Affects* (New York: Springer, 1962), and *Affect/Imagery/Consciousness: II. The Negative Affects* (New York: Springer, 1963), are very important. They have mapped out in a new way his "affective theory" of what the emotions are and how they function; shame is a part of this picture because it always generates one or another of the emotions. Further clarification on the distinction between shame and guilt is found in another significant volume, Leon Wurmser, *The Mark of Shame* (Baltimore: Johns Hopkins University Press, 1981). Some of the key theorists on shame are brought together in Donald L. Nathanson, ed., *The Many Faces of Shame* (New York: Guilford Press, 1988); he has further developed his own theories in *Shame and Pride: Affect, Sex, and the Birth of the Self* (New York: Norton, 1992). Narcissism has become a far more common personality disorder in the late twentieth century; three significant volumes that explore this are: Heinz Kohut, *The Analysis of the Self: A Systematic Approach to the Psychoanalytical Treatment of Narcissistic Personality Disorders* (New York: International Universities Press, 1971), which approaches it from the standpoint of "self psychology"; Otto Kernberg, *Borderline Conditions and Pathological Narcissism* (Northvale: Jason Aronson, 1975); and Andrew P. Morrison, *Essential Papers on Narcissism* (New York: New York University Press, 1986). For two more general studies that capitalize upon, and to a degree summarize, this other work, see Carl D. Schneider, *Shame, Exposure and Privacy* (Boston: Beacon Press, 1977), and Michael Lewis, *Shame: The Exposed Self* (New York: Basic Books, 1992). Two authors who have sought to rebuild their view of pastoral counseling around this new thinking on shame are Donald Capps, *The Depleted Self: Sin in a Narcissistic Age* (Minneapolis: Fortress Press, 1993), and Lewis B. Smedes, *Shame and Grace: Healing the Shame We Don't Deserve* (New York: HarperCollins, 1993).

From Guilt to Shame

Talking about the Self

In the previous chapter I sought to describe the two most important cultural changes that have happened in the twentieth century regarding our understanding of ourselves. These are the shift from character to personality and from nature to self-consciousness. Because of the first, we have slowly sloughed off the moral framework of life. Because of the second, a rampant relativism has been loosed on society, since no one's self-consciousness is exactly like anyone else's. A person's understanding about life, about his or her place in the cosmos, therefore becomes private and individualized. Implicit in these changes, however, is something else that is just as important: the vision of the self at the person's center.

In Western thought, it has principally been the philosophers who have kept alive the use of the word *self.* They have used it, at least from Descartes onward, more or less as a synonym for one's consciousness, and they have debated what the self can know, how that knowledge is derived, and what relationship it has to the actual world apart from the perceiving subject, though some have also used *self* to show that there is no such thing.[3] In the parallel stream of psychological thinking, interestingly enough, the use of *self* has, by comparison, been chaste and, until quite recently, rare. One can hardly find an instance of its use in Freud, for example. Psychologists have tended to favor a broader term like *personality,* which embraces the full continuum of being from what is biological to what is social, or the narrower term, *ego,* or the neutral term, *subject.*

What appears to have happened, then, is that technical psychological thinking has been somewhat overtaken by the flood of popular psychologizing spread far and wide in our society, often by rank amateurs. Beginning with Erik Erikson, and hastened in the work of psychologists Abraham Maslow and Carl Rogers (and supported by that of Heinz Kohut, Virginia Satir, and, to a lesser extent, Rollo May), the near obsession with the individualized self has spawned an industry whose watchwords are self-image, self-ideal, the true self, the false self, the inner self, and self-actualization. This language about the self has be-

---

3. See the account of some recent attempts along this line by Eugene Fontinell, "The Return of 'Selves'," *Cross Currents* 43, no. 3 (Fall 1993), 358-74. On more general and current philosophical thinking about the self, see Leroy Rouner, ed., *Selves, People, and Persons: What Does It Mean to Be a Self?* (Notre Dame: University of Notre Dame Press, 1992).

come central and dominant, and it appears to have forced the hand of
the theoreticians. They, too, are now talking about the self, and over
the last two decades psychologists have written extensively about it.[4]

Indeed, in America today the business of talking about the self is
big business. Sociologist John Rice has noted that the United States has
half the world's clinical psychologists, up from 12,000 in 1968 to 42,000
in 1990, when no other nation at that time had more than 400. We
have one third of the world's psychiatrists. In the fifteen years between
1975 and 1990, clinical social workers increased by 320 percent and
family counselors by 680 percent. By 1990, we had two psychotherapists
for every dentist and more counselors than librarians.[5] The plagues of
the self have come to nourish many a professional career as well as a
massive publishing industry.[6] The skepticism suggested in the title of
the 1992 book by James Hillman and Michael Ventura, *We've Had a
Hundred Years of Psychotherapy — and the World's Getting Worse,* appears
to be a minority viewpoint. It may be that many think that the world
is getting worse, but that has not taken the bloom off our love affair
with psychology.

We need, however, to linger with our cultural sense of what the
self is a little longer before taking up the central theme of this chapter.
Today, we typically think of the self as the "vast, stable, unique, important" interior world that provides the stuff of who we think we are as
well as who we would like to be. It contains, we believe, "thoughts,
feelings, intentions, personality traits, latent talents and capabilities, the
wellsprings of creativity, the key ingredients of personal fulfillment, and
the solutions to many of life's problems."[7] These typical and general

4. For a concise account of how the *self* has been thought about in psychology,
see Karl E. Scheibe, *Self Studies: The Psychology of Self and Identity* (Westport, Conn.:
Praeger, 1995), 23-54. See also the brief history of the understanding of person in
Michael Robbins, *Conceiving of Personality* (New Haven: Yale University Press, 1996),
27-36. On the philosophical side, see Troy Wilson Organ, *Philosophy and the Self:
East and West* (Selinsgrove: Susquehanna University Press, 1987).

5. John Steadman Rice, *A Disease of One's Own: Psychotherapy, Addiction, and the
Emergence of Co-Dependency* (New Brunswick: Transaction Publishers, 1996), 27.

6. See, for example, the listing of recent self-help books by Maria Heidkamp,
"Looking Out for Number One," *Publishers Weekly* 239 (February 3, 1992), 52, 54-57.
On women's use of this literature, see Wendy Simonds, "All Consuming Selves:
Self-Help Literature and Women's Identities," in *Constructing the Self in a Mediated
World,* ed. Debra Grodin and Thomas R. Lindlof (Thousand Oaks, Calif.: SAGE
Publications, 1996), 15-29.

7. Roy F. Baumeister, *Escaping the Self: Alcoholism, Spirituality, Masochism, and
Other Flights from the Burden of Selfhood* (New York: Basic Books, 1991), 3-4. A
comparable and equally typical understanding is found in Owen Flanagan, who uses

assumptions, of course, belie the current complexity of the more technical discussion over the self; this inner core, this center of our being,
this locus of the experiencing "I," it is argued, has its anchor dropped
into one of two entirely different waters. On the one hand, this sense
of "I," some say, is linked closely to our biology, which is something
unique to each individual. On the other hand, others say that this sense
of "I" is much influenced by our relations to others. The question of
connections concerns how far our identity is biologically given to us,
on the one side and, on the other, how far it is made up for us by our
roles in society, by relationships, and by the models we admire and seek
to emulate. Although these have become vexing questions among geneticists, sociologists and psychologists, they are not particularly pressing
matters in the wider culture.[8]

Here, the "I," the inner core of identity, is the focus; the roles
biology and society play are not large factors. The major exception,
of course, is the feminist contention that the self has been shaped in
a male-dominated culture from which it now needs to be redeemed.
More typically, though, the self is seen simply as having a potential
that, though not unlimited, is nevertheless still vast and largely un-
tapped. Deep within it are the springs from whence flow its own
healing waters. This understanding of the self implies an unwavering
faith in its capacities, as well as in our ability to tap into its capacities.
This sets us apart from many other cultures, in which it would be
inconceivable for people to imagine that they could look inside themselves for the answers to life. Even more remarkable is the thought
that buried within are the balms for our wounds and moral failures.
There is a touching innocence to this trust. It is almost as if no one
has told us that we now live east of Eden, that these internal streams
are also polluted waters.

---

the word *self* to mean "personality, character, an individual's central character traits,
the way(s) one carries oneself in the world, the way one represents oneself to others,
the dynamic integrated system of thoughts, emotions, lived events, and so on, that
make up who one is from the God's-eye point of view." See his *Self Expressions: Mind,
Morals, and the Meaning of Life* (New York: Oxford University Press, 1996), vii. A
sense of boundaries (I am not someone else) is also part of one's identity, and this
is central to self-preservation. See Daniel C. Dennett, *Consciousness Explained* (Boston:
Little, Brown, and Co., 1992), 173-82.

8. H. Ned Seelye and Jacqueline Howell Wasilewski, *Between Cultures: Developing Self-Identity in a World of Diversity* (Lincolnwood, Ill.: NTC Publishing Group,
1996), 105-06.

Home Alone

It is important to see what has happened if we are to understand where best to seek answers to the many dilemmas in contemporary life. Two problems in particular have come to the fore. First, we now have no transcendent reference point outside of ourselves. Second, sin has become a conceptual impossibility. However, since we continue to sin, much of our life has become inexplicable to us. These losses in understanding are lethal to our discovery of who we are as human beings and so to our identity.

The transcendent reference point for our life, the God who has spoken in Christ and in Scripture, has undergone two major relocations. First, in the Enlightenment, it was no longer believed that God had spoken, or that he wanted to speak, and so "truth" was sought out of relation to him. It was sought only in the natural world, not in divine revelation or, for those who had been raised as Catholics, in Church teaching. It was sought by reason in the absence of faith. Truth was thought to concern life, the meaning of things, but it was to be discovered strictly naturalistically. The truth discovered in this way, however, was assumed to have all the force of divine revelation, to be universally applicable, and this assumption is what cast so fraudulent a light on the whole ideology. Its authority really rested on stolen Christian assumptions, anti-religious though it was. And its latter-day children in our postmodern world have taken their revenge by disposing of every belief in "meta" truths, anything that can be used as a comprehensive umbrella of meaning that covers all situations in life. They prefer to have nothing to having fraud. Since "there no longer seems to be access to principles which can act as criteria of value for anything else," literary scholar Steven Connor writes, we are simply left with "the centerless universe of the postmodern."[9]

But what does it mean to be "decentered" in this way? It means that people have nowhere to stand cognitively in the world, no way to get their bearings, that life's experiences fall like pieces of confetti with no relationship to each other. Life is made up of a multitude of separate experiences that are without interconnections or meaning. We are without a framework within which their moral, aesthetic, and spiritual significance can be grasped. A rock concert in Boston, a bank robbery in Los Angeles, political scandals in Washington, civil wars in Africa,

---

9. Steven Connor, *Postmodern Culture: An Introduction to Theories of the Contemporary* (Oxford: Blackwell, 1989), 8.

watching a movie, buying new cosmetics, seeing one's physician — these are simply particles of information or experience that swirl around us each day, and there is no coherent way of knowing which are important and which are trivial, which are true and which are false, which are right and which are wrong. They are without meaning. In the twilight of the Western world, everything has become relative, and very little is normative any longer. We live in a world, Catholic scholar Gary Eberle notes, that is "without a map and without a center, a world in which compass bearings would be meaningless even if we could get them."[10] As this worldview collapses in on itself, we are simply left to stare blankly. The earlier protests against the rapidity of change in the modern world, its dehumanizing quality, its enforced anonymity, are not heard any more. These protests arose from some sense that things had gone awry, that something was terribly amiss. In the postmodern world, we have lost the standards that gave us the sense that things were awry and terribly amiss.

Along the way, however, the second transposition was taking place. As the skies of our culture filled with therapeutic clouds, the transcendent reference point for all of life now began to relocate itself from the external, natural world, and from naturalistic reason, to the world of the internal and psychological. Now, the self and its intuitions became our only means of understanding life's conundrums. But this "understanding" is often more sensed than thought-out. It is more about feeling than knowing. In the Enlightenment, the only unforgivable "sin," apart from being religious, was being irrational. Today, however, we traffic in the illogical and irrational without any misgivings and have become suspicious of those who are concerned with logic and rationality. Indeed, the irrational is often celebrated while the rational is denigrated. Then, the life of the mind was everything; now, the mind is trusted far less than the emotions, claims to truth far less than intuitions. And in the absence of any external authority, the line between right and wrong gets lost in the mists of self-desire and the mechanisms of self-justification. In the psychologized world we now inhabit, sin as the Bible thinks of it has become an impossibility.

What has disappeared is not sin itself but our cultural capacity to understand it. The Enlightenment dreamed of building societies in which everyone fit into the logic of the social machinery with no remainders. The reality, though, has been quite different; life has shown

10. Gary Eberle, *The Geography of Nowhere: Finding One's Self in the Postmodern World* (Kansas City: Sheed and Ward, 1994), 17-18.

itself to be unimaginably messy.[11] The construction of a society made efficient by technology, productive by capitalism, organized around cities, and driven by self-interest has not left people free of all constraints so that they can, without inhibition and regret, pursue their own happiness. Quite the reverse. If there was something to be said for replacing arbitrary power with the exercise of reason and violence with the legal state, the Enlightenment nevertheless grossly underestimated how many were the channels along which evil could run besides those of arbitrary power and violence. If the natural logic of Enlightenment thinking is the expressive individualism of our time, then that logic has brought us not freedom but a painful captivity to ourselves. And in the end, the collapse of this grand experiment in building a Kingdom of God without God was to be replaced by a new Kingdom, one in which the self has ascended the throne from which first God and then naturalistic reason had been dislodged.

However, we have imposed a severe penalty on ourselves in the process: a terrifying sense that while all we have left is the self, the self unfortunately does not amount to too much. The passion of believing and the passion of being have now been replaced by the empty stare, the ironic posture. Today, it is no longer right to care, because there is nothing to care about. It is not chic to care. The idealism of the young has been extinguished in self-preoccupation; for those who are older, the hope for change in the world has often died, too, because the world beyond the self is relevant only to the extent that it impinges on the self. This sense of meaninglessness is the signature of the depleted, minimal, and postmodern self. How, then, has this passage — away from a Christian sense of transcendence, through its Enlightenment replacement, and into our currently bleak world of the self — worked itself out psychologically?

Come, Join the Revolution

There clearly has been a revolution since Freud, who, one wag has observed, rediscovered the Christian doctrine of original sin! As it turns out, this revolution was accomplished by a number of the early popularizers of Freud who had been reared in liberal Protestantism. They found Freud's descriptions of dark, internal, instinctual drives to be quite uncongenial. They turned away from this and recast psychology in terms of the liberal belief that health and happiness are the natural

11. Alain Touraine, *Critique of Modernity* (Oxford: Blackwell, 1995), 138.

outcome to clean living and that instinctual drives are actually benign. Carl Rogers had been inspired as a young man by the idealism of the YMCA, and he found "Freud's pessimism as revolting and incomprehensible," Lasch writes, "as his spiritual forebears had once found Calvinism."[12]

Psychology in the Rogers/Maslow vein, then, is liberationist in its intent. As our expressive individualism has deepened and as their outlook has become culturally ensconced, especially among the seventy-five million baby boomers (those born between 1946 and 1964), what John Rice calls a "liberation psychotherapy" has been born. This is not so much a particular school of thought as a set of assumptions about human nature and culture that are shared by a number of schools. At the center stands the belief that others are the threat to our own reality. Thus the ethic of self-actualization "assigns ultimate moral priority to the self, over and against society" so that "any action governed by social convention rather than individual preference . . . is tantamount to self-violation."[13] Even one's deepest commitments, such as to one's spouse, children, friends, and faith, as well as one's obligations to institutions and society, all become matters of negotiation lest they become encumbrances to being more personally satisfied. This is truly revolutionary talk, whose goal is to liberate each person from all external constraints — societal, cultural, and moral — on the grounds that these can become sources of inward debilitation. Though expressed with some innocence, this view is radical in its rejection of society. And, interestingly enough, it has also produced in many people the counter-tendency to escape the self, because the bright hope that attended the liberated self turns into sour reality all around. The much sought emancipation from others does not yield a bountiful harvest of personal satisfaction but, rather, only loneliness and more disaffection. As Andrew Delbanco notes, this psychology, which "sanctified the rights of the self and charged malice to any obstructor of those rights," was bound to incite social strife, since "one man's good was likely to be another man's evil."[14]

The line between this psychology and the seeming utopia of cyberspace is quite thin. Cyberspace takes the central tenet of this psychology to its logical conclusion. Cyberspace is now being promoted

12. Christopher Lasch, *The Minimal Self: Psychic Survival in Troubled Times* (New York: Norton, 1984), 211.

13. Rice, *A Disease of One's Own*, 29

14. Andrew Delbanco, *The Death of Satan: How Americans Have Lost the Sense of Evil* (New York: Farrar, Straus, and Giroux, 1995), 107.

as the land of pure consciousness. Here one meets others simply and only at the point of mind; gender, class, race, and religion have vanished in this virtual universe. And so has sin, apparently. Because this is virtual reality, crime does not intrude as it does in the real world — at least, that is the claim. Many have dreamed of such a utopia, where our disembodied existence allows us to escape both the limitations and the flaws of real life. It plainly has taken liberationist psychology to a new level.

Baby boomers have been especially vulnerable to the appeal of liberationist psychotherapy and its technological incarnation in cyberspace. They have grown up in a world seriously wracked by marital discord. The older stabilizing cultural norms have gone, as has the older moral world that spoke of obligations outside the self. As the moral map has faded, nothing has come about to replace it. It is no coincidence, then, that this generation knows a lot about failed relationships and has experienced the moral ambiguity that modern culture inflicts upon those who feast at its table. For this generation, in particular, codependency groups and twelve-step programs have offered the way out.[15] They provide relationships, a community, and people who will listen — and a safe environment to practice liberationist psychology.

In these groups it is assumed, and often explicitly stated, that our innate drives tend not toward destruction, but toward growth, health, and happiness; and that society is burdensome and oppressive to the

---

15. The model established by Alcoholics Anonymous has been widely imitated to offer a cure for many other ailments. Among the groups cited by Rice who have grown astoundingly in recent years are Batterers Anonymous; Cocaine Anonymous; Co-Dependents Anonymous; Debtors Anonymous; Depressives Anonymous; Divorce Anonymous; Drugs Anonymous; Emotional Health Anonymous; Emotions Anonymous; Emphysema Anonymous; Families Anonymous; Fundamentalists Anonymous; Gamblers Anonymous; Grandparents Anonymous; Homosexuals Anonymous; Impotents Anonymous; Incest Survivors Anonymous; Marriage Anonymous; Molesters Anonymous; Messies Anonymous; Narcotics Anonymous; Neurotics Anonymous; Overeaters Anonymous; Parents Anonymous; Pills Anonymous; Potsmokers Anonymous; Prison Families Anonymous; Sex Addicts Anonymous; Sex and Love Addicts Anonymous; Shoplifters Anonymous; Smokers Anonymous; Spenders Anonymous; Workaholics Anonymous. Many chronic moral failings have now been co-opted by a treatment industry that views them as diseases, a development which Karl Menninger saw coming a long time ago. One of the anomalies, however, is that if the explanation of these maladies is the repressive nature of external society, then there is no moral difference between the man who abuses his wife and the woman who suffers that abuse, for they both suffer from the same problem. For both, there is a twelve-step program. Thus, among codependents, Rice says, "repression's consequences can and do run the gamut from inhibition through exhibition, producing both victims and victimizers" (Rice, *A Disease of One's Own*, 179).

self. Indeed, Carl Rogers lamented the influence of classical Protestantism, with its belief in original sin and in the necessity of regeneration
and conversion. Human nature, he countered, is not so flawed but
should instead be seen as "trustworthy." Its "redemption" lies not in
an internal miracle but in the more natural means of getting in touch
with one's self. The inevitable outcome of treating the self as the locus
of all meaning and of all moral values, however, is that both meaning
and values become relative to each self. If self-consciousness is private,
unique and individualized, then moral values, if they arise in the self,
are as private and individualized as the self in which they reside. A
sense of responsibility toward anyone outside the self dies, as does
integrity — that moral quality which secures continuity between what is
said or done in one moment and what is said or done in the future.
Moral integrity is simply at odds with the kind of personality makeover
that liberationist psychotherapy promotes.

A curious paradox is at work here. On the one hand, this movement is quite un-American; it is as subversive of American society as
the more secretive and hostile militia groups. On the other hand, this
widely believed psychology offers a vision for the cure of troubled souls
that is as American as apple pie.

This outlook simply replicates the expressive individualism that
has become ensconced in American culture, though it comes garnished
with some therapeutic additions. It is a way of thinking that echoes our
modern age with its dense cities, fearful stresses, painful anonymity,
and broken relationships. It also connects with our consumer culture,
for it offers personal growth and internal harmony as commodities that
can be bought as readily as cigarettes, cars, detergent, and houses.
Furthermore, in a society where loneliness is endemic, twelve-step
groups and the various psychotherapeutic enterprises offer personal
attention and understanding, which are in short supply in too many
people's lives. Finally, this psychology taps into the "can do" part of
the American spirit. Not even the most daunting and vexing of personal
problems will be allowed to triumph over our ability to control them.
There are techniques for the self that can be learned and that, it is
believed, will work. The result is that we are now about to conquer what
Philip Rieff has called "the last enemy" — not death, as the apostle
Paul declared, but our own personalities.[16] Consequently, American
psychiatrists and psychologists have proceeded to "work out ever more

16. Philip Rieff, *The Triumph of the Therapeutic: Uses of Faith After Freud* (New
York: Harper & Row, 1968), 391.

affirmative and uplifting therapies that promise not only personal regeneration but, in many cases, social regeneration as well."[17] They have replicated the liberal Protestant vision of a Christianized social order on strictly secular, humanistic assumptions.

A radical reversal of ends and means has passed almost unnoticed in this. The older kind of psychology sought to help the client to adapt to the outside world, to develop different ways of thinking about the self, different behaviors that would lead to less jarring and destructive consequences. The new liberationist psychotherapies shove society aside if it stands in the way. This is a transition, Rice argues, "from a body of theoretical knowledge and discourse *legitimating* a larger cultural vision to *being* that larger vision itself."[18] Liberationist psychology, then, is not simply a means of ministering to troubled selves; it is an alternative worldview in which the self becomes the fulcrum and what is good or bad is determined by whether or not the self is served. It is pursued in defiance of all external norms and expectations.

Guilt in Remission

This new thinking, which has steadily taken root in society over the last three decades, is throwing important new light, albeit sometimes unknowingly, on why guilt has been in remission and shame has emerged as the defining experience in our narcissistic culture. It is true, of course, that shame and guilt are also used interchangeably in our common parlance. Someone may say, for example, "The shame and guilt I felt over having an abortion was simply awful." However, the emerging consensus, especially among psychiatrists, is that guilt and shame should be distinguished even if, in experience, they often overlap and, I will presently argue, should overlap where moral matters are at stake.[19]

Here, however, is an anomaly. If shame, which up to now has been treated as a subset of, or as a synonym for, guilt is actually something different, then it is remarkable that "until very recently," Harvard psychiatrist Andrew P. Morrison says, shame has "been little explored in the psychoanalytical literature."[20] Elsewhere he says that "the absence of an extensive shame literature and the scant attention given to the

17. Lasch, *The Minimal Self*, 211.
18. Rice, *A Disease of One's Own*, 73-74.
19. Robert J. Stoller, "Pornography: Daydreams to Cure Humiliation," in Nathanson, ed., *The Many Faces of Shame*, 303.
20. Andrew P. Morrison, *Shame: The Underside of Narcissism* (Hillsdale: Analytical Press, 1989), 1.

existing work are perplexing phenomena."[21] This situation seems to be changing, though, and psychologist Gershen Kaufman can write that though "previously neglected and minimized, shame has finally moved center stage."[22] And this seems to be echoing the almost inevitable conclusions to which our modernized culture is also leading us.

The exact nature of guilt and shame, and their distinctions one from another, are hard to pin down. However, the difference I will be working with is that guilt is normally the emotional response to our violation of a moral norm, and shame is our disappointment with ourselves that we are not other than what we are. This is somewhat close to the distinction set up by pastoral psychologist Lewis Smedes. The difference between the two, he argues, is that we "feel guilty for what we *do*. We feel shame for what we *are*. A person feels guilt because he *did* something wrong. A person feels shame because he *is* something wrong. We may feel guilt because we lied to our mother. We may feel shame because we are not the persons our mother wanted us to be."[23] However, the divorce between shame and guilt suggested here is not wise. After all, the narratives I earlier recounted of Luther, Brainerd, and Owen all show rather clearly that they experienced guilt, not simply as an external violation of God's law, but also as internal embarrassment and mortification. The self was stricken before God. It was not simply that they had done something wrong; they were also wrong in themselves. I will return to the relations between shame and guilt later. They are far more complicated than Smedes allows. It is sufficient to say here that when guilt and shame are divorced from each other — as they have also been in contemporary experience — then the former is inevitably transformed into the latter. Guilt disappears and all that remains is shame. Psychiatrist Silvan Tomkins therefore says that today shame "refers more to feelings of inferiority than feelings of guilt, and therefore more to responses of proving oneself 'good' (in the sense of being superior) than to responses of proving oneself 'good' in the moral sense."[24] In other words, it is how we are being viewed by others, rather than by God, that weighs most heavily upon us. It is how we experience ourselves rather than how we stand in the moral world, and that is

21. Andrew P. Morrison, "The Eye Turned Inward: Shame and the Self," in Nathanson, ed., *The Many Faces of Shame,* 272.

22. Gershen Kaufman, *The Psychology of Shame: Theory and Treatment of Shame-Based Syndromes* (New York: Springer, 1989), 11.

23. Smedes, *Shame and Grace,* 9-10.

24. Silvan S. Tomkins, "Shame," in Nathanson, ed., *The Many Faces of Shame,* 135.

altogether a more manageable matter, for which abundant therapies are available.

Although it is possible to have false guilt and false shame — a matter to which I shall also return shortly — the basic distinction I have suggested helps us to understand why, in the contracted and flattened out mental universe we inhabit, it is so hard to make sense of our experience. Apologist Dick Keyes has located our inability to deal with shame and guilt right at the heart of our problems in identity.[25] Identity is a matter of knowing who we are, both as human beings and as individuals, and through this understanding arriving at some internal cohesion and coherence. The fact that we are made in the image of God, made as God's counterpoint, made to know him and, in the cultural mandate (Gen. 1:28-30), made for our roles as sub-creators in the world, means that this internal coherence will always elude us if we have no sense of life's worth, and no knowledge of its Creator. It will also elude us if we have no way to come to terms satisfactorily with what is wrong in our lives and with how we feel about that.

Guilt is the compass point that lines up our actions with the *moral world* in which we live. Whether people know it or not, this world is a part of that moral reality whose apex is the holiness of God and which is given verbal expression in the moral codes of Scripture. Shame has to do with our location in our *social world*. "The opposite of guilt is innocence, a state of being blameless or guiltless," Keyes writes. "The opposite of shame, however, is not innocence, but rather glory and honor."[26] Guilt is falling short of God's moral standards; shame is falling short of what we think we should be, what others expect of us, or of how others have modeled what we would like to be. Our guilt calls for forgiveness; our shame, for acceptance or self-acceptance.

In the biblical world, as we shall see, people understood who they were in terms of where they were born, who their father was, from which tribe or clan they arose, and the nation of which they were a part. To be held in high esteem by one's family, or in one's town or village, bestowed honor. Shame arose when one was seen by others to have acted foolishly, irresponsibly, or badly. One thus brought dishonor on one's self, on one's family, perhaps one's town. In so doing, a person had not lived up to what he or she expected of him or herself.

25. Dick Keyes, *Beyond Identity: Finding Your Self in the Image and Character of God* (Ann Arbor, Mich.: Servant Books, 1984), 5-72. See also J. Knox Chamblin, *Paul and the Self: Apostolic Teaching for Personal Wholeness* (Grand Rapids: Baker Book House, 1993).

26. Keyes, *Beyond Identity*, 53.

In America today, of course, the cultural environment is quite different. We do not think of our sense of identity as having much to do with our birth, our ancestry, or even our ethnicity (unless one is a minority). Shame for us works itself out in two rather different directions.

First, there is the matter of heroes and heroines. This has been developed helpfully by Keyes, who suggests that our imagination needs heroes and heroines, people who have embodied and acted on moral principle. Of course, these "heroes" may actually be antiheroes, people who epitomize, or give expression to, what is wrong and destructive. In his rebellion and apparent nihilism, the movie star James Dean was just such an antihero, and he stood out four decades ago as something of a novelty. Today, antiheroes or heroines who stand for nothing, and believe in nothing, are a dime a dozen; one runs into many of them in the world of rock music, where there seems to be a bidding war to see who can be the most outlandish and offensive.[27] Their function, however, is no different from that of heroes. They are equally emulated. The difference is simply in what is embodied and what is emulated. It is one thing, then, to know what honesty means; it is quite another to see honesty being worked out in life by others who are persons of such integrity that they cannot deny themselves and may even pay for it with their lives. Such a person was Sir Thomas More, a "man for all seasons" who has been a hero to some. It takes understanding to grasp what honesty is, but in our imaginations it takes fire when we see honesty modeled in this way by another. The decline of heroes and heroines who embody noble virtues and their replacement by celebrities, not to mention antiheroes, is an important ingredient in our difficulties with identity.

Some shame, then, is connected with a sense that we have fallen short of what our ideal is, as seen in a hero or heroine. We have not measured up to what we admire, what we see in them, and what we wish ourselves to be. Shame, however, also arises from a different direction. It is certainly still a sense of embarrassment — that we are not the people we thought we were or wanted to be — but the standard by which that becomes apparent may be something as impersonal as the voice of fashion, of what is "in" and what is "out." In another generation, people might have been ashamed of their poverty and have cringed at the thought of others knowing where they lived. Today, many young people feel ashamed if they do not have the right sneakers, or

27. See the brilliant history of America's popular music, especially rock, by Martha Bayles, *Hole in the Soul: The Loss of Beauty and Meaning in American Popular Music* (New York: Free Press, 1994).

if their pants are not baggy enough. Shame of this kind produces embarrassment of a strictly horizontal sort, and this is mostly how every experience of being unacceptable is understood. As external moral norms have collapsed, being unacceptable has come to mean being unacceptable only to *ourselves;* it is guilt that tells us we are unacceptable before *God.* These two realities, guilt and shame, now need to be illustrated further and their exact relationship defined more precisely.

On Feeling Ashamed

Exposed

At the root of all experiences of shame is the sense that we have been exposed and uncovered. We know ourselves to be something other than what we hoped. And this revelation often comes when others come to see, accidentally and without warning, a side to us about which we feel vulnerable and embarrassed.[28] We feel as if we have been wounded by what they now know, so the fear of scorn is part of the experience of shame, as is anxiety. This explains the painful urge to find some sort of cover when we are ashamed. We may literally cover our face with our hands or, at least, "put on a brave face," or we may avert our gaze from others as if, by doing so, we could pull down the shades on the windows through which they might have gazed into our self. When we feel ashamed, we feel low, alone, as if the wind had left our sails, sometimes depressed, humiliated, and empty. In the moment of being ashamed, we simply want to disappear, to fall through the floor. We want time to move on to other events as quickly as possible. Even those most hardened go through their ritual defenses. Often we see on television those who have been arrested, some for heinous crimes of cold-hearted brutality, in a remarkable contradiction, covering their heads with a coat as they are led off in handcuffs to a waiting police car. "No audience is needed for feelings of guilt," psychologist Paul Ekman says, "no one else need know, for the guilty person is his own judge. Not so for shame. The humiliation of shame requires disapproval or ridicule by others." This is true, provided we enlarge the seeing audience to include people who may only "see" us from within our imagination. However, when

---

28. Lynd, *On Shame and the Search for Identity,* 27-28. See also Jean Paul Sartre, *Being and Nothingness: An Essay on Phenomenological Ontology,* trans. Hazel E. Barnes (New York: Philosophical Library, 1956), 220-21.

Ekman goes on to add that if "no one ever learns of a misdeed there will be no shame, but there still might be guilt,"[29] he is divorcing shame from guilt in a way that is typically modern and that makes insufficient allowance for the fact that shame often also has a moral component and therefore overlaps with guilt.

Of course, shame also plays a rather different role; it stands guard over our own inner mysteries. This sense of shame protectively brackets what is private from what is public. It cordons off from the scrutiny of others our intimate knowledge, innermost feelings, disappointments, failures, weaknesses, and sometimes affections. And, as pastoral psycho-therapist Carl Schneider notes, an element of reticence is appropriate to human relations, for we need to remain only "half-open beings" to most of the people we encounter each day.[30] This reticence covers other matters as well, not simply our inner secrets and mysteries. Thus a mother, for example, might say to a young daughter whose clothes are altogether too revealing, "You can't go out looking like that! Have you no shame?" The mother, in this case, would be looking for a larger sense of sexual reticence than is apparently present in her daughter. Or perhaps the daughter is not fully aware of how she might be signaling that she does not want to be sexually reticent.

Today, reticence is now in full flight before all of the inquiring minds who want to know, who want to know everything and see every-thing. It is in full flight because, as far as moral matters are concerned, we seem not to care. In a ritualized acceptance of this reality, we often sanitize the personal revelations that we permit ourselves to make under the rubric of sharing. Sharing is, of course, a positive term, something that we instill into our children from the start as an antidote to their natural self-centeredness. So, to be willing to say to a person, or a group, "I just want to share everything I have been feeling recently" appears to be the essence of generosity. The reality, however, is often quite different. The secrets, perversions, struggles, and failures we reveal are not themselves ameliorated simply because they have been revealed, as we are inclined to imagine, and the listeners are often mildly violated by being offered these morsels and tidbits for processing. This, however, is now our cultural habit, and those who dispute it sound like hopelessly constricted people. We share. We feel an irresistible urge to expose

29. Paul Ekman, *Telling Lies: Clues to Deceit in the Marketplace, Politics, and Marriage* (New York: Norton, 1992), 65.

30. Carl D. Schneider, "A Mature Sense of Shame," in Nathanson, ed., *The Many Faces of Shame*, 200.

ourselves, almost as evidence of our humanity. We "let it all hang out." We empty ourselves, even before strangers, until little or nothing that is private remains unexhibited.

We are, of course, only doing what television and the movies have made legitimate. They have tilted the scales away from privacy toward exposure, away from bodily modesty toward public nakedness, away from the thought that grief and pain should be private and toward "the canonization of the intruding investigative reporter."[31] We want to see the stricken parents as they anxiously wait to see if their child survived a collapsed building. We want to see the family whose son was murdered. We want to watch their grief, and we think we have a right to know what they know and to see how they are feeling. And in movies, the American public wants to see nudity and wants to watch people having sex. A sense of shame that once would have stood guard over what is private and intimate is now largely gone, routed by our inclination to share and our voyeuristic hunger to watch. This, however, is a different sense of shame from what normally comes to mind when we hear the word.

Shame, more normally, is the feeling of having been exposed, of something having been revealed about us that we would prefer others not to see or know about. It happens when we act in a way that is inappropriate to a situation and, too late, realization breaks upon us. Our action reveals us to be someone we did not want to be. Our image of ourselves becomes disconnected from what we are seen to say or do. Suddenly a discrepancy or contradiction appears between the way we want to be seen and the way we appear. And the higher the expectation about ourselves — or the lower our behavior — the more likely, and the more severe, the contradiction will be. If shame has many different forms, there is nothing in the experience itself, however, that provides any discernment of whether the cause of that shame is legitimate or not. Do we feel embarrassed because we think we have been seen to be inferior or because we have been seen to have acted unethically? The experience of shame — the way it registers on us, the embarrassment that sweeps over us — is the same in each of these cases and so provides no answer. And that is what is so problematic about the current psychiatric and psychological evaluation of shame, not to mention the typical understanding of shame in the culture. The focus is on the *mechanism* of shame and not on its *content*. And we have now lost our ability to

---

31. Donald L. Nathanson, "A Timetable for Shame," in Nathanson, ed., *The Many Faces of Shame*, 5.

judge whether our shame has a moral dimension or not. All shame, therefore, tends to be viewed as if it has no such dimension and is treated accordingly. Let us consider some of the many different ways this mechanism of shame comes into play.

How Many Ways Can I Feel Ashamed?

Many people, for example, are sensitive about their bodies. They feel a sense of embarrassment if someone should call attention to their ears, which may be too large, their nose, which may be too prominent, or their weight, which may be outside national guidelines. Among younger women, the pressure to look more like a *Playboy* centerfold may be considerable. On university campuses, as sexual mores have become much more permissive, anorexia and bulimia have correspondingly increased; at the root of both is shame about an imperfect body. This is one kind of shame.

There are, however, other kinds. Some people are shy. "The presence of the stranger," Kaufman observes, "activates the feeling of exposure."[32] The stranger might stumble upon the sense of inadequacy or inferiority within a person, and so that person takes evasive action. Others conceal the same acute sense of inferiority, not by the mask of shyness, but by exercising steely control over those around them. "George," who manages a business, is like this. He makes sure that no situation will arise that would expose the inadequacy and inferiority he feels within. Were that to happen, he would be mightily ashamed, because he would be seen to be other than what he wants. He therefore makes sure that he is in total charge, that he controls access to as much information as possible, and that he delegates as little as possible. Dissembling and deceiving are key ingredients in presenting the self to others as something different from what it is felt to be.

Then there are life's embarrassing moments that, innocent though they may be, can also have a searing quality to them. Most people can recall moments that, in retrospect, were of no moral import at all but that nevertheless have never been forgotten. In one of the very first sermons I preached, in a rough urban setting in South Africa, I made a blunder that remains as fresh in my mind today as when it happened over thirty years ago. At that time, my knowledge of Scripture was small, since I had only recently come into Christian faith. It was my intention on that day to preach on the New Testament character Zacchaeus, the

32. Kaufman, *Psychology of Shame*, 24.

little man up in the sycamore tree as Jesus walked by. Unfortunately, I placed Zechariah — either John the Baptist's father or the Old Testament prophet of the same name — up in the sycamore tree! This mistake, needless to say, would have been immediately remedied had I paid closer attention to the passage on which I was preaching. The outdoor audience who heard me on that day was probably oblivious to my blunder, but I can still recall the sense of complete mortification I felt upon discovering my folly. In that moment, I had been revealed as an enthusiastic fool, an incompetent. Again and again I asked myself, "How could I have made such a mistake?" I felt ashamed of myself.

Then there is the problem of false shame.[33] In the strange mix of internal chemistry within every person, the external expectations of others, especially parents, can come to assume damaging proportions. The parents of "Mary" were enormously competent and gifted people, and they demanded of their children the same levels of achievement. These demands were compounded by regular attendance at a legalistic church that had evolved rules for all of life's contingencies. As Mary grew up, she developed an image of herself that was constructed out of what she knew was expected of her. The standards that resulted far exceeded her capacities to meet them. She was a very gifted person, but her gifts were in different areas. As the years passed, her "failures" to meet the expectations she felt resting on her so heavily became exaggerated in her own mind. These expectations also began to assume the force of God's moral law. This she applied even to shortcomings that had no ethical significance at all. Because her teenage children were difficult at times, Mary felt that she had failed entirely as a parent. Because her house was sometimes untidy, she felt completely incompetent. Because she did not hold an important job, as did her parents, she felt inferior, as if she had let everyone down. Each supposed dereliction excited fresh cries of self-accusation. Here was someone haunted by a sense of shame that was entirely unwarranted, but it was no less real than if she had been carrying on a seriously immoral life and had been caught red-handed.

The reverse side of this, however, produces something quite different. It is entirely possible to feel shame over doing something that is *right*. In the modern workplace, with its secular assumptions — not least of which is the marginalization of God and of his truth to the very

33. For an elaboration of the distinction between the real and the false self, see Stephen M. Johnson, *Humanizing the Narcissistic Style* (New York: Norton, 1987), 114-72.

edges of what is meaningful and relevant — it is easy to make oneself religiously anonymous but hard to bear witness to Christ. Indeed, it may seem so out of place to do so, even in the most appropriate way, that one feels embarrassed about one's faith. These were the undercurrents in the corporation where "John" worked. When he was asked one day whether he was religious and explained that he was, he became very uncomfortable. It was in doing what was right, witnessing to Christ and the truth of the Gospel, that he felt shame. And when he reflected later on why that was so, he realized how much he feared the scorn of others; he thought he would look unsophisticated, stupid, and narrow to them.

Finally, there is the case of the minister of a large, flourishing church, known for its fine biblical preaching and conscientious service in the community. It is a church that has spoken often of ethical issues, because this was one of the passions of its pastor, "Bill." In particular, the church often heard him decry the breakdown of the family, and he was especially concerned with the growing sexual permissiveness in society. In order to counter this in the church, Bill arranged a number of Sunday School classes on this subject, some for the young people and some for married adults. He led the class that addressed the place of sex in marriage, the danger signs that couples need to be aware of, and the peculiar sexual temptations of this time. The church deeply appreciated his concern and the strong leadership he provided in trying to preserve the sanctity of marriage.

This church, then, was caught entirely off guard when the news broke that Bill had, throughout this time, been having affairs with several married women. The contradiction between his public *persona* and his private life, between what he professed and what he did, was now so glaring and so painful that his congregation at first hardly even knew how to respond. Its initial incredulity, though, soon turned to anger as it came to realize that it had not really known its minister, that he was something other than what he appeared to be. It felt that it had been deceived and misled. That, however, was only a fraction of the pain that Bill himself now felt. As this contradiction set in, his sense of inferiority, inadequacy, and humiliation became almost unbearable. His cover had been blown. Now people saw the internal disorder in his life, which, until this time, he had successfully concealed even from his wife. It was not that he had never tried to resist his weakness. He had. But as opportunity arose, he found himself in the grip of an irresistible desire. He had known that it was probably just a matter of time before he would be exposed, but somehow he also thought that in this game of Russian roulette it was possible to turn up an empty chamber each time. Now his luck had run out. He was mortified and embarrassed, for even though he had tried to resist, he was now seen to be a complete hypocrite, a dismal failure. In that moment, he simply wanted to vanish.

What is interesting about all of these cases is that the *mechanism* of shame is the same. Whatever the experiences producing the shame, it is the self that is exposed, scarred, wounded, depleted, and left empty. Regardless of how it has happened, the result is that the person feels low, embarrassed, depressed, inadequate, foolish, or inferior. A person may become angry with himself, or feel contempt for herself, and all such experiences raise the level of anxiety. But the emotional repertoire called into play does *not* tell the person whether such feelings are warranted.

In the examples I have given, the only clear cases where shame would be warranted are those of "Bill," the minister, and "George," the controlling business man (who, in fact, acknowledges no reason for shame and conceals his feelings of inferiority from others). The minister, however, not only violated the external norms of Scripture, as well as his own marriage vows, but he also felt stricken before God for what he had done. He was guilty and filled with shame as a result. By contrast, "George," who over the years has developed ways of short-circuiting some of his feelings, actually feels quite self-righteous. Then, there is the case of "John," the Christian who witnessed to the truth of Christ's Gospel and felt shame, not for doing something wrong but for doing something *right*. Shame, then, may be false or it may be warranted. It may be hidden or it may be open. And it may arise from doing something morally right as well as morally wrong. This sets up several different relationships between guilt and shame.[34]

First, in the case of the minister, they converged. He felt guilty before God, and he felt ashamed because of what others now knew about him. In the case of "George," the controlling business man, they should have converged, but they did not. He experienced potential shame before others all the time, but he had expunged any sense of guilt before God or any external moral code for his treatment of other people and his dissembling.

Second, in my own case, guilt and shame diverged. It was not a matter of moral culpability to have made a simple mistake of confusing two names. Nor is it a moral failing to have large ears or a prominent nose. The feeling that results may be indistinguishable from guilt, but

34. Keyes, *Beyond Identity,* 53-54.

it is not guilt. The same can be said of "Mary." Her derelictions were experienced as if she had violated the moral law, but what she had really violated was only her expectations of herself.

Third, they can compete. In his place of work, "John" felt ashamed of witnessing to Christ, whereas he should have felt guilt for *not* doing so. Thus, sometimes guilt and shame can pull us in entirely opposite directions. We can feel ashamed of doing what is *right*.

What therefore needs to be injected into the discussion on shame is an understanding of guilt. This should be allowed to have a much larger role than it currently has in the clinical literature. What is in view here is not guilt feelings, which are subjective, but an understanding of guilt as worthiness of blame, which is objective. For shame that carries in itself this sense of guilt is quite different from shame that does not. Unless this is seen, "Bill," the minister who disgraced himself by his sexual dalliances, will be treated no differently from "Mary," whose ideal self is a little too large and overbearing. The mechanism of the shame in all of the above cases is the same, but the *content* is very different. And that content should include an informed sense of *conscience*.[35]

In the psychiatric literature, as well as in the wider culture, the transition to the language of shame from that of guilt really signals the secularization of our moral life. What it suggests is that any moral discomfort, any inward pangs that are the result of our actions, should be construed as *relational* problems, not moral ones. They should be resolved along the horizontal plane of psychological understanding rather than against the vertical realm of theological knowledge. It is we who will dissolve our own shame, not God. It is we who will do it by technique, for when all is said and done, what is awry is simply the way we are viewing ourselves.

Lost in Moral Space

Disoriented

Before leaving this present chapter, we need to reflect a little more on some of the consequences of our lost moral fabric. By a painful irony, the liberation psychotherapy that has taken root so widely in the culture, and that has made the cultivation of the self life's *summum bonum*, must

---

35. See Vladimir Solovyof, *The Justification of the Good: An Essay in Moral Philosophy*, trans. Nathalie A. Duddington (London: Constance and Co., 1918), 32-38.

now bear at least some responsibility for our lost sense of self-identity. We hear this loss in expressions (or in silent thoughts) such as "I am my genes," "I am my past," I am my sexual orientation," "I am my feelings," "I am my image," "I am my body," "I am what I do," "I am what I have," or "I am who I know." These alternative anthropologies have arisen in a time when the older ways of understanding who we are have dissipated, leaving behind a painful vacuum. The resulting identity crisis, Taylor observes, is "an acute form of disorientation, which people often express in terms of not knowing who they are, but which can also be seen as a radical uncertainty of where they stand."[36] If it is the case, as he says, that "to know who you are is to be oriented in moral space,"[37] the reverse is also the case, that not to be oriented in moral space is not to know who you are. This is the situation that is assuming epidemic proportions in our postmodern world.

This dilemma is not, of course, quite as simple as I have here suggested, because the loss of our moral world is part of a much larger loss, that of meaning in its entirety. This is what we mean by the postmodern condition. It has its intellectual expressions but, as we have seen, it is part and parcel of everyday life, too.

Identity and Style

Questions of identity today stand at the center of clashing perspectives on how we are to think about the human being. Sociologists are inclined to think of the person as a construct of factors like gender, social roles, socioeconomic status, level of education, and ethnicity. On this view, our identity is the "story" that we weave together out of the roles we fill, the people we know, the attention (or lack of it) we have received, what we have, and how we think of ourselves in relation to society. The interior space in the person, the place of stored memories and springs of motivation, may almost seem irrelevant. Likewise, geneticists may be inclined to dissolve this same interior space into its genetic roots, which, it is thought, provide the structure of being. For reasons beyond the scope of this chapter, neither of these modern forms of determinism can be accepted without some serious qualifications.[38]

36. Charles Taylor, *Sources of the Self,* 27.
37. Ibid., 28.
38. Two theologians who have worked with the new thinking in genetics but have resisted the determinism implicit in much of this work are Arthur R. Peacocke, *God and the New Biology* (San Francisco: Harper and Row, 1986), and Philip Hefner, *The Human Factor* (Minneapolis: The Fortress Press, 1993).

Yet personal identity is not simply a matter of cognition, or of our reading our own interior space. The sense of who we are, the "I" at the core of our experience, is built up in complex interaction between the shape of this interior space — which, in Christian terms, constitutes what is retained of the image of God — and three other matters. First, who we understand ourselves to be is significantly affected by interpersonal relations, beginning in the family, but also extending beyond that. There is constant affirmation or denial of who we are in these settings. It is here that we are first taught whether or not we have value and, if so, on what basis. It is here that we are learn or do not learn that we are created in the image of God. And it is here that we first experience or do not experience love. Second, our identity is affected by the workplace and the wider society. These provide us with roles and meanings through which our identity is partly forged and with the context in which we are to work out the cultural mandate, which is also essential to our identity. Third, our identity is affected by the values and beliefs that we come to hold as we move through life. These things being so, it is not hard to see how easily personal identity is damaged in a world of broken families and in a workplace fraught with alienation. It is, however, with the third factor that we are here mainly concerned, the effect of the loss of values on identity. In the identity crisis most common today, Roy Baumeister declares, "the person lacks sufficient commitments to make choices and lead a purposeful, directed life" and lacks the criteria "to determine which possibilities to commit to and which to reject."[39]

In such a situation, there is considerable pressure for people to adapt to each new situation, to reconstruct themselves, to reach into the world around them in order to extract some meaning for themselves, some sense of who the "I" is. The emptiness of the internal narrative is concealed behind the surface appearances. Irving Goffman speaks of modern people as often staging their own characters. By using the "techniques of impression management"[40] they are able to shape who it is that they want to be perceived as being. And style plays an important role in creating this impression.

Immigrants who came to America in waves during the last century quickly learned that they needed to look "American" as soon as possible if they were to avoid being cheated or ostracized. Their adaptations —

39. Roy F. Baumeister, *Identity: Cultural Change and the Struggle for the Self* (New York: Oxford University Press, 1986), 249.

40. Irving Goffman, *The Presentation of the Self in Everyday Life* (Garden City, N.Y.: Doubleday, 1959), 208. For a more contemporary study on the same theme, see B. R. Schlenker, *Impression Management* (Monterey, Calif.: Brooks/Cole, 1980).

forsaking European trousers and shoes for American, for example — reflected the fact that for them life was a series of encounters with those who were unknown, and in this context the art of survival lay in the ability to make quick and accurate judgments based on appearances. However, one not only judged outward appearances but was also judged by them.

The experience of the immigrant is also now ours. Native born Americans have become psychological immigrants, as alone in our huge cities and complex bureaucracies as the foreign immigrants who came ashore in New York. If a great many of those whom we see are unknown to us, we are unknown to them. We know ourselves to be aliens. We are defined, Stuart Ewen says, by a "sense of *self as alien*, as an object of scrutiny and judgment."[41] In our great centers of commerce, the cities, as well as in the thoroughfares of conversation like television and the movies, surface appearances take on a powerful, symbolic role and become commercially potent. Style is the "commerce in appearances." It uses what is a surface either to transform or to hide the person.

Perhaps style as it functions today was first made possible by the camera. The camera created a surface with an image that was different from the surface of the people or things in the picture. The image that would otherwise have been held in memory only was restored and preserved for posterity. Those who look at their pictures not only see what was captured but also remember the moment when it happened. Their memories become, in a sense, a commentary on that picture, seeing beyond it to relationships and events at best only hinted at in the picture by a smile, the holding of hands, the posture of the bodies. Style takes this one step further, because, unlike the picture, the surface image is now completely disembodied. Style, therefore, may be an act of cannibalization as we take from others to create our own surface, even though it may be entirely unrelated to who we actually are. It is, however, who we *want* to be.

The stylish person may borrow from across the entire social land-scape, indeed, may borrow entirely contradictory images, looking "like a duchess one week, a murder victim the next. Style can highjack the idiom of astronauts, or poach from the ancient pageantry of Guatemalan peasant costumes," says Ewen.[42] These illusions, diligently

41. Stuart Ewen, *All Consuming Images: The Politics of Style in Contemporary Culture* (New York: Basic Books, 1988), 72. Vance Packard was one of the first to sound this warning to the wider public in his book, *A Nation of Strangers* (New York: David McKay, 1972).

42. Ewen, *All Consuming Images*, 14. Of women's hair styles, Grant McCracken says that the "many styles in the world of hair represent a map of many, if not most, of

assembled and nonchalantly worn, are the ornaments of a life that must make ready adaptations to the constant change in our world. They are statements of who we are that day. With an extraordinary profusion of stylized goods to choose from — designer ties, designer scents, designer automobiles, and designer jeans — we now have a rich palette from which to paint our own meaning, to state our own *identity*. "The utility of style in this regard is to find oneself," says Ewen,[43] and perhaps more to the point, to create one's self.

Style also hints at, or provocatively suggests, a lifestyle. Style gives off an aroma. What is sumptuous suggests casual wealth; what is aggressive, indifference to convention; and what is conservative, obedience. The viewer is thus tantalized. Are the style and the lifestyle the same thing? That no one really knows is part of our modern mystique. However, this strategy of defining ourselves by what we are externally may diminish our sense of identity. This is especially the case where the "I" is disengaged from, and hides beneath, its changing masks.

Identity and Character

What strengthens the sense of identity, by contrast, are those things that require a person to be continuous with who he or she was.[44] A good illustration of this is the matter of the promise. Promises are, of course, of many kinds, ranging from those whose keeping is quick and easy,

---

the possible selves in the culture" and if all goes well with the hairdresser "each look is a new opportunity for the client's transformation and self-discovery." See his *Big Hair: A Journey Into the Transformation of the Self* (New York: Overlook Press, 1995), 123.

43. Ewen, *All Consuming Images,* 79. For a full discussion of the many facets of meaning and significance associated with dress, see Ruth P. Rubinstein, *Dress Codes: Meanings and Messages in American Culture* (San Francisco: Westview Press, 1995).

44. Owen Flanagan has suggested that there is an inherent contradiction between the idea of personal identity — that it is the *same* person in the body — and the reality of change, of intellectual and moral growth. This is, of course, a long-standing philosophical debate but also one that has its own theological track. The New Testament affirms that Christ was both the *same* divine Son, from incarnation to death, and that he grew in stature and wisdom. That would seem to imply that it is possible to preserve our personal identity in the midst of change. (See Flanagan, *Self Expressions,* 65.) On this same discussion of how the nature/nurture dynamic affects identity and whether we can have continuity of identity beneath different "personalities," see Thomas K. Fitzgerald, *Metaphors of Identity: A Culture-Communication Dialogue* (Albany: State University of New York Press, 1993), 23-56. A promise, Yale law professor Stephen Carter says, "is an open and unequivocal statement about how one intends to live" or behave (Stephen L. Carter, *Integrity* [New York: Basic Books, 1996], 33).

such as meeting someone for lunch, to those that are life long and sometimes hard, such as marriage. At their heart, however, all promises bind the person who makes the promise to be the same person in the future as the one who is doing the promising in the present. The husband who promises during the wedding ceremony that he will be a "loving and faithful husband, for better or for worse, in plenty and in want, in joy and in sorrow, in sickness and in health" has not the faintest idea what will be entailed in the keeping of that promise. The future lies before him unopened. As it unfolds, moment by moment, he comes to see what will be required for him to be a "loving and faithful husband." His intent to be the same person as the one who made that promise will be tested through misunderstanding, moral failures, illness, and the pressures of modern life. It is in the keeping of that promise, however, that identity is partly forged. In a curious paradox, the self-restraint and self-control that are inevitably a part of the keeping of that marriage promise are the very means of strengthening the self, rather than of diminishing it. Where a promise is kept, there is an unbreached moral relationship between the person who makes the promise and the person who receives it. What sustains that continuity, and what therefore underwrites a sense of identity, is the very thing most imperiled in the postmodern world: moral principle.

The breakdown of meaning in the modern world, following the bankruptcy of the Enlightenment experiment, has also created a dangerous moral vacuum. It is a vacuum that nourishes our rampant individualism, not to mention our many litigants, because it enflames our relativism and then requires that the fires started be doused by recourse to law. In the decline of the middle territory between law and freedom, that territory where moral restraint is self imposed, where there is "obedience to the unenforceable," we are losing both the moral fabric of life and our own identity as moral beings. This profound cultural disorientation is now providing the Church with an opening as large and as significant as it has seen in this century. What will it need to be able to seize this moment? This is the theme we must now begin to explore.

CHAPTER V

Contradictions

> As a sinner, man is a being whose nature has been perverted, one
> who has been severed from God, one who is remote from God. He
> is — whether he knows it or not — in conflict with the nature in
> which he was created; he is 'sick' with that 'sickness unto death'
> which, when it breaks out, manifests itself in the form of despair.
>
> Emil Brunner

From Amnesia to Memory

So far, this has been a one-sided analysis of the contemporary person.
The side that has been in view is that which has been emptied out,
which has lost the middle terrain between law and freedom, which is
adrift in moral understanding, and which has tried to dissolve guilt into
shame and to treat shame as simply a human malfunctioning. The new
preoccupation with shame, however, really reflects only an attempt to
secularize guilt. It therefore looks for help, not from the atonement,
but from psychological technique. There is, however, another side to
the contemporary person. All people, whether they understand it or
not, are moral actors, and their experience is replete with moral substance. Throughout the fabric of their life are woven threads of moral
consciousness, disconcerting as these often are. Here is a contradiction
of enormous importance both in understanding ourselves and in
developing an effective apologetic in our postmodern world.

As it turns out, these two sides to our experience, contradictory though they are, are really the two chapters in the human story, the first of which (odd though this may seem) actually lingers on in the pages of the second. For in the first, there is told the story of our creation in the image of God and in the second its wreckage by sin. However, this wreckage, this Fall, did not entirely undo what had been given originally, and the strains of moral experience that continue to be heard in our fallen world are constant reminders of who we once were. They are the best clues to the nature of our existence. They are "signals of transcendence," indicators that life is more than its natural processes, that human beings are anchored in a moral world to which they always have conscious connections. And listening to these signals can restore the memory of who we really are.

In speaking of "amnesia" in our contemporary culture, however, I am using the word advisedly, because it is a condition that psychiatrist M. Scott Peck rightly suggests is deliberately sustained (cf. Rom. 1:18). It is not as if we have actually lost some of our faculties. Rather, what seems to have happened, though Peck himself does not follow this line of reasoning, is that our culture — the habits, values, beliefs, and ways of looking at life that have become a normative part of the modern world — is actually at war with part of who we are as people. We are, as a result, frequently the depository of contradictions that we simply cannot resolve. At their center, for all of the reasons I have tried to adduce so far, is the belief that we inhabit our own private universe in which we are accountable to no one but ourselves in moral matters, whereas, in fact, we are also unable to escape the moral nature of our self. Harold Wilson, the former Prime Minister of Britain, had the reputation of being a particularly unprincipled politician behind his rather grave, moral exterior. In the House of Commons one day he was being upbraided by a Tory on the opposite side of the House. The problem with the Prime Minister, he was told, was that he was always wrestling with his conscience — and winning! What Peck describes takes this a step farther.

Our amoral culture greases the way for the emergence of what he calls, unflatteringly, the "people of the lie." These are people who refuse to "bear the trial of being displeasing to themselves."[1] They refuse to tolerate any moral recriminations within themselves. If they feel shame before others, they refuse to accept guilt within themselves. Peck then makes a telling observation. The "essential component of evil," he says,

1. M. Scott Peck, *People of the Lie: The Hope for Healing Human Evil* (New York: Simon and Schuster, 1983), 72.

"is not the absence of a sense of sin or imperfection but the unwilling-ness to tolerate that sense. . . . Rather than blissfully lacking a sense of morality, like the psychopath, they are continually engaged in sweeping the evidence of their evil under the rug of their consciousness."[2]

This internal dynamic explains why those who cannot bear the pain of any moral scrutiny are so often assiduous cultivators of their own image. The outward appearance of rectitude that they carefully cultivate serves as a counterweight to the jarring knowledge within that they are, despite all their efforts at denial, moral agents. They therefore become extremely sensitive to how they are being "read" by others, about who they know, who they are seen with, about what messages their "lifestyle" might be emitting, how they dress, what they buy. They are often careful about paying their taxes, working hard, being good neighbors. Often the next door neighbors of someone who is arrested for a crime remark on how quiet, decent, and upright this person seemed to be. They are shocked to discover that underneath the surface of life was serious moral disorder. Whether in an extreme case like this or in more benign forms, the rectitude of these people is all on the surface. That is why these are the people of the lie.

It is hard to know whether these people are nearer to the norm in this culture or whether they are still an aberration. Peck clearly thinks that they have become the norm, that this is no small pocket of people. He may be correct, because there is an unquestioned affinity between the narcissism of our culture, which is endemic, not to say epidemic, and the kind of behavior he describes. What both have in common is the denial or subjugation of the moral.

And yet here we encounter an enigma at the heart of our life. We try not to ask questions about our life, but those questions keep asserting themselves. Initially, we ask about the world around us, the shell within which we live, but then we start to ask about ourselves. Why can we not escape the pangs of remorse when we act unethically? Why is it that something seems to be disturbed within us? When we refuse to bear any moral scrutiny, why are we unable to silence completely our inner, moral sense? "Not only is the world full of riddles," theologian Emil Brunner says, but "he himself, who asks the riddles, has become a riddle." He continues:

All our problems are focused in this one question: Who is this being who questions — the one behind all questions? Who is this who per-

2. Ibid., 76.

ceives the infinity of the world? Who is this who is tortured by all life's problems — whether in human existence or outside it? Who is this being who sees himself as a mere speck in the universe, and yet, even while doing so, measures the infinite horizon with his mind? We are confronted here by the problem of the *subject*, separated by a great gulf from all problems of the objective world. What is this to which things are objects, which they are 'set over against'?[3]

In addition to the moral contradictions that run through our being, there is also the jarring sense that we are never quite able to make sense out of life. Theologian Reinhold Niebuhr argued that in its essence this loss of inner equilibrium stems from two seemingly contradictory aspects of who we are. On the one hand, we are part and parcel of nature, "subject to its vicissitudes, compelled by its necessities, driven by its impulses, and confined within the brevity of years which nature permits." On the other hand, the human being is a spirit "who stands outside of nature, life, himself, his reason and his world."[4] We have the capacity to stand apart from our world and think about it; indeed, to stand apart from ourselves and think of ourselves as objects. We transcend the natural world, knowing that it is more than simply the sequence of everyday events. This capacity is so disquieting because, as Niebuhr puts it, "the self which stands outside itself and the world cannot find the meaning of life in itself or the world."[5] Self-transcendence thus becomes the means of our self-damnation. Outside of the grace and knowledge of God, we are doomed to homelessness, to restless wandering, to wanting something that we can never find because of who we are.

In one sense, then, our experience of the modern world, which mightily disposes us against knowing ourselves as moral beings, and which has no place for those who are self-transcending beings, can also be an ally. In damning us to ourselves, in enclosing us in a culture without skylights, it provokes us to explore whether our culture and our behavior are not at war with who we were created to be and with who we know ourselves to be.

3. Emil Brunner, *Man in Revolt: A Christian Anthropology*, trans. Olive Wyon (Philadelphia: Westminster Press, 1947), 17-18.
    4. Reinhold Niebuhr, *The Nature and Destiny of Man* (2 Vols.; New York: Charles Scribner's Sons, 1964), 1:4-5.
    5. Ibid., 1:14.

The Moral Sense

Any suggestion that human beings are not simply loose accumulations of experience, not simply bare selves, but inescapably moral agents because they have a human nature (and one made in the image of God), is met with incredulity, even derision, in the academic world.[6] The idea has been battered from all sides for more than a century, though for different reasons. Those who followed in the wake of the Enlightenment found the religious framework intolerable. In the twentieth century, for reasons that have sometimes been psychological and sometimes philosophical, the idea that there is such a thing as human *nature* has come to sound highly improbable and quite unserviceable. Perhaps the three most influential debunkers in this tradition of doubt have been Nietzsche, Marx, and Freud.

By the end of his life, Nietzsche had gained widespread recognition throughout Europe, but for much of it he lived almost reclusively before being overtaken by madness. Although there are many angles to his thought, perhaps what laid the groundwork for his becoming the godfather to our morally collapsing world was his contrast between master and slave moralities. It was the latter he especially disliked, and he believed that it was the ethic of Christianity. It issued in resentment of life and of the rich, repression of the body, and opposition to reason. He sought to overturn it and replace it by a vision of a humanistic and unbelieving world in which what had widely been taken as normative, morally speaking, would all perish.

The irony in the cases of both Freud and Marx is that while their thought has been highly destructive of moral life in this century, they both retained a sense of the indubitable correctness of their own views. Marx dismissed morality as something that the socially powerful had contrived in order to keep the weak and oppressed in their place, but no one who has read him can miss the sense of moral outrage in which his own social judgments are delivered. There can be no doubt that, in his own mind, he was marching in a cause of world righteousness in opposition to all entrenched unrighteousness. However, Marx's assumption that internal moral corruption can be made to disappear by simply reorganizing society so greatly trivialized the tragedy of fallen life that its moral consequences could no longer be counted.

6. For an excellent, though brief, review of the major competing anthropologies, see Leslie Stevenson, *Seven Theories of Human Nature* (Oxford: Oxford University Press, 1974).

And Freud allowed that morality was necessary but showed no further interest in the idea. His real focus centered on the development of "conscience." This is the superego, developed early on, in the boy's case, as the barrier against his lust for his mother and his jealous anger of his father. There is apparently not a shred of evidence to support such a theory,[7] but it has been immensely successful in giving people a reason to forsake what is moral on the supposition that self-restraint is not good for one's psychological health. Freud never counted the cost of what he was doing in this area. He argued that it is only as external authorities such as parents and God recede that a moral sense can emerge as an *internal* authority. The problem with this is, however, that in the absence of an external authority the line between right and wrong easily gets erased under the pressure of what we want, and what we want may be quite venal at times. And with the disappearance of God as the standard of what is right, it becomes impossible to sustain the idea that what is wrong is *sinful*. Despite Freud's role in not only routing out religious belief but, in effect, demolishing the possibility of a responsible moral life, it is nevertheless hard to miss the strains of assumed righteousness on his part. He proceeded to uproot religious wishful thinking with the aura of scientific detachment but also with all of the fervor of a cause.[8] The currents of skepticism about human nature have flowed into the twentieth century, gathering strength from the modernized culture into which they have flowed, and are now spilling into our postmodern world.

This, however, has produced an enigma of no small size. On the one hand, we have abundant evidence of the disordering of life that has accompanied modernization, such as soaring crime rates, illegitimacy, and the breakdown of the home, not to mention the escalating levels of anxiety and the stress provoked by a competitive and insecure workplace. It is also clear that a culture which allows the thought, however subtly or indirectly, that what is not illegal is probably morally permissible, is also one in which truth telling, honesty, civility, generosity, self-restraint, and self-discipline are all going to be frequent casualties. On the other hand, even as moral life is thus eroded in the culture, we continue to experience ourselves as moral beings. We are part and parcel of the one world and trapped in the other. That is the enigma.

7. See Seymour Fisher and Roger P. Greenberg, *The Scientific Credibility of Freud's Theories and Therapy* (New York: Basic Books, 1977).

8. See Paul Crittenden, *Learning to Be Moral: Philosophical Thoughts about Moral Development* (London: Humanities Press International, 1990), 12-25.

While many of our cultural critics have, in study after study, shown the corrosive effects of modernity, James Wilson has picked up the other side of this enigma. He has canvassed the significant body of research conducted over the last three decades that shows how inextricably woven through our sense of life are moral threads. In our everyday experience, we know ourselves to be moral agents, and the explanation he offers is that we do have such a thing as human nature.

Consider the evening news. It is usually filled with stories that assault one's sensibilities: a child is abducted and then murdered; African warlords squabble over territory and expose millions to slow death by starvation; ethnic differences spark an urban riot; teenagers shoot some of their gang rivals in cold blood; ancient rivalries in Palestine burst into fresh hatreds. Why is this considered "news"? The answer, Wilson argues, is that these events are not normal, however often we may have seen them. They go against our residual sense that these things should not be. If life were nothing but unrelieved darkness, endless brutality, and complete moral chaos, and all of this were considered completely normal, then the opposite of what we now see would be counted as news. The real newsmakers would be — far more often than they are today — the parents who sacrificed for their children, the person who gave an anonymous gift to someone in need, or the church that cared for those on the margins of society. These are the things reporters would search for each day, because they would be unusual — not the riots, bloodletting, hatreds, and political corruption we currently see. The darker realms of life catch the attention of the news industry because these are the things that catch *our* attention. Starving children, battered bodies, and callous killers may be commonplace, and we may accommodate ourselves to seeing them or knowing about them, but "in our calm and disinterested moments we discover in ourselves an intuition and powerful aversion to inhumanity."[9]

There is a side to this interest that Wilson has not discussed. Evil is usually far more graphic than goodness. For that reason, television is an especially powerful tool in its portrayal. The commercial interests driving television are not averse to exploiting such a fact. Furthermore, in a fallen world, evil is often far more interesting than goodness. Indeed, it is interesting precisely because it is not good. One of the great challenges that novelists have to face, not to mention television producers, is how to make the goodness in a character compelling. This is why a play or a movie about Christ will always be intrinsically flawed;

9. James Q. Wilson, *The Moral Sense* (New York: Free Press, 1993), 2.

no matter how many technological tricks are pulled in presenting him, he will always come across as infinitely less than he was.

Even as we feel a certain interest in, even fascination for, evil, we nevertheless retain our "moral sense." That is Wilson's argument. After all, if there were no moral sense, how can we account for the universal rejection of murder as being wrong? How can we explain the universal rejection of incest? And how can we explain the sense that most mothers and fathers have that they should care for their children, despite the inconvenience and hardship involved? In a study done in England on hardened men who had numerous criminal convictions, the overwhelming percentage of them said that they would be "angry" if their children acted as they had done. Despite what they had done and, given a chance, would probably do again, they had enough interest in their children's well-being to assert that they should not follow in their fathers' footsteps.

These norms regarding murder, incest, and the care of children have their violators, but these people are violators precisely because the common assumptions, in every culture, run the other way. The sanctions imposed on perpetrators of such crimes may vary from culture to culture, but what is universal is that people have the moral intuition that they should not commit murder, or incest, and that they should care for their children.

This is not all. Research has shown that buried within the human being are constructive moral intuitions about how life should be lived. These have been uncovered in cultures that are different from one another. Wilson considers four of these inward motifs: sympathy, fairness, self-control, and duty.

Sympathy, he suggests, is "the human capacity for being affected by the feelings and experiences of others."[10] For the most part, sympathy does not lead us to act altruistically, but it can prevent us from acting with harshness and cruelty. We sometimes take account of the impact of our actions on others. In Truman Capote's *In Cold Blood,* a Kansas family was slaughtered by a pair of drifters as loathsome as the family was wholesome. These young killers, whom the author interviewed, had no feelings for their victims, so it was not hard to kill them — a situation confirmed again and again in studies done on killers. Yet because we recognize this absence of sympathy as a moral aberration, we also affirm the ethic of its alternative, so sympathy is "an important source of the moral standards by which we judge both others and

10. Ibid., 30.

ourselves."[11] This is even evident when we suspect that a person has been altruistic for the wrong reasons. Someone who makes public his or her donation of a large gift for cancer research may, we think, simply want to reap the publicity that such an act generates. And yet, the person is still admired for this act of sympathy. Why? The answer apparently is that even though we know how flawed human motivations can be, we nevertheless wish to reward such behavior by our approval; and in our disapproval of those who have no regard whatever for the feelings or plight of others, we are affirming a measure by which we also judge ourselves.

If human nature were devoid of a moral sense, we would be hard-pressed to explain the considerable body of research showing that we have an ingrained sense of fairness. This notion includes a belief in equity. In one experiment, for example, proofreaders were all offered the same wage for their work. When they received their pay, however, some had been underpaid and others overpaid. Those who had received less than they should expressed their dissatisfaction in the follow-up questionnaire, but so too did many of those who had been overpaid. Fairness also includes the thought of reciprocity. This belief in the virtue of reciprocity — that I should help those who have helped me — is found in every culture and is a naturally discovered variant on the Golden Rule. Even in the context of the selfishness in which we all live, there are social sanctions against disregarding this belief. Fairness, finally, includes the idea of impartiality. It is what every employee hopes for, that he or she will be judged on his or her merits, and when this does not happen a sense of outrage is the typical response. In one study, even serious criminals felt more positively toward the judicial system when they believed that they received a fair trial than when they thought that they had gotten a lenient sentence.

It is perhaps harder to identify convincingly the third strand in this "moral sense," that of self-control, or what Aristotle called temperance. Partly, this is because the research has not been done on it and partly, I imagine, because this virtue is probably more vulnerable than any of the others in a culture such as ours. Self-control becomes a problem, Wilson notes, "when one is faced with a choice between an immediate pleasure and a more distant one that is of greater value."[12] In an age that demands immediate gratification, the pleasure at hand has a far more compelling attraction to it than the pleasure that is afar.

11. Ibid.
12. Ibid., 80.

This is unfortunate because worthy goals and accomplishments all require that we forego immediate pleasures. Parents who wish to nurture their children must often set aside their desires to spend time on something else; those who wish to be proficient in some occupation must first put years into training for that occupation; those who wish to retire in some comfort must be willing to save for that day. The fact that we approve of such restraint, even though we also muddy the picture by our chronic self-indulgence, suggests that at least remnants of this aspect of the "moral sense" remain.

Finally, there is the matter of duty. This is "the disposition to honor obligations without hope of reward or fear of punishment."[13] It is, of course, difficult to discern sometimes why promises are kept, loyalties preserved, and taxes paid. The motives could be base and pragmatic. It could be that a promise is kept because of the consequences of developing a bad reputation by not doing so. Taxes may be paid, not out of a sense of citizenship, but only out of fear of the Internal Revenue Service. In other cases, however, there are disincentives, or no tangible rewards, to the expressions of duty. A sense of obligation to what is right, for example, led several researchers in the tobacco industry to speak out about the addictive power of nicotine even though they placed themselves in some jeopardy by doing so. And some people take it upon themselves to honor a deceased's wishes even though there is nothing to be gained from having done so.

By itself, duty is often a weak sense. It is easily overrun, for example, by our desire for sociability. When the honoring of an obligation, such as being truthful with a person, collides with our desire to be liked by that person, we easily resort to the evasions we call "white" lies. However, when duty is allied with other parts of our moral makeup, it can become a potent reality. In a study done on Gentiles in the Second World War who rescued Jews from their Nazi enemies, it was discovered that most did so, despite the danger to themselves, out of a sense of sympathy for the Jews. About 10 percent, however, acted out of a sense of duty because of their revulsion over the Nazi brutality.

That there are those who are uncaring about the impact of their actions on others, that there are murderers, swindlers, cheats, liars, and cowards, in no way invalidates the argument that there is within human nature a "moral sense." It is precisely because there is this moral texture to life that we find those who violate its norms reprehensible. This dynamic, in fact, is at work in every area of life. We recognize those

13. Ibid., 100.

who are mad because the contrast with those who are rational is so striking, those who are dull because of the contrast with those who are brilliant, those who are lazy because of those who are hard-working, and those who are parsimonious because of those who are generous.

Our "moral sense" does, of course, need to be instructed. But while its nurture is important, its roots clearly reach down into nature. That is the unmistakable conclusion to which the work of psychiatrist Robert Coles leads us. He has spent a lifetime studying the emotional, spiritual, and moral lives of children, some of them very young.[14] It was, however, his experience in the South during the Civil Rights crisis in the 1960s that transformed his views. He was there to study the Black children who were walking into schools that had been desegregated. To get there, they had to walk "past grown men and women who were calling them the foulest of names, who were even threatening to kill them."[15] Psychologists who examined many of these young people were not sympathetic. They judged the children to be "sick," "delinquent," "troubled," "sociopathic," and "psychopathic." Indeed, Coles himself fell into this same attitude. Of the children he observed, Ruby was from a "culturally deprived" family, Tessie's grandmother was "illiterate," Martha "projected" a lot, Jim had a "character disorder," Fred would probably become psychotic later. And yet they acted with courage and with character. That was what began to trouble Coles. The case of Ruby Bridges took the phenomenon even further. The daughter of sharecroppers, only six years old, but church-going, "this child had to brave murderously heckling mobs, there in the morning and there in the evening, hurling threats and slurs and hysterical denunciations and accusations."[16] Ruby not only acted with resolute courage but smiled at her adult tormentors and at night prayed for them. Coles says elsewhere in the book that the comments of children, "some extremely poor, some extremely rich, remind us that boys and girls are constantly at work noticing what is just, what is unjust, rendering their judgments,"[17] sometimes with little or no instruction from parents or teachers, and often in defiance of conventional academic wisdom about what they are likely to think. They see life, he says, in a moral perspective, and this begins at a very early age.

14. See his series of books under the general title of *Children of Crisis* (5 vols.; Boston: Little, Brown, 1967-1980).

15. Robert Coles, *The Moral Life of Children* (Boston: Atlantic Monthly Press, 1986), 140.

16. Ibid., 22.

17. Ibid., 15.

The Biblical Perspective

What this research has discovered, of course, is what all along has been described in the New Testament. Paul, in the epistle to the Romans, speaks to the same dilemma I have been describing. On the one hand, people then, as now, experienced themselves as moral beings. On the other hand, Gentile society then was disintegrating morally, as contemporary American society appears to be doing now, and these two realities seemed not to be consistent with one another.

The moral sense we have as human beings has, as it were, two coordinates, one external and the other internal. What is external comes from the fact that we live in the theater of nature in which God, its creator, can be glimpsed. Nature is a parable that, in its structure, orderliness, beauty, and design, points beyond itself to its creator (Rom. 1:18-20; Acts 14:17; cf. Ps. 19:1-2). There are footprints in our world whose size and shape speak of Another. He is out of all proportion to what is merely natural and is the only explanation of what is natural. That is the external coordinate. What is internal comes from the fact that our human nature brings to our consciousness the disquieting realization that we are not only moral beings but also morally accountable (Rom. 2:14-15). This sense of the moral character of reality may never be fully understood, but nor is it ever fully evaded, and literature is full of characters who are haunted by their own confused, unrequited moral sense.

In Albert Camus's novel *The Fall*, for example, a successful Parisian lawyer, Jean Baptiste Clamence, had an experience one night that forever changed his life. Prior to this time, he had been embarked, against his will, on a slow process of self-discovery. Although he was an upright person, who took no bribes and aided the poor, he began to realize that his rectitude was entirely self-serving. It was a kind of exhibitionism. He was "always bursting with vanity. I, I, I, is the refrain of my whole life,"[18] he said. He came to see that he was not only vain but also just skimming along the surface of life, women and alcohol being his only solace. True "debauchery," he said, "is liberating because it creates no obligations."[19] That night, however, changed everything.

It was late when he crossed over a bridge on his way home to the Left Bank. He passed a slim woman dressed in black who seemed to

18. Albert Camus, *The Fall*, trans. Justin O'Brien (New York: Vintage International, 1957), 48.
19. Ibid., 103.

stare into the water. Shortly after passing her, he heard the sickening thud of her body striking the water. A few cries followed as she was swept away by the river, and then the night was silent. He stood motionless for a minute, stabbed by recrimination over the lost opportunity to save her, but then he moved on and never reported this event to anyone. Although this incident disappeared into his memory, its effects within him were only just beginning. His guilt now began to take hold. Soon he would not cross bridges, so painful had the memory become. On an ocean liner, he imagined that he saw a body floating in the water, but on closer inspection it was only garbage. He began to feel a deep need to confess his sins as the fear of death began to intrude into his life. An unconfessed sin, after all, became an indelible mark. But to whom should he confess his sin?

When religion was flourishing, he said, one confessed to the priest. But, now? With the passing of religion, "soap has been lacking, our faces are dirty, and we wipe one another's noses." And he went on to say that we "should not wait for the Last Judgment. It takes place every day."[20] The fact, however, that we are left only to confess to ourselves means not only that the stain of guilt is left untouched but that our very contrition becomes the cause of self-righteousness. "The more I accuse myself, the more I have a right to judge you."[21] His self-righteousness began to elevate him over everyone else. "How intoxicating to feel like God the Father,"[22] he sighed finally to himself. And so, after this long process of self-examination, he finally came back to the scene on the bridge in his mind. When he revisited his memory of this fatality, he decided that, after all, he would not dive in to rescue her.

The starkness of Camus's godless world is not softened at all in this book. For Camus, there was no one to whom confession could be made even though his character, Clamence, had a deep need to confess. He could not understand why he could hear the rumble of divine judgment in his world, the sound, he thought on one occasion, of God laughing at him. And he finally could not escape himself and his self-righteousness, which was the problem with which this whole process of self-discovery began.

Despite his concluding despair and emptiness, Camus is otherwise close to Paul's own analysis at some points. For Paul speaks not only of

20. Ibid., 111.
21. Ibid., 140.
22. Ibid., 143.

an indelible moral sense, but also of the rumble of divine judgment that could be heard in the culture of his day and that, if we listen carefully, we will also hear through ours today. He speaks, too, of the self-righteousness that is not simply an occasional visitor but a permanent resident in the self.

The external coordinate of this moral sense, then, is in the disclosure God has made of his "eternal power and deity" (Rom. 1:20) through nature. By "deity" Paul appears to have in mind God's moral splendor. The revelation God has made of this in the fabric of things is not complete, but it is sufficient. It delivers enough knowledge about him for us to know that he should be worshipped and honored.[23] We reach this conclusion by inferring back, however inchoately, from the results of his creation to their cause in the Creator. What "can be known about God is plain to them," Paul says, "because God has shown it to them" (Rom. 1:19).

If this external coordinate gives us the knowledge of God's existence, our first-hand knowledge of his moral character comes most immediately from the other coordinate, the fabric of moral life within. For it is the peculiarity of man, Emil Brunner says, that "he is responsible to God, whose Voice he hears, whose claim he recognises";[24] more than that, whose Voice and whose claim are sufficiently clear that they have to be actively resisted. This inner sense may be misinterpreted, may even be sublimated for stretches of time, but it remains a source of dis-ease.

Here is "truth" that, in our fallen human world, is suppressed (Rom. 1:18). In Scripture, as has already been noted, what is true and what is morally right are often bracketed (e.g., John 3:21; 2 Cor. 4:2). And that seems to be so here. Truth about God and about what is morally right are always implied in each other, and these are made of

---

23. Melanchthon suggested that the knowledge that remains in human experience derived from creation and the *imago Dei* is this: "There is one God, of immeasurable power, wise, just, good; the founder and preserver of nature; punishing the unjust and criminal; hearing and saving — not *gratis*, not those guilty of sin — but the righteous and pure; that God must be obeyed; that he commands what is honorable, and prohibits shameful deeds; that he implanted in our minds the distinction between what was honorable and what is shameful. These are the things known by nature, which we constantly hear speaking to us in our conscience. . . . It judges that only those who are without sin please God. This is the natural voice of conscience." Philip Melanchthon, *Commentary on Romans*, trans. Fred Kramer (St. Louis: Concordia, 1992), 75.

24. Brunner, *The Divine Imperative: A Study in Christian Ethics*, trans. Olive Wyon (London: Lutterworth Press, 1937), 153.

no account by men and women who are in their nature fallen. A more precise description of modern, secularized society would be hard to find. And so, right here are sown the seeds of our own internal contradictions. From the creation, we have a twilight knowledge of the kind of God before whom we are standing, and we have some sense of how we should comport ourselves in life, but from within ourselves we find only the urge to disregard what we know and to dismiss what we should do. And, in our society today, this inner compulsion to disregard what we sense is true is made to seem very plausible by our culture, which, for all of the reasons I have suggested, has emptied itself out of moral life. It is this inner contradiction, however, that renders us, in Paul's words, "without excuse" (Rom. 1:20).

This device of suppressing inconvenient or unwanted knowledge is the tell-tale sign of a nature that is fallen. Although it is clear from Romans that the knowledge suppressed has to do with the reality of God and of our moral standing before him, it may be that in every culture this device needs to work a little differently. We certainly see this propensity in the "people of the lie," those who simply refuse to bear any moral recriminations. Would it be amiss to think that it is also at work among those in our culture who have buried their knowledge of their human nature and replaced it by a self that can be controlled, cultivated, and satisfied? Would it be amiss to see this inward device behind our loss of interest in character and behind its replacement by personality, which can be manufactured in a way that inward virtue cannot? Is the same mechanism not at work in those who have supplanted virtue by values and then proceeded to think about values in an entirely value-free way? And is not the disappearance of guilt in our culture and its replacement by shame also evidence of those who "by their wickedness suppress the truth" (Rom. 1:18)?

When people turn away from the truth about God and the moral implications of that truth, God turns away from them. This is the dialectic of life. When we dismiss what is good, we only sell ourselves to what is bad. When the mind "turns from the one," Luther observed, "it of necessity becomes addicted to the other."[25] Thus is the worship of God overtaken by the worship of the self.

Twice, therefore, Paul says that God "gave them up" (Rom. 1:24, 26) to a fuller experience of their own decadence as he withdraws his restraints and allows the sin of idolatry — now taken to an art form and

25. Martin Luther, *Commentary on the Epistle to the Romans*, trans. J. Theodore Mueller (Grand Rapids: Kregel Publications, 1954), 44-45.

into high commercial enterprise in our society — to aggravate itself and take its toll on those who are in its sway. His displeasure is registered in society through its decadence. In that moral chaos, his judgment is being rendered. Although sin, for the moment, becomes its own judgment (Rom. 1:25), this is far from being simply cause and effect at work in the moral world. No, this is also the judgment of God on those who do not love the Judge. It is his "wrath." It is his "No" thundering out against the whole order of our existence. It is his rejection of the self-oriented world that has rejected him. Far from working some remedy, however, this experience of our own dissolution only hardens our contempt for God and for his will (Rom. 1:32).

All of this, however, collides with our knowledge of ourselves as moral actors. It has always been thus. The Gentiles, Paul says, live and die "outside the law" (Rom. 2:12). Would this mean, then, that since they are not recipients of biblical truth, they have not heard the moral law, that they cannot be held culpable for their moral lives in the absence of a clear standard that has been violated? This is, indeed, a logical question, but it overlooks an important fact. There is a law that is written into human nature. "When Gentiles . . . do by nature what the law requires, they are a law to themselves" (Rom. 2:14). Paul apparently means that there are certain things the moral law requires that seem to be right simply by the light of nature. These people, therefore, do "by native instinct or propension, by spontaneous impulse" what is right, says theologian John Murray, and therefore they "confront themselves with the law of God. They themselves reveal the law of God to themselves — their persons is [sic] the medium of revelation."[26] Their conscience, as a result, "also bears witness and their conflicting thoughts accuse or perhaps excuse them" (Rom. 2:15). Wilson summarized some of this evidence, though he focused only on what is moral and did not consider what is religious. He argued that not only is there a universal sense that murder and incest are wrong, and that parents should care for their children, but also buried in human nature, apparently, are the norms of sympathy, fairness, self-control, and duty. They are norms in

26. John Murray, *The Epistle to the Romans* (London: Marshall, Morgan, and Scott, 1967), 73. After a very careful review of the exegetical options, Käsemann concluded that for Paul "everything depends on the fact that the Gentiles also experience the transcendent claim of the divine will and thus become, not *the* law or *a* law, but law to themselves. . . . They sense that a person is set in question and that a demand is laid on him from outside, and paradoxically they do so in their inner beings." Ernst Käsemann, *Commentary on Romans*, trans. Geoffrey W. Bromiley (Grand Rapids: Eerdmans, 1980), 64.

the light of which thought about our own action either accuses or excuses us. So, in the very moment when our own culture is lifting moral restraints, and emptying life of its moral reality, our own nature, sometimes to our great discomfort, is declaring that it is unable to adapt to this flattened out, trivialized, morally vapid world. Our very nature is signaling the fact that it has connections with moral reality that transcend the culture.

We are in some ways, then, inwardly at odds with our disintegrating culture — and also inwardly at odds with our own selves — even though the permission our culture often gives to what is morally wrong is happily accepted by what is fallen within us. We find that against all of our wishes, we cannot live as if there were no moral absolutes even though we may declare our firm belief that there are no such absolutes. And the more morally threadbare our life becomes, the more our nature cries out against us. It is in these contradictions that we find the real clues to the nature of existence, because there is memory running through these experiences of a world we now no longer know.

This contradiction is the contradiction between creation and sin. It is not one that lies outside of ourselves but one that we bear within our very being. Indeed, we have not understood ourselves at all until we have come to know why this contradiction lies buried beneath all our experience and why it asserts its presence in ways that elude our control. "Only he who understands this contradiction," Brunner said, "understands man as he actually is, and only he who comprehends the depth of the contradiction comprehends the depth of man as he actually is."[27] At the heart of this existence-in-contradiction is autonomous reason, our self-proclaimed emancipation, not only from God, but also from any world outside of ourselves. For in setting off to live and think as we will, we find that we have run headlong into the hard wall of reality, a wall that God himself sustains despite all of our most energetic assaults. Seeing ourselves as sinners is simply another way of saying that we now know the nature of our inner contradictions.

27. Brunner, *Man in Revolt*, 478.

Honor and Shame

Then and Now

It is true, of course, that honor and shame were "pivotal values"[28] in the ancient world of the Bible, and there has been some renewed interest in reading what the Bible has to say from this angle.[29] Since the experience of shame has become such a crippling phenomenon in America, it is worth revisiting the Bible with this in mind. Does the way that it treats honor and shame shed any light on the inner contradictions we experience in our modern world? I believe that our experience of shame today is rather different from the experience of shame then, that guilt is in remission now in a way that it was not then, and that in any case the cultural patterns of that time do not prescribe what is honorable and shameful in God's sight, nor do our ways of ascribing importance or denying it to people today coincide with what is and is not important to God. In exploring these differences, however, we will encounter interesting connections with our own time.

The Old and New Testaments were born in a world quite unlike our own today. This is true not only in the obvious ways, such as the fact that we are surrounded by the processes and results of modernization and they were not, but it is also true of the ways in which people came to understand themselves. Ours is a highly individualized culture, and theirs was not. We think of our individual consciousness as being unique, as something unlike anyone else's, and we express this in a

28. The pioneering anthropological work done on this theme is found in Jean G. Peristiany, ed., *Honor and Shame: The Values of Mediterranean Society* (Chicago: University of Chicago Press, 1966); Jean G. Peristiany and Julian Pitt-Rivers, eds., *Honor and Grace in Anthropology* (Cambridge: Cambridge University Press, 1992). See also David D. Gilmore, *Honor and Shame and the Unity of the Mediterranean* (Washington, D.C.: American Anthropological Association, 1987). This work has been mediated to the world of biblical scholarship principally by Bruce J. Malina, *The New Testament World: Insights from Cultural Anthropology* (rev. ed.; Louisville: Westminster/John Knox Press, 1993). See also Lewis M. Hopfe, ed., *Uncovering Ancient Stones: Essays in Memory of H. Neil Richardson* (Winona Lake, Ind.: Eisenbrauns, 1994); Halvor Moxnes, "Honor and Righteousness in Romans," *Journal for the Study of the New Testament* 32 (1988), 60-77; Jerome H. Neyrey, "Despising the Shame of the Cross: Honor and Shame in the Johannine Passion Narrative," *Semeia* 68 (1996), 113-37.

29. David DeSilva, "Despising Shame: A Cultural-Anthropological Investigation of the Epistle to the Hebrews," *Journal of Biblical Literature* 113, no. 3 (Fall 1994), 439. This approach he has worked out fully in his *Despising Shame: Honor Discourse and Community Maintenance in the Epistle to the Hebrews* (Atlanta: Scholars Press, 1995).

multitude of ways: how we dress, what we buy, how we look, and how we make decisions. Whatever sense of identity we have is woven together within our own inner, private sense of reality from whatever materials we choose. The biblical world was very different.

Then, people thought of themselves, not as free-floating, isolated individuals, but as belongers. Theologian Bruce Malina and New Testament scholar Jerome Neyrey have pointed out that individuals were understood then from within their social matrix. People were known, first, as members of a family or clan. Jesus was called "the son of Joseph" (John 1:45); Simon was the "son of John" (John 21:15); David, "the son of Jesse" (Acts 13:22); James and John, the "sons of Zebedee" (Matt. 10:2; 26:37). Knowing something of the family meant, people believed, that one knew something of the child. Second, people were also understood in terms of the place where they had been born, and some places were more honorable than others. Jesus was from Nazareth and Paul from Tarsus. Where one was born said something about who one was. Third, people were understood in terms of their ethnic origin, and it was common to stereotype the behavior of those in the group. Thus Paul can quote an unnamed prophet who said that "Cretans are always liars, evil beasts, lazy gluttons" (Tit. 1:12). Fourth, people were understood in terms of their craft or occupation, some crafts being more honorable than others. These, however, were not matters of choice, as they are for us today, but were roles handed down from father to son. It is no surprise to learn that Jesus' father, Joseph, was also a carpenter (Matt. 13:55; Mark 6:3). Finally, people were understood in terms of any group to which they might belong, such as the Pharisees, Sadducees, Herodians, or Epicurians, for this revealed who the person was.[30] We, today, think that the place where people were born and the family in which they were raised probably tell us little about them. Their occupation and affiliations may tell us more. But we also want to think that people cannot be contained within, and are not completely defined by, these associations and connections. In the ancient world, these factors were thought to provide a large sense of who a person was.

That world held no place for what to us is a virtue, that of "standing on one's own two feet," being autonomous, and being an individual. In that world, one stood by and within one's group, and it was from this group that one derived prestige. And since honor was of

30. Bruce J. Malina and Jerome H. Neyrey, "First-Century Personality: Dyadic, Not Individual," in *The Social World of Luke-Acts: Models for Interpretation* (Peabody, Mass.: Hendrickson Publishers, 1991), 74-75.

far more worth than money, which is exactly the opposite of their respective values in our society today, revenge and vendetta became the common coin of social relations.[31] This also meant that if others read a person in terms of these connections — to family, place, ethnicity, occupation, or associations — so, too, did that person. It was from these connections that a person's identity was forged and not from within a self disengaged from its social matrix.

It is now becoming rather clear, then, that if ours has become a "shame culture," it is so in ways that are quite different from the traditional shame cultures. It may be that shame has become our pre-eminent source of emotional distress,[32] but its substantial loss of *moral content* sets us apart from cultures in Asia, Africa, the Mediterranean world, and South America that, since Margaret Mead's work first at-tracted attention, have been thought of as shame-oriented, rather than guilt-driven. In those cultures, at least prior to the onset of modernity, there has been a thick weave of moral convention within the social fabric that is no longer present in America. Moreover, these other societies have all stressed the family, community, and nation over the individual in a way that Americans do not. In Japan today, for example, children are rarely praised, because it is believed that this might undermine the value of group accomplishment by reinforcing individual achievement. In these societies, when failure occurs, it is experienced as failure in the *group*, rather than as something purely private. It is the relationship to others that defines how failure is understood — hence the expression "losing face." To lose face is to suffer embarrassment because others see the offender as having let them down, or having dishonored their family, or town, or the business. Shame and dishonor become inter-twined, the one hardly ever happening without the other, because of the sense of *responsibility* toward others.[33]

---

31. Duncan M. Derrett, *Jesus' Audience: The Social and Psychological Environment in Which He Worked* (New York: Seabury Press, 1973), 40.

32. This is the argument in Robert Karen, "Shame," *Atlantic Monthly* 269 (February 1992), 40-43, 46-49, 52, 55-58, 60-62, 64-65, 68-70.

33. Gabriel Moran has attempted to use the notion of responsibility as a bridge across five distinct moral domains, even though he is swimming against a strong cultural tide. First, it reaches across the chasm between "ought" and "is"; second, between what is collective and what is individual; third, between what is human and what is not; fourth between what is past and what is present; finally, it can be a bridge between those divisions created by the collision of competing cultures. Responsibility has seldom been classified as a virtue before, which suggests that some of the moral weight that it has today was once carried by other virtues. That leaves Moran's book open to the charge that he expects responsibility to express

However, in our highly individualized, narcissistic American culture, the sense of moral responsibility to the groups in which we have connections has now worn thin. A person caught falsifying a business's charge sheet may worry about possible prosecution but will give hardly a thought to the firm's reputation. Someone who abducts a young woman from his town may fear the police, but he will give not a single thought to how this action impinges on the town's residents. If we have few sensitivities about our moral responsibilities toward others, we are nevertheless easily embarrassed by how our self is being read. In our interactions with others, our question is not how our actions have affected them but how we *appear* to them. That is the trailing edge of our narcissism.[34] Is their evaluation of me different from my evaluation of myself? How will they understand what I have just done? Will I appear to have been awkward, foolish, unsophisticated, incompetent, inadequate, or ignorant? The victim is not the group — be it family, community, or business — but the *self*. It is how we think of ourselves, how we perceive ourselves as being perceived, that calls into play the emotional repertoire that we associate with shame, feelings such as inferiority, anger, contempt, anxiety, and sadness. In experiences like these it is the *self* that is diminished and depleted. In a narcissistic culture, Donald Capps sums up, people "do not experience guilt to any significant degree" in the sense of having failed objective moral norms, and yet, despite this fact, they still do not feel whole and happy. They are, instead, burdened by "a deep, chronic, and often inexplicable sense of shame." It is this, rather than guilt, that makes them feel "that something is seriously wrong with them."[35] This sense, though, is internalized. It is psychological, not social. This is what makes us different from traditional "shame cultures," even though today shame is very much on the surface of our relations with others.

That there is, in the postmodern world, a "deep, chronic, and

---

more of the moral life than it is able to. Nevertheless, his book is valuable in pointing out that moral bridges need to be built across the domains that, in a postmodern world, are frequently lost to one another. See his *A Grammar of Responsibility* (New York: Crossroad, 1996).

34. For a review of the major psychiatric theorists who have explored the connections between shame and narcissism, see Andrew P. Morrison, *Shame: The Underside of Narcissism* (Hillsdale: Analytic Press, 1989), 48-67, 134-51. See also Leon Wurmser, "Shame: The Veiled Companion of Narcissism," in Donald L. Nathanson, ed., *The Many Faces of Shame* (New York: Guilford Press, 1988), 68-74.

35. Donald Capps, *The Depleted Self: Sin in a Narcissistic Age* (Minneapolis: Fortress Press, 1993), 39.

often inexplicable sense of shame" is a powerful indicator of how we have both secularized our moral life and failed in that attempt. Our folly lies in exchanging theology for psychology and truth for therapy, so it is no surprise that we are fumbling in our attempt to understand our own inner dis-ease.

Faith as Subversive

As we start to see the differences in the cultural patterns between the first-century world and our own, we also begin to notice how the New Testament distances itself from those same ancient patterns. Much of the new anthropological work brought into the field of biblical studies has proceeded on the assumption that the cultural patterns of honor and shame, central to societies in the Mediterranean world, can explain honor and shame in the New Testament.[36] This, however, is quite fallacious. For with the intrusion of the Kingdom of God, the inauguration in Christ of the "age to come," a way of looking at life has been introduced that turns the patterns of the ancient world on their head. What caused shame or produced honor in the ancient world is by no means always the explanation of what the Bible sees as shameful and honorable. What was culturally honorable then might be quite dishonorable in the sight of God now. What seemed shameful then, such as being born among the lower levels of society — "the dregs of the populace," as historian Edward Gibbon would later say of Christians, people such as peasants, women, beggars, and slaves — could go hand in hand

---

36. Some of this new work, however, has thrown interesting light on the biblical narrative. Crucifixion, for example, was a barbaric way of carrying out capital punishment. It was also an exquisitely designed means of bringing total, humiliating shame upon the accused as they slowly made their way toward death. It entailed public "status degradation," destroying every vestige of a person's standing in society before he died. The condemned frequently were flogged as a prelude to crucifixion and, perhaps, blinded to underscore their helplessness. They were forced to carry the cross beam upon which they would die, which added insult to the injury they were about to sustain. Their clothes were parceled out to others so that they had to bear the humiliation of being naked in public. Once nailed, they were exhibited as powerless, and this provided much public entertainment. The victim was ridiculed, and the possibility of vengeance, which might have rectified such dishonor, was publicly withheld. The humiliating body contortions and excretions were in public view, and often the bodies were not buried but left on the cross until the birds had done their work. Crucifixion meant death with great dishonor, with public degradation, and that is what Hebrews has in mind when it says that Christ "endured the cross, despising the shame" (Heb. 2:2). See Jerome H. Neyrey, "Despising the Shame of the Cross," 113-14.

with great honor in the sight of God (see, for example, James 1:9-10; 2:1-7; Rom. 12:16).[37] The Bible, after all, is not simply a repository of cultural habits. It is also a *theological* document, for it records not only cultural patterns but also divine intrusions in the flow of redemptive history, intrusions that often overturn the values implicit in those cultural patterns. There are many occasions when this occurred, but one especially germane to this study is that of the way *conscience* is understood by the apostles.

Those who think that the patterns of a "shame culture" always describe how the biblical authors viewed the world are obliged to think that conscience has nothing to do with the pain that we feel within ourselves over our sin. It has none of the "introspective conscience of the West" derided by Krister Stendahl and summarized by Bruce Malina as ranging from "some sort of internalized standard of morality, some sense of personal guilt, to a self-punitive, self-critical reaction of remorse and anxiety after the transgression of some commandment of God."[38] On the contrary, conscience was construed, Malina thinks, as "sensitivity to what others think about and expect of the individual, pain one feels because others consider one's actions inappropriate and dishonorable."[39] On any reading of the biblical material there will, of course, be

---

37. Although there were such "dregs," from a historical point of view Gibbon's picture was also unbalanced. It is apparent from the pages of the New Testament that Christian faith embraced people in all of the social strata. There were the common people who gladly heard Christ, but among his friends were "Joanna, the wife of Chuza, Herod's steward, and Susanna, and many others, who provided for him out of their means" (Luke 8:2-3). Zacchaeus was greatly despised by the Jews, but Luke observes that he was also "rich" (Luke 19:2). Jesus had followers in high places, not simply among the uneducated. Joseph of Arimathea, "a respected member of the council," asked Pilate if he could have Jesus' body. He was a man "looking for the kingdom of God" (Mark 15:43), and he is described by Matthew as being "rich" and a "disciple of Jesus" (Matt. 27:57). Further, "many of the authorities believed in him, but for fear of the Pharisees they did not confess it" (John 12:42). In the book of Acts, we have land holders like Barnabas of Cyprus, Ananias and Sapphira, and the mother of John Mark, in whose house in Jerusalem the first church met. Early on, "a great many of the priests believed" (Acts 6:7) A little later, Manean "a member of the court of Herod the tetrarch" was converted (Acts 13:1), and eventually members of Caesar's own household. If Christianity spread horizontally, from Jerusalem into the far corners of the Roman world, it also spread vertically, up the social ladder, until by the third century Tertullian could boast that the pagan, unbelieving world had been left nothing but its idolatrous places of worship. See James Orr, *Neglected Factors in the Study of the Early Progress of Christianity* (London: Hodder and Stoughton, 1899), 95-162.

38. Malina, *The New Testament World*, 65.

39. Ibid., 88.

sins of this kind, because some actions impinge harmfully on others or will be viewed negatively by others. Some actions put us in a bad light. There are references to *conscience* that might perhaps be understood this way (Heb. 13:18; 1 Pet. 3:16; Rom. 13:5-7), but the vast majority cannot.[40] What seems rather clear from the New Testament is that it is one's interior moral reality to which conscience is attuned, and how one is viewed by others is not part of its functioning except in the cases, such as I discussed in the previous chapter, of false guilt or shame (1 John 3:20-21).

For Paul, the point of reference of the conscience, again and again, is *God,* rather than any group in which a person is socially embedded. At his trial, Paul defined his "good conscience" in terms of having "lived before God" (Acts 23:1; cf. 2 Tim. 1:3; Acts 24:16). The conscience is the jury in the inner court of appeal where morally dubious action must be judged (1 Cor. 8:7, 10, 12; 10:25, 27, 28, 29). In the Pastorals, as a result, Paul can elaborate on the moral nature of faith by saying that some, "rejecting conscience," had made "shipwreck of their faith" (1 Tim. 1:19; cf. 1 Tim. 4:2), which could not possibly be a reference to some group dynamic of shame. Again, in his letter to Titus Paul places the conscience in parallel to the mind, not to the group to which a person belonged. To "the corrupt and unbelieving nothing is pure; their very minds and consciences are corrupted" (Tit. 1:15). Paul argues elsewhere that the conscience is at the source of love and that it must be bound to "the mystery of faith" (1 Tim. 3:9).

It is therefore no surprise to note how Hebrews explores the conscience. It does so, not from the viewpoint of a person's sociological status, such as class, family, or economic standing, but from a Christological perspective. Even the Old Testament sacrifices could not remove "the consciousness of sin" (Heb. 10:2), it declares. A clear conscience is a blessing bestowed only by Christ, on account of his substitutionary death on the Cross (cf. 1 Pet. 3:16), and it simply cannot be bestowed

---

40. When the social conventions about shame are used as a grid through which to read God's acts, much that is incomprehensible results. Lynn Bechtel, for example, claims that in the Old Testament an understanding of guilt, as opposed to shame, is unknown, despite the elaborate sacrificial system in which there was a guilt-offering (Lev. 6:1-7; 19:20-21). The purpose of the sacrificial system was to provide atonement, covering for sin, and it is hard to see how this can be construed as somehow related to the dynamics of group shaming when the worshipper, except in the case of national sacrifices, killed the animal himself, laying his hand on it by way of identification. See her essay, "The Perception of Shame within the Divine-Human Relationships in Biblical Israel," in Hopfe, ed., *Uncovering Ancient Stones,* 79-92.

by self-effort or social approval. And, by extension, it cannot be wrested out of our own psychology by any ten- or twelve-step program. It is the "blood of Christ" alone that can "purify your conscience from dead works to serve the living God" (Heb. 9:14; cf. 10:22). It is not the clan, family, community, or nation that can lift this burden of dead works and release the conscience. Paul could have said of these things what he said of the false teachers, that "they are of no value in checking the indulgence of the flesh" (Col. 2:23).

These, however, are all references to conscience from within a Christian framework. They are speaking of conscience as Paul and the apostles knew of it. This is important, because it tells us, from within the framework of revealed truth, exactly what its nature is. Yet conscience clearly also functions in those who know no such truth and who may well be inhospitable to its warning sounds. The difference between these two experiences, one inside truth and the other outside, lies in the capacity of the person who has been prodded by his or her conscience to understand it, to align it with the transgression that has triggered its cry, and to measure the gravity of the offense. Conscience in itself is less active than passive, less rational than emotional. It is the sense, Brunner writes, that man "feels himself in the center of his existence to be disturbed, injured, affected by the contradiction, the consciousness that 'things are not right with him', that they 'are out of order', a knowledge which comes to him involuntarily."[41] Conscience, then, is more like the moaning of a prisoner in his cell than the discourse of a professor at his lectern. It is an alarm signal whose noise can be turned down but not off. It is our interior reality, which is inexplicable in the absence of God and inconsolable apart from his grace.

That the New Testament aligns our moral nature with God by creation and grace means that it gives to honor and shame a meaning quite unlike the one that was conventional in the world in which it came to birth. In Scripture, honor and shame, in their deepest and truest meanings, have to do with our standing before God. They have to do with the way in which the "age to come" is, or is not, sending its clarifying light into our lives now. They have to do with whether or not we are in Christ's Kingdom, are living by his Word, are the children of his heavenly Father. At the heart of Christian faith stands this fundamental relationship to God himself through Christ; it is a relationship that is moral at its center because God is holy in his being, not one that is sociological and determined by those in our family or tribe.

41. Brunner, *The Divine Imperative*, 156.

Honor, as a result, is not what we bestow upon ourselves. It is not derived by our social connections. It is *God* who bestows honor (2 Cor. 2:8). And he first bestowed this honor on us at creation. At creation, for a short while, we were "made lower than the angels" and were crowned "with glory and honor" (Heb. 2:7). The writer to the Hebrews does not elaborate on this, but it seems rather obvious from the context that he was speaking of our creation in the image of God and of the cultural mandate that followed. With this creation came the capacity to know God and to live out our lives on his terms in this world, serving the Creator rather than the creature. This honor was partly lost in the Fall.[42] Therefore, at the center of the moral world there now stands the

42. The *imago Dei* presents a tantalizing problem in Scripture; while its importance is beyond doubt, its exact nature has to be constructed piece by piece from the biblical testimony. The traditional Christian response has been that it consists in internal *capacities*, although some in the Reformed tradition have wanted to emphasize *functions* in the fulfillment of the creation mandate. These capacities would further be distinguished as natural and moral. The ability to reason, for example, would be a natural capacity, and the ability to reason in a wholly obedient way is a moral capacity. At the time of creation, all our capacities were directed by what was holy; after the fall, they were not. Thus, we retain our natural image and lose our moral image. What remains, Brunner says, "is the formal element: creative power in virtue of the perception of ideas, self-consciousness and self determination, as characteristics of man's being which cannot be lost" (Brunner, *Man in Revolt*, 229). The most important reason for establishing the distinction in the *imago Dei* between that which is natural and that which is moral comes from the New Testament. It asserts, first, that Christ himself was the *imago* (2 Cor. 4:4; Col. 1:15) and, second, that in union with him, we begin to recover the lost moral dimension of the *imago*. We have been "predestined to be conformed to the image of his Son" (Rom. 8:29); we are slowly being changed into his "likeness" (2 Cor. 3:18); we are to put on the "new nature, created after the likeness of God" (Eph. 4:24).

This was the position of Brunner argued in his debate with Karl Barth, though it was also modified by his existentialism. Yet Brunner was rebuffed as being Pelagian. In other words, because Brunner argued that we have lost part of the image of God (what I have here called the moral), he was charged with saying that we are only half fallen. This charge is inaccurate. We are still in the image of God (James 3:9) but not, as fallen beings, in his moral image. We are fully fallen although we have not lost our natural image. See Emil Brunner and Karl Barth, *Natural Theology: Comprising "Nature and Grace" by Professor Dr. Emil Brunner and the Reply "No!" by Professor Dr. Karl Barth*, trans. Peter Fraenkel (London: Geoffrey Bles, 1946). More generally, see David Cairns, *The Image of God in Man* (London: SCM Press, 1953). Valuable historical material is still to be found in the older study of Sydney Cave, *The Christian Estimate of Man* (London: Gerald Duckworth, 1949). See also the useful sections on the *imago* in Anthony A. Hoekema, *Created in God's Image* (Grand Rapids: Eerdmans, 1986); Charles Sherlock, *The Doctrine of Humanity: Contours of Christian Theology* (Downers Grove, Ill.: InterVarsity Press, 1996), 27-91. Paul K. Jewett's study, *Who We Are: Our Dignity as Human* (Grand Rapids: Eerdmans, 1996), is more wide-ranging and explores the theme of human nature in its many relations.

Cross of Christ. Christ has covered the moral and spiritual shame of those who believe, and they need never fear being exposed again (Rom. 5:5). Christ's shame upon the Cross is God's means of both buying back the lost honor of sinners (1 Cor. 6:20; cf. 7:23) and exposing to public shame their spiritual enemies (Col. 2:15; cf. Heb. 6:6; 10:32-33).[43]

In the shadows of this moral world, where guilt has not been covered and the offense of sin rises up daily before God, we find those "with minds set on earthly things" (Phil. 3:19), and this is what is truly shameful in the biblical view. It is those who live stubbornly and insistently in their sins who are shameful before God (Jude 13; Rom. 1:27; 6:21; 2 Tim. 2:15; Eph. 4:19). By contrast, it is those who serve Christ, who have been reconciled to God by his death in their place, who please him. It is they who, "by patience in well doing," seek "glory and honor and immortality" (Rom. 2:7; cf. 2:10).

In texts like these we see that the coming of the Kingdom of God shattered the ancient ways of thinking about honor and shame. It overturned many of the cultural habits of the day, even as it overturns many of the cultural habits of our time. This, however, is exactly what we should expect. Jesus said his Kingdom was not of this world (John 18:36). This, however, is simply a small part of a long line of biblical texts that have far-reaching implications for the relation of biblical truth to this fallen world. Is this truth simply a reflection of cultural norms? Is it merely the last piece in a jigsaw puzzle, the rest of which we have been able to assemble ourselves? No. This Kingdom, in its nature and outworkings, is utterly different from the realms of cultural convention in which we live and is frequently at odds with them.

It is ever the tendency of human rebellion to reduce what is divine to what is manageable. More than that, it supposes that human habits, which have not been subjected to the judgment of God and refuse to accept that judgment, are therefore emancipated to become our guides to what life means. Culture becomes our revelation. The truth is that these habits and this culture are not the building blocks out of which

43. Gustav Aulén argued that the conquest motif suggested in this text was the "classical" model of understanding in the New Testament's view on the death of Christ, and he then made the others, such as redemption and justification, subservient to it. He went on to deny the penal element in justification and substituted for the idea of a declared righteousness that of a restored filial relationship. In the absence of imputation, this conquest motif easily lends itself to universalism, which is the path along which Karl Barth moved. See Aulén's *Christus Victor: An Historical Study of the Three Main Types of the Idea of Atonement*, trans A. G. Hebert (London: S.P.C.K., 1965). I have explored the connections between these ideas in my *Search for Salvation* (Downers Grove, Ill.: InterVarsity Press, 1978), 30-32, 53-73.

the Kingdom of God is built. In the presence of God, they must die. They must die as long as they lay claim to being unbroken and un-tainted, as long as they do not stand upright in the presence of God. His Kingdom is made of different stuff. It is at this nexus between truth and culture that many Christian paradoxes are born.

These paradoxes are rooted in Christ himself who, though he was rich, made himself poor for our sakes in the incarnation (2 Cor. 8:9). He who had been robed with all of the insignia of divine majesty removed those tokens of power and position and assumed the lowly garb of an insignificant servant (Phil. 2:5-11). Though he was a Son, he had to learn "obedience through what he suffered" (Heb. 5:8). This is exactly the opposite of what we would naturally think would be the case. And the consequence, for those who are Christ's, is that they also come to live in a way that is exactly the opposite of what a culture might naturally expect. They find that worldly expectations have been over-turned.

Will there not be those like Lazarus, who are treated with contempt in this life, who know its want and deprivations, but who will neverthe-less come to enjoy the presence of God forever (Luke 16:19-31)? At the same time, will there not be those who enjoyed the world's abundance, who are bathed in the power and privilege it confers, who will, neverthe-less, be abandoned by God in the end (cf. Luke 18:24; Mark 4:19)? Is this not the upending of expectations, of normal worldly patterns, which we hear celebrated in the *Magnificat*?

God, Mary saw, is the great reverser of what we think is normal. From a human perspective, there is a contrarian twist to God's actions. They do not follow the paths of convention. In this case, does it make sense that Mary, a poor, inconsequential teenager (in all likelihood), is remembered today, for she said, "Henceforth all generations will call me blessed" (Luke 1:48)? And they have — while the rich and powerful of the day have more or less vanished from memory. Who today knows of the great celebrities of Mary's time, women like Livia (who married Augustus Caesar), Octavia (whom Mark Anthony divorced in order to marry Cleopatra), or Antonia (who was poisoned by her emperor grand-son, Caligula)? They had their season at the pinnacle of power and at the center of attention. They lived in great honor; Mary, in great obscurity and social shame. The wind, however, has blown them away, but Mary will be remembered forever. Why is this?

Mary experienced two of the contrarian principles in God's work-ing. First, he opposes the proud but lifts up the humble (whereas we typically fawn over the rich and powerful and disregard those who are judged to be insignificant). God scatters the proud "in the imaginations of their hearts," and he puts down "the mighty from their thrones" (Luke 1:51-52), but his mercy reaches out to those who fear him and those of "low degree" whom he exalts (Luke 1:50-51). This violates every canon of what constituted honor in that society, even as it violates every canon of what constitutes importance in ours. Second, he passes by those who are full. The "rich he has sent empty away," but "he has filled the hungry with good things" (Luke 1:53). This hunger is not simply psychological need. It is, rather, owning inward moral bankruptcy and wanting some resolution to it. It is what led Mary to rejoice in "God my Savior" (Luke 1:47). In one of the contradictions we know as the beatitudes, Jesus tells us that "blessed are the poor in spirit, for theirs is the Kingdom of God" (Matt. 5:3). The qualifier in Matthew (that it is the poor "in spirit" and not simply the economically poor) indicates that what Jesus had in mind is what Mary herself knew. It is not the self-righteous, not those who find their confidence in the honor they enjoy, that Jesus calls to himself, but sinners (Matt. 9:13). It is the weary and heavy-laden that he calls to himself, sometimes the outcast and those who are unacceptable, not the self-satisfied (Matt. 11:28). And there will be those with whom Christ has eaten and conversed, whose expectations of acceptance are unbounded, who believe they are worthy of honor and not of shame, who will find the door closed upon them with the words, "I tell you, I do not know where you come from; depart from me, all you workers of iniquity" (Luke 13:27). For here, there are surprises of the most profound kind. Here, "the last will be first, and the first last" (Matt. 20:16).

It is paradoxical that those who know they have failed God are made to succeed, those who have fallen are raised, those who are bankrupt are made rich, those who are empty and depleted are satisfied, and those who are, in their own eyes, of no account are made to stand beside the Lord of the universe. This overturns all human calculations. Standing in this world brings no standing with God, regardless of family, wealth, or connections. We can acquire a massive number of goods, be showered with honor and prestige, but despite all of the earthly security we can buy or negotiate, the day comes when we lose our own soul, because what elevates people in this life may also contribute to their shame in the next (Luke 18:18-25).

Sometimes, God does accommodate himself to our ways, as he did when he guided the ancient astrologers, the wise men, by a means they understood (Matt. 2:1-12), but more commonly, and especially in matters of salvation, he is in the business of overturning what we expect.

Looking back at the Cross, Paul could say that those who were known for knowing — the philosophers who thought that the problems of human existence could all be solved by rational means, as well as the religious leaders of the day — had all been shown up as ignorant and unknowing. "Has not God made foolish the wisdom of this world?" he asks. The Cross seemed inconsequential and wrong-headed to them, but to God it was the means of conquest and the portal through which Christ passed en route to his glorification. "For the foolishness of God is wiser than men, and the weakness of God is stronger than men" (1 Cor. 1:20, 25).

This completely different angle of vision, this breaking of our human conventions, can help us to think about our postmodern world in a new way. How are we to find honor, and how are we to attend to our shame? In America, honor is not supposed to come by birth. Honor by ascription was one of the casualties of the American Revolution, though habits of this kind die slowly, as the Kennedy family knows. In America, honor comes by achievement, especially in the marketplace. Honor and financial reward are frequently joined in this preeminently commercial culture. Honor, in the sense of social attention, is also manufactured in our celluloid fantasies and in the business of making celebrities. Honor of this kind, however, is often fleeting and always insubstantial, perhaps lasting no more than the fifteen minutes Andy Warhol mockingly said it would. And what about shame? The truth is that we have no answer to this. It is, apparently, our most vexing emotional problem. Our only answer is to indulge in the illusion that the self can, in fact, be reconstructed, that the empty and depleted self can be transformed by purchase, by style, by technique, by inward reconstruction. This is where the secularization of our moral life shows its complete bankruptcy.

In God's reverse world, however, honor does come by birth — by *rebirth*.[44] Through our adoption, the change in our status wrought in the death of Christ, we have received all of the rights attendant upon being in God's family (Rom. 8:15). We now share in the divine inheritance (Rom. 8:17). This is honor, indeed. And shame, which is dealt its death blow at the Cross, is also understood in an ultimate way. If shame is the experience of knowing that we are not the people we should be,

---

44. Bernhard Citron's *New Birth: A Study of the Evangelical Doctrine of Conversion in the Protestant Fathers* (Edinburgh: Edinburgh University Press, 1951) treats conversion more or less as a synonym for the Christian life but includes a discussion of regeneration.

of being exposed or revealed as such, then is it not the case that our deepest shame will be experienced before God? And is not a covering for such shame held out to us in the death of Christ? The New Testament doctrine of justification declares that through trust in Christ we can be covered and clothed in a righteousness not our own, one that Christ gives by grace alone to those who trust, not in their own psychology or in their image, let alone in their family or town, but only in his death in their place at the Cross. That is a powerful message for those who are ashamed of themselves! And the reverse of this is that on the last day, those who have no such covering are going to be truly wounded, for they will be exposed before all. Their every dark secret, every idle word, every hidden intention, every act will be made known (Matt. 12:36; 1 Cor. 4:5). If shame is the experience of knowing we are not the people we should be, then on that day this private knowledge, now deepened in the presence of God, will become public knowledge. We will be seen to be the flawed, broken, and vain people that we are. The judgment of God will be the ultimate experience of being shamed, and it will be borne, not by Christ, but by those who have refused to bow before him and accept his death in their place. Their shame will be eternal.

What remains of the image of God within us, then, is what accounts for the presence of a moral sense that has never been quite erased. Given the reality of our inward moral pollution, this sense is sometimes diverted, silenced, and suppressed. And yet, its light is not wholly extinguished, its presence never entirely stifled. It is this fact that accounts for the many inward ambiguities that we experience.

Slicing through life, then, is the contradiction between creation and sin, between what we were and what we are now. This contradiction becomes the Church's most powerful apologetic weapon. The postmodern world has destroyed logic, dispensed with history, discarded meaning, but deep within itself, as a Trojan horse, is its betrayer. What betrays it is the ineradicable sense of being part of a moral order that has never been pushed aside entirely successfully, of having to use language in a meaningful way in order to deny that meaning exists, of finding that in the moment in which the triumph of the emancipated self seems supreme, its own sickness becomes most serious. Fallen life is, indeed, in full flight from reality, and part of Christian responsibility in this fallen world is to illumine that flight. The further the flight, the larger the inability to live in this world, and the deeper the despair. This fact preaches sin in our postmodern world without ever using the word, because, in the end, this inability, this flight, and this despair only become comprehensible in the presence of God. Only here does that sin which has been inchoate become sin revealed as sin — in the bright presence of God's holy light.

CHAPTER VI

Faith of the Ages

The Incarnation shows man the greatness of his wretchedness through the greatness of the remedy required.

Blaise Pascal

The contemplation of God, and heaven, is a kinde of buriall, and Sepulchre, and rest of the soule; and in this death of rapture, and extasie, in this death of the Contemplation of my interest in my Saviour, I shall finde my self, and all my sins enterred, and entombed in his wounds, and like a Lily of Paradise, out of red earth, I shall see my soule rise out of his blade, in a candor, and in an innocence, contracted there, acceptable in the sight of his Father.

John Donne

Today, the Church finds itself in the midst of a culture whose moral fabric is rotting and whose spirit is troubled. But as evening descends upon America, the prospects for Christian faith, I believe, could be bright. The Church, however, will have to have its moral vision restored in two principal ways if it is to seize this moment successfully.

First, it will have to become courageous enough to say that much that is taken as normative in the postmodern world is actually sinful, and it will have to exercise new ingenuity in learning how to speak about sin to a generation for whom sin has become an impossibility. Without an understanding of sin — sin understood within a powerfully conceived moral vision of reality — there can be no deep believing of the

Gospel. This, then, is not an optional task but an essential and inescapable one.

Second, the Church itself is going to have to become more authentic morally, for the greatness of the Gospel is now seen to have become quite trivial and inconsequential in its life. If the Gospel means so little to the Church, if it changes so little, why then should unbelievers believe it?

It is one thing to understand what Christ's deliverance means; it is quite another to see this worked out in life with depth and reality, to see its moral splendor. It is one thing to know the Gospel; it is quite another to see it lived. That is when its truth catches fire in the imagination. That is what makes the Gospel so attractive. The evangelical Church today, with some exceptions, is not very inspiring in this regard. It is not being heroic. It is exhibiting too little of the moral splendor that Christ calls it to exhibit. Much of it, instead, is replete with tricks, gadgets, gimmicks, and marketing ploys as it shamelessly adapts itself to our emptied-out, blinded, postmodern world. It is supporting a massive commercial enterprise of Christian products, it is filling the airways and stuffing postal boxes, and it is always begging for money to fuel one entrepreneurial scheme after another, but it is not morally resplendent. It is mostly empty of real moral vision, and without a recovery of that vision its faith will soon disintegrate. There is too little about it that bespeaks the holiness of God. And without the vision for and reality of this holiness, the Gospel becomes trivialized, life loses its depth, God becomes transformed into a product to be sold, faith into a recreational activity to be done, and the Church into a club for the like-minded. In this chapter, then, I am asking whether the Church is sufficient for this time. Will it be able to be faithful to its moment? Will it rise to the occasion?

Whatever Happened to Sin?

It is impossible, of course, to speak about the Gospel without speaking about sin, though if there were a way, our church marketers, with their boundless ingenuity, would have found it. They have often come close to passing the Gospel off as if it had more to do with what we want than with who we are, more with consumption than with repentance. The closer they have come, the closer they have come to a self-defeating strategy, because if there really is no danger from which deliverance needs to be sought, then there really is no necessity for anyone to take the Gospel seriously and believe it. What has happened here, and in many other ways, is that the Church has accommodated itself to a culture in which sin now makes no sense. So, how can the Church talk about sin without actually talking about sin? In order to understand this, we need to revisit some of the cultural terrain that I have already covered, though from a slightly different angle. We need to ask three questions. First, what has befallen the idea of sin? Second, what is it in ourselves that accounts for this cultural transformation? Third, what is the Church's entrée to the postmodern spirit in which sin has died?

The Cultural Transformation of Sin

The disappearance of sin in the modern world is not, of course, an actual disappearance. It is not sin that has vanished. What has been lost is our capacity to understand our life as being sinful. So, what has happened?

We should begin by noting that this is not a problem of recent vintage. "By 1900," Andrew Delbanco writes, "it was impossible to reattach the word 'sin' to its original sense, because the target of the violation — God — was gone."[1] He had ceased to be a reality to be reckoned with in the culture. Churches nevertheless continued to use the word, but in the windowless world in which the language was heard, it ceased to have meaning. Its use created the same kind of dilemma that a promissory note might today where the financial accounts of the person making the promise are discovered to be empty. The promissory note is seen to have nothing behind it to give it meaning. And this situation has continued down to the present. While we deplore the fracturing of life, its robberies and rapes, its abuses and cruelties, its assaults and catastrophes, we can no longer measure its darkness in the presence of God. All we can do is weep. We cannot make confession. There is no one to whom to confess. We cannot bring our sin before God, because he is gone. In our failures, we are not able to penetrate the real character of our sin, because we cannot take its measure, see its nature, in relation to *God*. We cannot say, as did David after his adultery, "Against thee, thee only, have I sinned, and done that which is evil in thy sight, so that thou art justified in thy sentence and blameless in thy judgment" (Ps. 51:4). All we can do is wipe each other's noses.

Only 17 percent of the American public defines sin in relation to God. The consequence is that the nature of sin is now much obscured.

1. Andrew Delbanco, *The Death of Satan: How Americans Have Lost Their Sense of Evil* (New York: Farrar, Straus, and Giroux, 1995), 156.

It is reserved only for a few minor infractions, perhaps some church rule, or the inconsequential matter of "living in sin." When our culture has to reach for a word to describe something that is morally repugnant, it turns to *evil*. We will not call a terrorist action that maims dozens of people "sinful," for that would say altogether too little. No, it is "evil."

The convenient thing about evil as a word, however, is that it expresses moral repugnance without needing to make clear the standards by which the action is seen to be repugnant. Where cold-blooded murderers are concerned, or brutal dictators, or drug lords, the moral violations are so obvious that the standards perhaps need not be declared. And yet this is the Achilles' heel of modern thought, that it has been chronically unable to explain evil and that its attempts to do so have invariably been attempts at explaining it away. Why is this so? It is so partly because its acknowledgment can only come at the cost, Emil Brunner said, of believing in our own essential innocence and of the hope of progress on our own terms.[2] And it is also the case, as Delbanco argued, that the language of evil becomes meaningless when the standard by which an action is judged repugnant has vanished. And that standard has vanished in our postmodern world. It has vanished for both sin and evil. Today we can neither explain evil, nor even sustain our belief in its existence. It is, however, language that has to be preserved; otherwise, we are left entirely speechless before life's brutalities and atrocities.

The difference between the cultural use of *evil* and the Christian use of *sin* is that while both words may be used to describe the same phenomenon, *sin* deliberately understands this in relationship to God. That is the standard by which what is wrong is measured. When poor character or hurtful action is read and measured in God's presence, it becomes altogether more serious than when it is not. In our culture, the use of *evil* simply expresses our abhorrence of something; in the Bible, the word *sin* expresses God's abhorrence of it. In the absence of God and his moral law, there is no reason why we should not cheat, lie, defraud, and injure others. Why should we *not* do such things if there is some perceived advantage to doing them? In the absence of God, these things really cannot be evil; they can only be called evil.[3] What is

---

2. Emil Brunner, *The Mediator: A Study of the Central Doctrine of the Christian Faith*, trans. Olive Wyon (New York: Macmillan, 1934), 122-38.

3. If God does not exist, William Craig correctly argues, "then it is plausible to think that there are no objective moral values, that we have no moral duties, and that there is no moral accountability for how we live and act." William Lane Craig, "The Indispensability of Theological Meta-ethical Foundations for Morality," *Foundations* 5, no. 2 (Spring 1997): 12.

called evil, however, becomes sinful when these actions are seen to violate what God has commanded. As God has disappeared from our culture, the realm of sin has correspondingly become contracted. As God vanishes, so too does sin.

The result, as Karl Menninger saw quite clearly,[4] is that in the modern period some sins have become crimes and others have become diseases. Menninger was writing a quarter of a century ago. And he was far from being the first or, for that matter, the last to notice the conceptual banishment of sin from our world. What he did see, however, has mightily accelerated. Today, the domain where the language of sin makes any sense at all has been reduced almost to the point of nonexistence. In our therapeutic culture, the notion of what can be classified as a disease has grown exponentially, and moral responsibility has been diminished in proportion. The dynamic in society that I have called the dance of law and freedom has also cut into the territory of sin; we tend to think that what is within the bounds of the law is morally permissible and therefore not susceptible of being named as sin. At the same time, what is illegal has ceased to be sin and become a crime! Thus disease and crime have supplanted and replaced much sin in our culture because of our profound loss of moral consciousness. As we have already seen, this loss is not complete, and this is a significant point to which I will return.

The Spiritual Transformation of Sin

So why is it that sin is now forgotten in our culture? Why is it assumed that the idea of sin is so irrelevant to understanding our postmodern world? Why does sin live such a precarious existence even in the understanding of the Church? The answer is no doubt many-sided. I have tried in this book to trace out the many cultural dynamics that might explain the erosion of our moral consciousness. To these cultural answers, however, I now want to add a spiritual one. The cultural and the spiritual transformation of sin are not alternative ways of answering this question. They are complementary ways. They are both necessary to our understanding, and together they show how inextricably connected is our inner life with the outer culture in which we live. The reason that sin has been obliterated in the postmodern awareness is partly that it makes no sense in the world in which we live and partly because its nature has been transformed and disguised by our pride.

4. Karl Menninger, *Whatever Became of Sin?* (New York: Hawthorn Books, 1973).

We tend to think that we encounter pride only in boastful words, arrogant actions, or contempt for others, but these are not its only expressions. There are far more common expressions that we tend to miss. Pride, theologian Cornelius Plantinga says, "is a blend of self-absorption — that is, narcissism — with an overestimate of one's abilities or worth — that is, conceit. So a proud person thinks a lot *about* herself and also thinks a lot *of* herself."[5]

Are we self-absorbed and conceited? Much of this book has consisted in a prolonged analysis of why it is that all reality has become contracted into the self. Indeed, the liberation psychology I have described has made of self-absorption and self-centeredness both a virtue and a necessity. And the plagues of the self nourish a massive industry. As everything outside the self becomes thin and empty, the self becomes the only reality that remains standing. Self-absorption becomes as natural as water running down hill. And what about the other aspect of pride, conceit? When all external moral standards have collapsed it becomes easy to think a lot of ourselves. After all, we have only ourselves as a comparison. Culture and pride thus blend their voices in a remarkably harmonious song, and the preoccupation of each is the self.

The conventional wisdom says that our major problem is not conceit but a lack of self-esteem. This lack supposedly explains hostile behavior, discipline problems in school, underachieving, the refusal to learn, street violence, sexual depravity, marital conflict, drugging out, zoning out, and copping out. In 1997 in Massachusetts, there was anxious public discussion about the wisdom of continuing the spelling bee because children who misspelled a word often cried. Their self-esteem had obviously been shattered. There was also talk about ending little league because children who came up to bat often struck out. Again, a blow to their self-esteem. On this view, few of the myriad problems that beset our society today cannot be traced back, at some point, to the loss of self-esteem. We do not think of ourselves well enough. That is the problem. We have poor self-image. We are always undermining ourselves, depreciating ourselves, thinking that we are scum. Not only so, but in many ways we are also victims — undermined, depreciated, and treated as scum by others. We are thus subjected to this twin assault, one from the inside and the other from the outside, which combine to tell us that we are worthless. Not that self-esteem is

5. Cornelius Plantinga, *Not the Way It's Supposed to Be: A Breviary of Sin* (Grand Rapids: Eerdmans, 1995), 80.

to be disposed of too lightly. It is worth remembering, though, that self-esteem may have little or no relation to actual character and accomplishments. Social critic Henry Fairlie observed that "it is possible to feel good about yourself in states of total vacuity, intoxication, and self-indulgence, and it is even possible when you are doing wrong and know what you are doing."[6]

Undoubtedly, there is poor self-image around, perhaps a lot of it. But is so much of what goes awry to be charged to its account? Is our world falling apart only because we do not think highly enough of ourselves?

The reality, actually, is quite the reverse. Part of the problem is that we think too highly of ourselves. We imagine that in many matters we are well above the average, and that when things go wrong it is almost invariably someone else's fault. This is the thesis that psychologist David Myers has advanced. He cites a variety of studies that have, at an empirical level, demonstrated the self-centered and self-congratulatory bias to human nature. For example, of almost one million American high school students who were studied, 70 percent rated themselves "above average" in leadership ability, and only 2 percent thought themselves to be below average; in their ability to get along with others, none rated themselves below average, 60 percent rated themselves in the top 10 percent, and 25 percent in the top 1 percent! In another survey, 94 percent of a college's faculty thought that they were better than their average colleague, so when pay increases based on merit were announced, there were many who felt that injustice had been done! Experiments have also been done in which people have to cooperate with someone else in order to make money, but most blame their partners when failure occurs. Other experiments show that when people admire a particular trait, they are quite likely to think that they have it in some abundance. They are also more likely to think they possess qualities they admire if the quality is hard to measure. People also see themselves as more cooperative, more competitive, more likable than most others. What is at work throughout this pattern of behavior, rather obviously, is self-deception, a deception made all the easier where standards are vague or absent. And self-deception leads easily into self-justification, the inner mechanism of exculpation, and each feeds into conceit. We enter our own private moral universe where we are above average and where responsibility for what goes wrong rests, almost invariably, with

---

6. Henry Fairlie, *The Seven Deadly Sins Today* (Notre Dame: University of Notre Dame Press, 1979), 40.

others.[7] We refuse to bear the pain of moral recrimination, or accept the reproach that such self-scrutiny may entail.

This business of thinking much about ourselves and much of ourselves is what pride is all about. Actually, it is also about the desire for power, the self grasping power for itself, and what results works itself out in our knowledge, virtue, and religion. Niebuhr's analysis of this pride goes beyond the rather circumscribed usage of the language of pride in the Bible to see in its outworking what is more generally ascribed to sin.[8] In the New Testament, for example, pride often shows up simply in lists of sins (e.g., Rom. 1:29-31; Gal. 5:19-21; 2 Tim. 3:2-5) but there can be little doubt, as Augustine and the Protestant Reformers argued, that pride is at the heart of both our rebellion against God and of our blindness to ourselves.

The essence of pride is the self forsaking God in order to find in itself what it had once found in God. Why does the self thus turn to itself? The answer, of course, is that this is the nature of sin, but sin is not without its rationales. Here, the answer is that the self imagines that it has power enough, in and of itself, to find security amidst all of the vicissitudes of life and to manage the moral breaches that are such a constant theme in life. This is the "can do" part of the American spirit working itself out in a deleterious way. The self "does not recognize the contingent and dependent character of its life and believes itself to be the author of its own existence, the judge of its own values and the master of its own destiny,"[9] says Niebuhr. This presumption, the presumption of sin, is present in all but is expressed differently in different people.

In those who have access to power, pride often expresses itself as a lust for more power. And because the retention of power is a precarious matter in this life, this lust is often attended by fearful insecurities that are usually pacified only by further reaching after power. The cycle into which pride of this kind leads is quite vicious. In the therapeutic culture of our time, however, the same yearning for power takes different forms. It expresses itself more commonly as a confidence in self-mastery, the belief that the self can be reconstructed, that its aches and pains, its bewilderment, its confessions, can all be healed with the right technique. This same search for inner power is even evident in the hymnody of

7. David G. Myers, *The Inflated Self: Human Illusions and the Biblical Call to Hope* (New York: Seabury Press, 1981), 20-30.
8. Reinhold Niebuhr, *The Nature and Destiny of Man* (2 vols.; New York: Charles Scribner's Sons, 1964), 1:186-203.
9. Ibid., 1:188.

the postmodern Christian spirituality analyzed in chapter one, though its source is thought to be God and not the self. The same interest in the self, however, is there.

This inward disposition of the self to seek in itself what, in fact, it can only find in God insinuates itself into our intellectual life, too. All human knowledge, in fact, is tainted by its origin in corrupted human minds. What pride does, however, is to pass off that knowledge as being more certain, more ultimate, more indisputable, and more authoritative than it really is. It thus claims for itself a transcendence that actually only belongs to God. And it refuses to see in itself the limitations that it sees so quickly in opposing views and philosophies. "Professors," Plantinga notes dryly, "still leave faculty meetings feeling less enlightened by what they heard than by what they said."[10] The problem is that such aggressive self-regard, however vexing it is in the context of personal relations, is also treated in the culture as a necessity of inward health and is therefore indulged rather than restrained.

That there is a moral aspect to this kind of intellectual pride is rather clear. Yet pride in the moral sphere is usually more evident in overt expressions of self-righteousness. This is the attempt to establish the private standards of the self as universal norms to which others should be subject. When others fail to meet these standards, this form of pride renders its judgment on them, along the way mistaking its judgments for God's. Thus Paul said of unbelieving Jews in his day, "They have a zeal for God, but it is not enlightened. For, being ignorant of the righteousness which comes from God, and seeking to establish their own, they do not submit to God's righteousness" (Rom. 10:2-3). "Moral pride," says Niebuhr, "is the pretension of finite man that his highly conditioned virtue is the final righteousness and that his very relative moral standards are absolute."[11] This was the struggle of Jesus with the Pharisees, of Paul, who argued for salvation by grace alone through faith alone so that all human boasting would be excluded (Rom. 3:27), and of Luther in the sixteenth century, who saw that our unwillingness to be judged as sinners in the light of God's righteousness, rather than our own, was at the heart of what it meant to be a sinner.

In moral pride there is self-deification, but this pride finds its fullest expression in our religion. We find it in the attitude of those who may acknowledge themselves to be under the judgment of Christ but

10. Plantinga, *Not the Way It's Supposed to Be*, 82.
11. Niebuhr, *The Nature and Destiny of Man*, 1:199.

who also find in his righteousness a striking resemblance to their own. "Thinking of ourselves what can only be thought of God," writes theologian Karl Barth, "we are unable to think of him more highly than we think of ourselves." Being "to ourselves what God ought to be to us, he is no more to us than we are to ourselves."[12] Thus does the little god topple the great God. And thus salvation becomes a "final battle-ground between God and man's self-esteem,"[13] in Niebuhr's words, because the condition for consciously receiving God's grace is the shattering of our self-will and the abasing of our pride, so that the self is stripped of its pretensions to being God and becomes simply the created being that it is and then acknowledges its own defilement.

Pride, of course, is not the only sin, but it is at the heart of sin; what we see in it, as theologian Langdon Gilkey put it, is "an ultimate religious devotion to a finite interest." Sin is an overriding, overweening fascination with the self, with its senses, its prestige, its demands. That is its utter folly. Pride makes of the small, tawdry, paltry, human preoccupations of life ultimates that must be served with a devotion that should be reserved for God. From this "inordinate love of self," Gilkey continues, "stem the moral evils of indifference, injustice, prejudice, and cruelty to one's neighbor, and the other destructive patterns of action we call 'sins'."[14]

If pride is thinking much of ourselves and much about ourselves, elevating our judgments, ourselves, and our righteousness to divine heights, then it is no mystery why this particular culture, with its therapeutic texture and its loss of moral absolutes, has made pride its characteristic sin. Pride is not the only sin, but it is the essence of sin. And the interesting thing is that most people can see its presence in others in these ways without even having to name it as sin. So, what is the difference between how the Bible views this pride and the way it might be viewed in our postmodern world?

The difference, of course, is that in the Bible all sin, including that of pride, is understood in relation to *God*, whereas in the postmodern world it is simply understood in relation to *ourselves*. We may dislike the sins of others, but our dislike has none of the condemnation that God's dislike has. For he sees sin in its moral connections, while

---

12. Karl Barth, *The Epistle to the Romans*, trans. Edwyn C. Hoskyns (New York: Oxford University Press, 1976), 45.

13. Niebuhr, *The Nature and Destiny of Man*, 1:200.

14. Langdon Gilkey, *Shantung Compound: The Story of Men and Women Under Pressure* (New York: Harper and Row, 1966), 233.

we see it only in its psychological pains and relational disruptions. Before God, we become *guilty* of our sin; at worst, in the postmodern world we may become *ashamed*.

In the biblical perspective, God's character and his moral law are the measure of sin; in their light, the nature of sin is revealed for what it is. Sin is not merely a crime, like breaking the law against burglary, for in such a case it is only the state that is offended, and through prison time a burglar's debt to society can be paid off. Sin is different. Sin is both the breach of moral law and an offense against *God*. Furthermore, the debt owed to God can never be paid off by the offender. Sin is a moral infraction that is deeply *wrong*.[15] Sin is defiance of God. In Brunner's words, it is "defiance, arrogance, the desire to be equal with God, emancipation, a deliberate severance from the hand of God."[16] Man, he says elsewhere, "*is* a sinner; he does not only commit sins. Insubordination towards God, the state of being alienated from God, is not the determination of certain moments" but "the character of man's existence."[17] Sin is the reordering of existence around the self so that it becomes its own creator, sustainer, and healer. All sin therefore involves idolatry, and all idolatry, even that of the modern self-move-ment with all of its psychological undergirding, is deeply offensive to God.

Much has been made of the pictorial nature of the biblical vo-cabulary for sin. Sin is missing the target, falling short of a standard, and transgressing boundaries. However, the target that is missed, the path that is abandoned, the authority that is defied, the law that is transgressed are in each and every case *God's*. Sin is therefore going contrary to God, dismissing him, taking issue with him, defying him, refusing to submit to him, displacing him from the center of existence, ignoring him. It is, in short, arrogating to the self the place that only God should have. All of this lay in embryo in the first temptation, "You will be like God" (Gen. 3:5). Paul had this in mind when he said that the unregenerate mind, which "is hostile to God," does not "submit to God's law, indeed it cannot" (Rom. 8:7). This mind is disaffected with God's rule, resents his claims, is hostile to his Word, and is determined to pursue its own values, pleasures, and goals in defiance of him.

15. Wayne Grudem, *Systematic Theology: An Introduction to Biblical Doctrine* (Grand Rapids: Zondervan, 1994), 490-92.

16. Emil Brunner, *Man in Revolt: A Christian Anthropology,* trans. Olive Wyon (Philadelphia: Westminster Press, 1947), 129.

17. Brunner, 143.

Within this overall picture, different words convey slightly different nuances of meaning. The most general language used implies the whole range of experience, from the violation of a single commandment to the ruin of one's personal existence, and this language is usually translated as "sin." It is what we most commonly find in contexts of forgiveness. It is there in the prodigal's resolve to say, "Father, I have sinned against heaven and before you" (Luke 15:21) and in the Pharisees' indignant rejection of Jesus in the words, "Who can forgive sins but God only?" (Luke 5:21). This is Paul's language in his general indictment of humanity in Rom. 3:23: "All have sinned and fall short of the glory of God." And it is in this general framework that we find Paul working out his doctrine of Christ's saving work. All are "under the power of sin" (Rom. 3:9), knowledge of which comes through the law (Rom. 3:20). As sin has abounded so has grace (Rom. 5:20), and in Christ's substitutionary death on the Cross, sin was condemned and vanquished in the triumph of grace.

Other language is more focused in its range of meaning. To sin is to act unjustly toward others, and so the idea of unrighteousness is part of this vocabulary. We read of the "unjust" steward (Luke 16:8) and the "unjust" judge (Luke 18:6). In Romans, Paul links this unrighteousness with ungodliness (Rom. 1:18) and contrasts it with obeying the truth (Rom. 2:8). There are some who take pleasure in unrighteousness in its opposition to truth (2 Thess. 2:12), but love does not do that (1 Cor. 13:6).

The image of turning aside and transgressing provides yet another strand in the biblical understanding of sin. The almost spatial sense that this language suggests is retained in the description of Judas' fall. Two candidates were chosen to replace Judas, only one of whom could actually be selected, and he was chosen by lot "to take the place in this ministry and apostleship from which Judas turned aside, to go to his own place" (Acts 1:25). Sin is turning aside from what is true and right in order to settle down elsewhere in what is wrong and false. These departures are revealed for what they are by the law. It "was added because of transgressions" (Gal. 3:19) to induce self-knowledge and so prepare sinners to understand their need of Christ's death.

Sin is also spoken of as lawlessness. John says that "every one who commits sin is guilty of lawlessness; sin is lawlessness" (1 John 3:4). Sin is also described as going astray, falling, deceiving oneself, and acting in an ungodly way.

Sin, Plantinga says, "has a thousand faces."[18] The Old Testament

---

18. Plantinga, *Not the Way It's Supposed to Be*, 9.

prophets knew it when they saw it, because they also had a vision of what life should be like. Their vision was of a life that was wholesome, in which things flourished, in which there was justice and delight. This is what sin has rent. It has torn apart the world that God made. Sin is not simply a matter of private attitude but invades all of a person's life. It enters every nook and cranny; nothing is immune to its touch. If, as Plantinga says, God "binds things together: he binds humans to the rest of creation as stewards and caretakers of it, to himself as bearers of his image, and to each other as perfect complements,"[19] then sin works to unbind all of these linkages. It has created a deep chasm between God and sinners over which no bridge can be humanly constructed; it drives the carelessness with which the environment is treated; it scars and mutilates marriages; it stirs up the ambitions and greed, the hatreds and distrust, that lead nations to break the peace and make war on one another. It brings in its wake folly, self-deception, and hardness. And knowledge of its work, indeed profound dismay over the ease with which we serve its impulses, as well as the precarious position in which we stand before God, and the false confidence that our pride lends to everything we do, all have to be understood if we are to begin to grasp the meaning of life.

In a highly pluralistic, commercially driven, secular culture such as ours, this kind of understanding of the human predicament seems to be a remote possibility, because all of its coordinates are gone. Gone is the God against whom sin is measured. Gone is the understanding, though not the experience, that we are all made to be moral actors by creation. Gone is truth and, as part of that, moral norms. It is this cultural reality that is bending Christian thinking and evangelistic strategy but, as I will suggest, bending them in the wrong ways. A Christian faith that tries to adapt itself to this culture in order to win a "hearing" is a Christian faith that will be left with nothing to say. The ally of faith is not culture but creation, not the ethos and trends of modernity, but the stubbornly present *imago Dei*. For it is the image of God that persists in raising the questions that must be answered, even as it is modernity, in union with our fallen proclivities, that works to obscure these questions.

Disaffection with Postmodernity

The Church's best entrée into the postmodern world, then, is found in the indelible moral contradictions that penetrate all of life. These

19. Ibid., 29.

contradictions arise from the fact that, on the one hand, we are moral agents by creation and, on the other, that we are living as if we have detached ourselves from moral reality. We are, as a result, caught. We are condemned forever to the jarring uncertainties that come from being morally and spiritually out of step with who we are by creation. The more we sin, the greater the contradiction with what we are in the image of God; the more consistently we try to live by the moral sense imparted by creation, the more inexplicable and frustrating our moral failures will be. Exactly what phase of his life Paul was describing in Romans 7 has been debated, but there is a sense in which the struggle he describes, in different ways, is present in both Christian and pre-Christian experience: "I do not understand my own actions. For I do not do what I want, but I do the very thing that I hate. . . . For I do not do the good I want, but the evil I do not want is what I do" (Rom. 7:15, 19). It is this frustration, I believe, that gives Christian faith its best access to a postmodern culture that has given up on serious thought, rational argument, and historical defenses. The nature of this frustration now needs to be explored a little further.

Fallen man, Emil Brunner says, "makes himself independent over against God, instead of over against the world,"[20] and so he has no way to address his dis-ease, because there is no exit from the culture. There is no way to settle what persists as unsettled within. At the end of life's trajectory is death, which only serves to heighten this sense of uneasiness. The Puritan poet and preacher, John Donne, spoke of "this bell tolling softly for another, says to me, Thou must die." Who does not attend to such a bell, he asks, "which is passing a piece of himself out of the world"?[21]

It is, of course, in the conscience that premonitions of a judgment to come are felt, for the conscience is tuned to the moral universe that we inhabit. Our supposed emancipation from God, then, is illusory. As the medieval thinker, Anselm, observed to his student, Boso: "Even though a man or a fallen angel is unwilling to submit to the divine will and plan, still he cannot escape it; for if he wants to escape the dominion of the will that commands, he rushes under the dominion of the will that punishes."[22] And yet the uneasiness of the conscience also serves

20. Emil Brunner, *The Divine Imperative: A Study in Christian Ethics*, trans. Olive Wyon (London: Lutterworth Press, 1937), 62.

21. Roberta Florence Brinkley, *English Prose of the Seventeenth Century* (New York: W. W. Norton, 1951), 106-7.

22. Anselm, *Why God Became Man and the Virginal Conception and Original Sin*, trans. Joseph M. Colleran (New York: Magi Books, 1969), 1:15.

to point fallen human beings in a direction different from the one in which they are traveling, because this inward disjointedness defies all resolution. It cannot be forgotten, nor can it be bought off with the fruits of our modern abundance. It cannot be assuaged by religious diligence, nor yet by Eastern meditation. Like some horrible virus, it is stubbornly resistant to all of our cures.

In the opening lines of John Calvin's *Institutes*, the apologetic significance of this inward struggle is briefly addressed. There he says, perhaps surprisingly, that "the knowledge of God and of ourselves" belong together. In understanding God, we understand something of ourselves, and in understanding ourselves, we understand something of God. The connections between these two sides of our knowledge are many. But important among them is that our experience discloses "an immense series of disgraceful properties" so that "every man, being stung by the consciousness of his own unhappiness, in this way obtains at least some knowledge of God." The consequence of this is that every person, "on coming to the knowledge of himself, is not only urged to seek God, but is also led as by the hand to find him."[23] Our postmodern spiritual disjunctions, our inward contradictions, on which we place such a morally neutered assessment, can be the very hand that leads us to God, because they lead us back into moral reality.

That these internal contradictions are painfully felt in our post-modern world is evident, I believe, in the new search for spirituality.[24] The original secularization thesis was that religion and religious interest would retreat before the patterns of life spawned by modernization. To some extent this has been the case. However, it is not the total picture. And perhaps the best way to understand the new spiritual hunger is to see it as the protest of the human spirit against a life now so stripped down, so leveled off, so emptied out, so banal, so enclosed, as to have become intolerable. This search for spirituality is an unwitting defiance of postmodernity as well as an expression of the difficulty of living as if the *imago Dei* had itself been removed.

Evidence that we are now in a bull market for spirituality is every-where. It is there in the interest in angels upon which some movies have capitalized. Sophy Burnham's *A Book of Angels* started it, and many

23. John Calvin, *The Institutes of the Christian Religion*, trans. Henry Beveridge (2 vols.; London: James Clark, 1953), 1:i.

24. These contradictory interests are pointed out in an unpublished address by Lane Dennis, "Evangelical Publishing and the Crisis of Our Day: Evangelical Christian Publishers Association Chairman's Address, May 1996."

others have followed. There is evidence of this interest in spirituality in the recent torrent of books on near-death experiences as well. This was initiated by Raymond Moody's *Life After Life: The Investigation of a Phenomenon, Survival of Bodily Death* in 1977, and was followed by Elisabeth Kubler-Ross's various books, including *On Life After Death*. Betty Eadie's *Embraced by the Light* has been a best-seller for four years and has sparked a small industry in books about this "light." The proliferation of New Age habits, from listening to the divine within, to seeking psychics without, to the use of crystals and other New Age paraphernalia, also speaks to the void now left in human experience. What this means is that the Church finds itself once again in the Areopagus. If only it were more stirred by today's idolatry (cf. Acts 17:16) it would be more compelled to say as Paul did long ago: "Men of Athens, I perceive that in every way you are very religious. . . . What therefore you worship as unknown, this I proclaim to you" (Acts 17:22-24).

This spiritual yearning and the inability of human nature to live comfortably in a world evacuated of meaning, is the best Christian "point of contact" with postmodern culture. However, it must not become the first step in a natural theology. In other words, the awkward discovery that we are spiritual beings and that a moral nature is part of that spirituality does not mean that salvation then becomes a matter simply of paying more attention to the moral life and seeking to live in more principled ways. This discovery of our moral self is not the first stair in the slow ascent to God. Nor does the sense of spiritual need itself disclose what "product" the Church should offer as its satisfaction, as the Church marketers appear to think. Quite the reverse. All that we are discovering in our culture is what we are by creation and what we have become by sin. Our contorted inward life gives us the clue to the kind of world in which we live; it does not provide us with the building blocks out of which we can construct our own salvation, nor does it tell us how we can reconstruct or satisfy the self.

God both reveals himself to us and hides from us. He calls and yet is also silent. His revelation in nature and in our conscience is his call, and it is sufficient for Paul to declare that, given its voice, men and women "are without excuse" (Rom. 1:20) when they ignore it. And yet, this voice does not lead us out of the labyrinth of life in which we are spiritually lost. In that sense, God is not at the end of our moral and spiritual life waiting to be discovered if we try hard enough. He hides from us because he will relieve our inward contradictions only on his terms and in his way at the Cross.

There is, then, no doubt that the knowledge of God and of the

Good, which is naturally discovered, can thus be misused. The problem is not that what God reveals through nature and through the conscience is untrue. The problem is that fallen human beings misuse what they sense. These things simply become pieces of information that circle in their universe, whose center is still the self.

Especially in a therapeutic culture such as ours, where happiness is abundantly marketed and the two great healers of our times — psychotherapy and advertising — join in a common enterprise, it is not unnatural to think that the self can be molded, changed, and satisfied by our own effort, even in our quest to become spiritual. And if the moral sense is heeded, it may seem quite natural to suppose, as Kant did, that "I ought means I can." This view assumes that although we may fail in some of our conduct and responsibilities, the inner core is good. It is this, in the liberationist psychology, which holds the hope of life. Mistakes and miscalculations may be made, but at the core of our existence is this corrective, this power for Good.

Nowhere is the difference between a Christian view of the Good and a naturalistic one further apart than at this point. The difference does not lie on the surface but in the depths. On the surface, a morally-minded secularist may be quite moral, indeed as moral as the average born-againer. The Gentiles, after all, "do by nature what the law requires. . . . They show that what the law requires is written on their hearts" (Rom. 2:14-15). The great difference lies well beneath the surface. While the secularist may fail on the surface, he or she thinks that beneath it, in the self, is goodness. The Gospel, by contrast, declares that though the surface may be exemplary, beneath it, in the self, there is corruption (cf. Matt. 23:25). This is what explains the thunderclap of judgment that rumbles through Paul's words in Romans: "None is righteous, no, not one . . . no one seeks for God. All have turned aside, together they have gone wrong; no one does good, not even one. . . . There is no fear of God before their eyes" (Rom. 3:10-12, 18).

That being the case, there is always, in all natural morality, the taint, the disease, of *self-righteousness*. The moral life that is lived out on a basis of self-confidence over its inward source of goodness, whose standards are self-referential, and whose confidence is in the self, is a moral life that is suffused by sin. In this way the real domicile of evil is so often obscured. When, in this culture, we speak of evil, we speak of *actions*. We speak of stores robbed, children murdered, women raped, and the elderly defrauded. In other words, we look for evil in the life of vice in our society. The last place we would naturally look for it is in the life of *righteousness*, in what is morally right.[25] However, the same self from which this righteousness springs is also the headquarters of evil. It lives in the self. It is the heart, the core of our being, that "is deceitful above all things, and desperately corrupt; who can understand it?" (Jer. 17:9). And out of the heart "flow the springs of life" (Prov. 4:23).

This is the dilemma of the modern world. Indeed, it has been the dilemma of all time. We cannot elude our own moral nature or its corruption. We know ourselves to be moral agents, but there is always a residue of moral unease when the day is done. Our experience is thus shot through with ambiguity. Spates of pleasure-seeking are followed by seasons of regret; well-meaning actions, by those that are malicious, vindictive, or craven; hope in our ability to take hold of life in good ways, by despair that we have not succeeded in doing so. We party on Saturday and repent on Sunday. This tangle of contradictions we are unable to untangle because of both the power of sin and the intent of God. It is this inability that points us back, even in our state of advanced postmodernity, to the Cross, because there simply is no other place of resolution.

If, then, we in this generation have lost our ability to name our sin — and we have — we have nevertheless not lost our sin. We may call it by other names, we may not even recognize it at all, and we always misinterpret it. Our moral radar is defunct. And yet, moral reality keeps intruding into our experience; the threads of a moral existence are ever present. It is thus that creation is the great ally of the Gospel, while culture and the fallen self are its great enemies. This is the awful contradiction that cuts through all of life, and it offers the most telling entrée for the Gospel into the postmodern soul.

Whatever Happened to the Church?

Irony is never far from the life of the Church. Scripture speaks of the Church in exalted terms, but what we see of it in the world is often quite disappointing. On the one hand, the Church is the community called into existence in eternity. Now joined together in Christ, who is its head, it is the people of God. With the Spirit's marks upon it, it is entrusted with the Gospel and is the embodiment of God's truth in this world. This is where we hear the confession of Christ. This is where we

25. Brunner, *The Divine Imperative*, 71.

hear the Word of God preached. It is here that we expect to see manifested the power of the Spirit, the grace of Christ, the hope of life everlasting. On the other hand, this is a very human community, too. If we see the Spirit's power, we also see alongside it the power of sin. We see God's power but also human frailty. We see Christ's grace but also pride in its many forms. Here, in an even more intense form, are the contradictions of the postmodern world. Whereas there the knowledge of God is seen through creation and so is veiled, here it is seen in Christ and so is intensified. There, sin registers as a disturbance within, but here this voiceless disturbance is named and judged in the light of the Cross. That is an altogether different matter. We are, Luther said, at one and the same time both justified and yet sinners. That is our irony. And yet, when the contradictions become too glaring, or are too sustained, the capacity of the Church to speak to the contradictions of fallen life is greatly diminished. It is to some of these contradictions in the Church's life, these ironies, that we must now turn.

The biblical revelation with which the Church has been entrusted is clear and insistent on the nature of sin, its consequences, and, of course, its cure. Since this is a matter that is inextricably bound up with the nature of the Gospel and, behind that, with the work of Christ on the Cross, it might be supposed that on this, at least, the Church would be as clear and insistent as Scripture is. This, however, does not take account of its frailty. The German biblical scholar, Christof Gestrich, has spoken of the "embarrassment many modern theologians feel about their task of making accurate, thought-provoking statements about sin."[26] They are not alone. Many people today are embarrassed. Undoubtedly, one reason for this is the pressure people feel to be civil in this secularized society, but it is also the case that the Church's moral fabric has been worn bare and that its own sin in failing to grasp what sin is all about is apparently lost on it. Examples abound, though here I will simply take three illustrations. As it happens, two are psychologically driven and the other is commercially inspired. The healers of our time — psychotherapists and advertisers — have extended their long reach into the life of the Church as well. Our secular healers have populated the Church with their close cousins. Given the Church's chronic worldliness today, is this surprising?

First, from the world of psychology, there is the case of Princeton's

---

26. Christof Gestrich, *The Return of Splendor in the World: The Christian Doctrine of Sin and Forgiveness,* trans. Daniel W. Bloesch (Grand Rapids: Eerdmans, 1997), 11.

Donald Capps, a mainline Presbyterian pastoral psychologist. Since he is a psychologist, his angle of vision and his expertise are a little different from others, but the outcome to his thought is not.

Capps begins his book, *The Depleted Self,* by acknowledging that the very subject of sin has become passé among members of the psychological fraternity. Among them, his discussion about sin might well be viewed as retrograde, like taking "a small but fatal step backward into the dark ages from which our predecessors worked so hard and tirelessly to free us."[27] What he decided to do, therefore, was to translate what has been understood as sin theologically into the language of psychology, so that it might be more acceptable.

Capps takes the framework for understanding sin from the pioneers of the new thinking on shame, rather than from Scripture. When we feel shame, which Capps somehow blurs with the idea of sin, three things happen. First, the self becomes divided against itself, parting into what is ideal and what is real. Second, those who have been shamed by others will often develop defensive strategies as their means of protection. These may include blaming others, withdrawing inwardly, or striving for power as a means of self-protection. Third, shame experiences leave people feeling empty. They find that they have no zest for their work, they take refuge in routine because their initiative has dried up, their emotions are dulled, and they feel themselves to be less than fully real.[28] This, then, is Capps's description of the way sin is experienced today, and the Gospel — what he calls "the therapeutics of the self" — must, correspondingly, be hatched afresh to match this.

Capps uses the biblical story of Jonah to illustrate how this might be accomplished. After a complex analysis of the exchanges between Jonah and his shipmates and then with God, Capps shows that all the signs of shame eventually appear in Jonah. He becomes divided, depleted, and defensive. God's business then becomes simple. By a mixture of goading, of being indifferent to Jonah, and of raising doubts in Jonah's mind about his own character, God is finally able to confront

27. Donald Capps, *The Depleted Self: Sin in a Narcissistic Age* (Minneapolis: Fortress Press, 1993), 2.

28. Ibid., 100. Capps's approach is typical of what has happened to pastoral care in the twentieth century. Care has become increasingly psychologized, and in understanding what is central to spirituality there has been a shift from self-denial before God toward self-affirmation within humanly framed experience. This shift has been traced out by E. Brooks Holifield, *A History of Pastoral Care in America: From Salvation to Self-Realization* (Nashville: Abingdon Press, 1983).

and address him in such a way that he is saved, that is, brought to "the discovery of his true self."[29]

Feeling divided, defensive, and depleted, however, is simply not an adequate translation of the biblical language about sin, because sin concerns our moral relation to God as holy, not our relation to ourselves. Sin has to do with being bad, not with feeling bad about ourselves. The standard by which we measure sin is *God*, not the self. It is his revelation in Scripture that is the standard, not our feelings. Furthermore, the discovery of our true self will be a happy discovery only if we can make Pelagian assumptions about its innocence. The truth is, though, that the discovery of our self is always an ambiguous and painful matter; we inevitably discover as part and parcel of the self what is selfish, cruel, conniving, manipulative, hateful, and uncaring. These threads are woven throughout the self, and they are there, in potential, at all times. Capps has substituted the psychological self for the moral self, the dynamics of shame for the workings of sin, therapy for the Gospel, and psychological wholeness for biblical justification. What he has done is now being echoed throughout the Church, both liberal and evangelical: buying passing cultural acceptance at the cost of real relevance. The meaning of *sin* is lost, defined away amidst a fog of psychologizing and a yearning for cultural relevance.

Does the Church have the courage to become relevant by becoming biblical? Is it willing to break with the cultural habits of the time and propose something quite absurd, like recovering both the word and the meaning of sin? Is it sagacious enough to be able to show how the postmodern world is trapped within itself? There is plenty of evidence that this kind of courage is now missing from large sectors of the Church. Let me cross the theological aisle and take up the second illustration, also psychologically inspired, which is what we encounter in the Crystal Cathedral.

Robert Schuller, the cherubic preacher from California, is probably unique in his ability to produce visual extravaganzas in the Crystal Cathedral at high times in the Christian year, with angels descending on invisible wires, Pilate and his domesticated tiger, Roman soldiers in full battle regalia, the inevitable camels and sheep all coming and going through a recreated Holy Land at one end of the auditorium. Flair and imagination there is, and audiences delight in it. However, behind this

---

29. Capps, *The Depleted Self*, 161. For a further exploration of some of these themes, see Richard Fenn and Donald Capps, eds., *On Losing the Soul: Essays in the Social Psychology of Religion* (Albany: State University of New York Press, 1995).

Christian parroting of Disneyland, which is a stone's throw away, stands a message that is thoroughly American and ubiquitous in the culture. It is a message, not about sin, but self-esteem.

As the air became clogged with therapeutic nostrums like this, in the late twentieth century, the real meaning of Christianity finally emerged — in the Crystal Cathedral, as it happened. Sin, Schuller discovered, is really nothing more than poor self-image, and salvation is its reversal. That was the message sent gratis to thousands of pastors in Schuller's *The New Reformation*. Presto! In a flash, in the twinkling of an eye, all the tension between Christ and culture was dissolved away in happy feelings. The language of sin was quickly banished from the Crystal Cathedral, as were all penitential prayers, and in their place came the therapeutic language. Many of the Psalms could therefore not be read in public, because they are unhappily forthright about sin and God's judgment upon it. Indeed, in his spectacular drama put on at Easter but also available on pay-per-view television, Schuller found it necessary to change the Lord's Prayer. The part about sin was unacceptable. "And forgive us our debts" became "Forgive us those who have wronged us."[30] This certainly sounds like a needless confession, since it is those who wrong, not those who are wronged, who need to seek forgiveness. But never mind. Logic is a lost art in this culture, and few probably stumbled over this oddity.

This is just a small part of the confusion that results when biblical language is displaced by the psychological. Soon, guilt becomes bad and pride becomes good. No one remotely within a Christian framework has imagined this before, though some of the earlier Protestant liberals came close. And the Christian virtue *par excellence* at the Crystal Cathedral now becomes enthusiasm.[31] This is, of course, exactly the sort of psychological substitute for real moral virtue that one would expect. Tacitus saw in first-century Rome "a reign of terror in which no virtue could live." In place of terror we have enveloped ourselves in a sugary therapeutic atmosphere, which is, of course, much more comfortable but no less lethal to virtue than was the vice of ancient Rome. The problem with all of this is that where sin has lost its moral weight, the Cross will lose its centrality, Christ will lose his uniqueness, and his Father will no longer be the God of the Bible. This process of unraveling

30. Michael R. Linton, "Smoke and Mirrors at the Crystal Cathedral," *First Things* 74 (June/July 1997), 13.

31. Robert H. Schuller, *Self Esteem: The New Reformation* (Waco, Tex.: Word Books, 1982), 50, 65-69, 106-21.

is now well afoot, not simply in the televised programs of Schuller's Disneyland Christianity, or in the liberalism that inhabits some churches in the mainline denominations, but it can also be seen across the vast evangelical landscape as pastor after pastor adds to the confusion by trying to learn how to market the Church.[32] This is the third illustration, and its inspiration is the world of commerce.

The wisdom common to many of our marketers is that, if it wants to attract customers, the Church should stick to a positive and uplifting message. It should avoid speaking of negative matters like sin.[33] Not only so, but what has distinguished the Church in its appearance and functions should now be abandoned. In order to be attractive to people today, church buildings should not look different from corporate headquarters, malls, or country clubs. Crosses and robes should go; dress should be casual; hymns should be contemporary and empty of the theological substance by which previous generations lived, because this is incomprehensible today; pews should be replaced by cinema-grade seats, organs by synthesizers and drums, solemnity by levity, reflection by humor, and sermons by light dialogues or catchy readings. The theory is that people will buy Christianity if they don't have to deal with what the Church has traditionally been.

The best construction that can be put on this is that these market-driven churches have become like hermit crabs, which walk around concealed within a shell. Hidden beneath the outer shell — the corporate style that disguises the churchly business that is supposed to be going on, the mall-like atmosphere in which faith is bought and sold like any other commodity, the relaxed, country club atmosphere — is the little animal who supposedly is really evangelical. As it moves from rock pool to rock pool, all we can see are the little legs — the most minimal doctrinal substance — that protrude from under the shell. Is this substance enough to sustain people amidst life's fierce trials? Is it enough to preserve biblical identity in these churches in the decades ahead? I think not.

32. I have tried to analyze the theory of church marketing in my *God in the Wasteland: The Reality of Truth in a World of Fading Dreams* (Grand Rapids: Eerdmans, 1994), 72-87.

33. Even though his critique of Willow Creek's seeker services is extremely mild, sociologist G. A. Pritchard notes that it is impossible to get away from "the idolatry of personal fulfillment" in market-driven churches like Willow Creek. He also suggests that this is not a biblical idea. See his *Willow Creek Seeker Services: Evaluating a New Way of Doing Church* (Grand Rapids: Baker Book House, 1996), 249-57.

This marketing approach to church life raises questions of a most profound kind that seem not to have occurred to any of the movement's apostles, who remain blissfully ignorant of the havoc now germinating in the churches. Can churches really hide their identity without losing their religious character? Can the Church view people as consumers without inevitably forgetting that they are sinners? Can the Church promote the Gospel as a product and not forget that those who buy it must repent? Can the Church market itself and not forget that it does not belong to itself but to Christ? Can the Church pursue success in the marketplace and not lose its biblical faithfulness?

This strategy for marketing the Church obviously sounds admirable to a lot of people. It sounds like its pioneers have placed themselves on the cutting edge, and this may be true from an advertiser's standpoint. However, the movement's most prominent advocates rarely show any cultural acuity at all. What they usually have is an eye for what might work. The raw pragmatism that is foundational to their thinking is embraced as if it were part and parcel of the divine revelation; the serious questions that need to be asked about how this process of adaptation might affect the content of faith simply go unanswered. The result is that biblical faith is beginning to erode in many of these churches.

The issue, of course, is not whether Christian language is being used. The issue is whether that language can function in its full biblical scope in the churchly contexts that we have created for it. And it is not only the trendy marketers that have a corner on this confusion. Think of the more conventional pastors whose preaching on the prodigal son, as examined by Marsha Witten, we recounted in chapter one. Did they not demonstrate how easily the Christian message can be lost amidst the use of good, Christian language? The language used in preaching — sin, redemption, forgiveness, grace, God, Christ — must be used within the framework of truth in which it arose, or else it becomes meaningless. It cannot be co-opted and employed in a secular or psychological framework, or in a marketing context, and retain its original meaning.

In the cases examined by Witten, preachers were caught between the secular assumption that the self can be found, crafted, molded, and actualized and the biblical notion that it is corrupted, fragmented, and incapable of healing itself. Furthermore, many in their congregations had also bought, perhaps unwittingly, the secular assumption that God is remote from our world and is not a moral presence in it. To people like this, nothing is more incomprehensible and offensive than preaching about sin as the contradiction of God's character and law, not to mention any references to the consequences of not believing. This is not what they want to hear. What they want is an uplifting, exciting, fun, inspirational time, so that when they emerge they can feel better about themselves and their prospects.

Preachers know this, and they either dance around the subjects that our age finds most trying to hear about — like sin as a violation of God's character, and the judgment that rests upon it — or they simply plunge in and recast the meaning of Christian faith in therapeutic terms. The sermons examined by Witten used ploys to soften the whole sorry business of letting modern congregations in on what they should know about their moral standing before God. The biblical truth about sin, which is at the heart of the parable of the prodigal son, was treated ever so delicately and impersonally, with the result that few would have imagined that the parable was speaking to any but society's basest offenders. Alternatively, the parable was psychologized so that the brothers' moral offenses could be seen simply as personality flaws or interesting foibles demanding no moral connections. As God's moral nature has faded from view and as his transcendence has receded, his immanence and relatedness have obviously grown in the modern period. The sermons reflected this; in 82 percent of them God was portrayed in terms of the positive benefits he can have for men and women today, principal among them being that through the Gospel we can experience how he relieves negative feelings like doubt and anxiety. And that, by a different route, is also what happens when the Church is marketed, for no one buys a displeasing product.

This transformation of Christian faith is enormously appealing to modern people who are typically preoccupied with their own inward worlds and want "fixes." What is uppermost on their minds is not the moral fabric of life but how to cope with their wayward personalities, self-doubt, the stages of life, marital stress, as well as calamities like job losses and the soaring cost of college tuition. These are the things that are intensely real to them and that drain their psychological energy. However, while these are not inconsequential matters, they are not the burning moral issues with which the Bible is concerned. What is central to the Bible is the true and the right, sin and grace, God's wrath and Christ's death; what is central to so many people today is simply what offers internal relief. Biblical truth, even in the Church, is in a different universe of meaning from that into which modernity has led us and where we now so often comfortably reside.

Much of the Church today, especially that part of it which is evangelical, is in captivity to this idolatry of the self. This is a form of corruption far more profound than the lists of infractions that typically pop into our minds when we hear the word *sin*. We are trying to hold at bay the gnats of small sins while swallowing the camel of self. It is an idolatry as pervasive and as spiritually debilitating as were many of the entanglements with pagan religions recounted for us in the Old Testament. That this devotion to the self seems not to be like that older devotion to a pagan god blinds the Church to its own unfaithfulness. The end result, however, is no less devastating, because the self is no less demanding. It is as powerful an organizing center as any god or goddess on the market. The contemporary Church is whoring after this god as assiduously as the Israelites in their darker days. It is baptizing as faith the pride that leads us to think much about ourselves and much of ourselves.

The most urgent need in the Church today, even that part of it which is evangelical, is the recovery of the Gospel as the Bible reveals it to us. This is often quite different from the ways in which we have reconstructed it through psychology, the fashions of this culture, or our commercial life. The Church needs to recover some old habits now much discarded, like learning to think of sin as moral failure before God and the self as needing to be restrained, displaced, and forgotten, and seeing God not for his value to us as consumers but for the value he has in himself. His glory should be a matter of more profound interest to the Church than its self-satisfaction. The emancipation that the Gospel offers, after all, is not only from the judgment of God but from the tyranny of self as well. Its freedom is, in part, the freedom to be forgetful of the self in its imperious demands and its insatiable appetite for attention, the freedom to think that God is important in and of himself and not simply in relation to what he can do for us. This freedom lies at the heart of the New Testament understanding of humility. Humility has nothing to do with depreciating ourselves and our gifts in ways we know to be untrue (cf. Col. 2:18, 23). Even "humble" attitudes can be masks of pride. The English, it has been said, take pride in not praising themselves! Rather, humility is that freedom from our self which enables us to be in positions in which we have neither recognition nor importance, neither power nor visibility, and even experience deprivation, and yet have joy and delight. That is the pattern of humility modeled in the incarnation (Phil. 2:5-11). It is the freedom of knowing that we are not in the center of the universe, not even in the center of our own private universe. Those who have best learned this kind of godliness know that what may seem like the most awful loss is actually true liberation.

Alongside the success of much Church marketing, and in the midst of much of the psychologized faith in the evangelical world today, a profound secularization of faith has taken place, and this despite the continued use of good biblical words like sin, grace, Christ, and atonement. This secularization is appealing because it buys the appearance of success, but it also forfeits the nature of biblical faith. The seeds of a full-blown liberalism have now been sown, and in the next generation they will surely come to maturity.

The Courage to Believe

It was the contention of the Protestant Reformers that Christian faith will always be misunderstood if the Cross is misunderstood. Or, to put the matter positively, those who understand the Cross aright, grasp the meaning of Christ aright and can then see the entire purpose of revelation clearly. For Christ and his Cross stand at the center of God's disclosure of his moral will and saving ways in Scripture. Indeed, without the Cross we are without the magnifying glass through which his love and holiness are most keenly seen. To stand beneath the Cross is to stand at the one place where the character of God burns brightest and where his resolution of the problem of sin is sounded for all time.

It is hard to stand here, though. The cost of admission to this place is the humbling of our pride — intellectual, moral, and religious. For to stand here is to repent of our proclivity to elevate our own standards of what is right and wrong to universal norms and to accept the judgment of God in their place. It is to repent of our trust in the innocence of the self, which is the fount of our self-righteousness, and to acknowledge instead the corruption of the self. It is to displace ourselves from the center of the universe we inhabit and to elevate Christ to that place of honor. It is to see in our chronic self-absorption nothing other than chronic self-centeredness. It is to accept the sobering evaluation of God on fallen life rather than the rosy assessment we are inclined to register upon ourselves. This is a hard place to stand, and few choose to stand here. That is why so many have dismissed the Cross. It is why in the last century liberal theology claimed that Paul had perverted the original doctrine of Christ's death to give us this kind of Cross. It is why in our own time, much contemporary theology is proposing, in one scheme after another, that since the Cross achieved universal salvation, there is no price of admission to its benefits. No humbling, no repenting, no believing is necessary.

The reality, however, is that in the postmodern world the enmity sustained is toward God and not toward our fallen selves and their extension in culture. Indeed, wherever the Church has lost its sense of sin, and much of it has, this antithesis toward the self and culture naturally disappears on the mistaken assumption that it can all be lost without an antithesis toward God, his Christ, and his Word replacing it.

That is as profound a mistake as any Christian can make. In this fallen world, the issue is not whether we will sustain this sense of antithesis. The issue only will be who is its object. Is the antithesis against God or against the world?

The evangelical Church today imagines that this choice does not have to be made, that it can be on friendly terms with both. This attitude, more than anything else, accounts for the Church's diminished spiritual stature — for why it appears as a moral pygmy among the dilemmas of the modern world, which seem to be giants. Amidst enormous pain and confusion, evangelical faith seems by comparison to be trivial, as it indulges itself with "happy clappy" praise songs, light Sunday morning dialogs or, worse yet, drama in their place. Contemporary evangelicalism places a premium on being amused and, like a petulant consumer, makes its sales people in the pulpit tremble. The consumer, after all, is always right. Unless it recovers some spiritual gravity, some seriousness, some authenticity, indeed, unless it recovers the substance of classical spirituality, the evangelical Church will rapidly become an irrelevance in the modern world.

Scripture is clear in its teaching that the "old man," who has lived comfortably in the fallen world, must die with its entire understanding of the self and of its relationship to God, if the "new man" is to emerge in Christ. Faith lives in the midst of this polemical context. It lives between the ways of death in culture and in the self, on the one hand, and the ways of life in Christ, who is above it, on the other.

Faith thus requires both a transition in loyalties and in enmities. The transition from the existence of the "old man" to that of the "new" is one from faith in one's self to faith in Christ, but it is also a transition from enmity toward God to enmity toward the world. That is why the Church's idolatry is so profoundly wrong. The enmity that should be expressed toward the self in its fallenness — Jesus, after all, did speak of the necessity of crucifying the self if one is to become a follower — must inevitably be redirected against God if the self is going to be indulged rather than crucified. This is why James asks indignantly: "Do you not know that friendship with the world is enmity against God?"

(James 4:4). The problem of idolatry is always a problem of both misplaced love and misplaced enmity. So, how can we exchange the enmity we have for God by one for the world? How can we exchange the love we have of self and the world by a love for God?

We ask this question assuming that the answer has to be complex. How could it not be? The Church, after all, is living in the late twentieth century, in a culture with no cognitive horizons and with a moral core that has crumbled. Should we not then use new languages for translating the Gospel into the contemporary vernacular, either the psychological or the contemporary? Do we not have to have at our finger tips all of the latest information about Baby Boomers and Generation X if we are to be relevant?

The fear of which I am speaking is an old one; it has everything to do with our unbelief and nothing to do with the complexities of making the Gospel known in the late twentieth century. The only way that our love of self can be exchanged by a love of God is through believing the Gospel. The only way that a moral enmity toward God will be replaced by a moral enmity toward fallen human life is through the supernatural work of the Holy Spirit remaking fallen nature, on the basis of Christ's atoning death, so that the recovery of the *imago Dei* might begin as we are "changed into his likeness from one degree of glory to another; for this comes from the Lord who is the Spirit" (2 Cor. 3:18). The Church must find the courage to recover both the language and understanding of sin. It must reinhabit the universe of meaning given in Scripture. It must recover its enmity toward fallen human nature and fallen culture and stop mumbling on these subjects. It must care more about truth than its success, more about faithfulness than being culturally at home. It must find the strength to believe that modernity poses no problems that are insurmountable to the grace and power of God. Despite all of our sophistication and wealth and knowledge and information, the dilemmas of life in the postmodern world are still addressed in God's economy by the same Gospel the Church has always proclaimed to confront human dilemmas. The Church's problem today is simply that it does not believe that, without tinkering, the Gospel will be all that interesting to modern people. This is not even an accurate assessment. Furthermore, it has nothing to do with the intrinsic nature of the Gospel and much to do with the flaws of those who are hesitant, or embarrassed, to proclaim it undiluted. Why should the postmodern world believe the Gospel when the Church appears so unsure of its truth that it dresses up that Gospel in the garments of modernity to heighten its interest? It is a self-defeating strategy. What the Church needs is not more of these strategies but more faith, more confidence that God's Word is sufficient for this time, more confidence in the power of the Holy Spirit to apply it, and more integrity in proclaiming it.

In the long section of Paul's description of the ministry in 2 Cor. 2:17–6:10, one thread is apparent throughout. It is Paul's confidence in what God will do through the ministry. "Such is the confidence that we have through Christ toward God" (2 Cor. 3:4); "Since we have such a hope, we are very bold" (3:12); "Therefore, having this ministry by the mercy of God, we do not lose heart" (4:1); "So we do not lose heart" (4:16); "So we are always of good courage" (5:6); "We are of good courage" (5:8). Today, the Church does not share Paul's confidence, it does not have his courage, and it is not bold. It cannot see the bankruptcy of postmodern culture, nor does it see that understanding sin in biblical terms unlocks so many of the painful dilemmas of life that would otherwise remain closed and inexplicable. It thinks, instead, that new strategies are called for, when all too often these strategies entail new evasions that make it look increasingly likely that the gates of hell will, indeed, prevail. And what it has forgotten is the greatness of God's power to liberate people from their blindness and to remake life. Today's churchly trendiness is really yesterday's unbelief.

Men and women of faith have always been confronted by the insurmountable task of proclaiming what seems absurd in a world of unbelief. That, however, is why the sovereign grace of God is necessary. Consider, for example, the remarkable discovery in the Jerusalem temple, toward the end of Judah's existence as a nation, of "the book of the law" (2 Kings 22:8), which may have been Deuteronomy. The young king Josiah, great grandson of Hezekiah, had set out to renovate the temple, which was in a state of much disrepair. This was part of the reform that the king had slowly begun initiating over the prior decade (2 Chron. 34:3). It was in connection with this work that the high priest, Hilkiah, made his momentous discovery, which greatly sparked the impetus for reform.

The king's own reaction to the reading of this book was immediate contrition (2 Kings 22:11; cf. Neh. 8:1–9:38). He realized that the idolatry and social abuses of which Judah was guilty would bring down upon it the full weight of God's judgment. Josiah, full of sorrow and repentance, sent a commission to the prophetess Huldah to learn how the fate of Judah would be worked out. Her reply was that Josiah would die at peace before the awful sentence would fall on his people. This notwithstanding, Josiah called the people together. They, too, heard God's Word. They were moved to repentance. It is clear from the prophecies of Jeremiah that this repentance was not heartfelt enough (Jeremiah 2–6). Nevertheless, the people of Judah did follow the king in renewing their covenant (2 Kings 23:3). Josiah also restored the Passover Feast (2 Kings 23:21-23), drove out the spiritists and mediums (2 Kings 23:24-25), and destroyed the pagan cult shrines and places of sacrifices (2 Kings 23:11, 14-15, 19). An important reformation followed.

This description of Josiah's reform is so sparse in its details, unfortunately, that we are left ignorant of its inner mechanics. What we can say is that the cultural darkness that prevailed at that time was very great and that the cultural pressure to capitulate was also very great. It is also clear that those who had domesticated the abominable practices of the pagan religion in Judah had lost their moral sensitivity. Their consciences had apparently become singed, and the moral fabric of life had worn very thin. The book of Deuteronomy was strange and alien to those who heard it, for Judah's religion at that time was in complete shambles.

Josiah knew of the preaching of the prophets Jeremiah and Zephaniah. Perhaps this had encouraged him. The Word of God was able to penetrate the conscience of the most rebellious and obtuse. Against all odds, and in the midst of a troubling world situation, this Word brought back what had long since disappeared: a sense of sin, the understanding of how morally offensive to God we are when we do not live by and within his law.

And thus it has been, again and again, across the ages. In the hand of God, the biblical Word is a fearsome weapon, "sharper than any two-edged sword, piercing to the division of soul and spirit, of joints and marrow, and discerning the thoughts and intentions of the heart." And thus it is, Hebrews says, as we stand in the presence of God by its work, that everything is "laid bare to the eyes of him with whom we have to do" (Heb. 4:12-13). Is it too much to hope that the evangelical Church can yet again recover its moral seriousness, that it can recover its vision of the holiness of God, its trust in the greatness of his power? This is the key, strange as it may seem, to Christian effectiveness in the postmodern world. It is the reform of the Church of which we stand in need, not the reform of the Gospel. We need the faith of the ages, not the reconstructions of a therapeutically driven or commercially inspired faith. And we need it, not least, because without it our postmodern world will become starved for the Word of God.

Bibliography

Anderson, Digby, ed. *The Loss of Virtue: Moral Confusion and Social Disorder in Britain and America*. London: Social Affairs Unit, 1992.

Anderson, Walter Truett. *Reality Is Not What It Used to Be: Theatrical Politics, Ready-to-Wear Religion, Global Myths, Primitive Chic, and Other Wonders of the Postmodern World*. San Francisco: Harper Collins, 1993.

Anselm. *Why God Became Man and the Virginal Conception and Original Sin*. Translated by Joseph M. Colleran. New York: Magi Books, 1969.

Arendt, Hannah. *Eichmann in Jerusalem: A Report on the Banality of Evil*. New York: Viking Press, 1963.

Aulen, Gustav. *Christus Victor: An Historical Study of the Three Main Types of the Idea of Atonement*. Translated by A. G. Hebert. London: S.P.C.K., 1965.

Baker-Fletcher, Garth. *Somebodyness*. Minneapolis: Fortress Press, 1993.

Bancroft, E. H. *Christian Theology: Systematic and Biblical*. Edited by Ronald B. Meyers. Grand Rapids: Zondervan, 1925.

Barth, Karl. *The Epistle to the Romans*. Translated by Edwyn C. Hoskyns. New York: Oxford University Press, 1976.

Baumeister, Roy F. *Escaping the Self: Alcoholism, Spirituality, Masochism, and Other Flights from the Burden of Selfhood*. New York: Basic Books, 1991.

———. *Identity: Cultural Change and the Struggle for the Self*. New York: Oxford University Press, 1986.

Bayles, Martha. *Hole in the Soul: The Loss of Beauty and Meaning in American Popular Music*. New York: Free Press, 1994.

Bellah, Robert. *The Good Society*. New York: Alfred A. Knopf, 1991.

Bellah, Robert, et al. *Habits of the Heart: Individualism and Commitment in American Life*. New York: Harper and Row, 1985.

Bennett, Arthur. *The Valley of Vision*. Edinburgh: Banner of Truth Trust, 1975.

212 LOSING OUR VIRTUE

Bennett, William. *The Index of Leading Cultural Indicators*. Washington, D.C.: Heritage Foundation, 1993.

Berger, Peter L. *The Heretical Imperative: Contemporary Possibilities of Religious Affirmation*. New York: Anchor Press, 1979.

Berman, Ronald. *Advertising and Social Change*. London: SAGE Publications, 1981.

Bernstein, Richard. *Dictatorship of Virtue: Multiculturalism and the Battle for America's Future*. New York: Alfred A. Knopf, 1994.

Black, Jim Nelson. *When Nations Die: America on the Brink: Ten Warning Signs of a Culture in Crisis*. Wheaton, Ill.: Tyndale House, 1994.

Blais, Madelein. *In These Girls, Hope Is a Muscle*. New York: Atlantic Monthly Press, 1995.

Bloesch, Donald G. *The Crisis of Piety: Essays Toward a Theology of the Christian Life*. Colorado Springs: Helmers and Howard, 1988.

Boorstin, Daniel. *The Image; or, What Happened to the American Dream*. New York: Atheneum, 1962.

Bork, Robert. *Slouching Towards Gomorrah: Modern Liberalism and American Decline*. New York: HarperCollins, 1996.

Boyd, Stephen B., W. Merle Longwood, and Mark W. Muesse. *Redeeming Man: Religion and Masculinities*. Louisville: Westminster/John Knox Press, 1996.

Brainerd, David. *The Diary and Journal of David Brainerd*. 2 vols. London: Andrew Melrose, 1902.

Brunner, Emil. *The Divine Imperative: A Study in Christian Ethics*. Translated by Olive Wyon. London: Lutterworth Press, 1937.

———. *Man in Revolt: A Christian Anthropology*. Translated by Olive Wyon. Philadelphia: Westminster Press, 1947.

———. *The Mediator: A Study in the Central Doctrine of the Christian Faith*. Translated by Olive Wyon. New York: Macmillan, 1934.

Brunner, Emil, and Karl Barth. *Natural Theology: Comprising "Nature and Grace" by Professor Dr. Emil Brunner and the Reply "No!" by Professor Dr. Karl Barth*. Translated by Peter Fraenkel. London: Geoffrey Bles, 1946.

Brzezinski, Zbigniew. *Out of Control: Global Turmoil on the Eve of the Twenty-First Century*. New York: Charles Scribner's Sons, 1993.

Cairns, David. *The Image of God in Man*. London: SCM Press, 1953.

Calvin, John. *The Institutes of the Christian Religion*. Translated by Henry Beveridge. 2 vols. London: James Clark, 1953.

Camus, Albert. *The Fall*. Translated by Justin O'Brien. New York: Vintage International, 1957.

Capps, Donald. *The Depleted Self: Sin in a Narcissistic Age*. Minneapolis: Fortress Press, 1993.

Carlson, Allan C. *From Cottage to Workstation: The Family's Search for Social Harmony in the Industrial Age*. San Francisco: Ignatius, 1993.

Carr, Karen L. *The Banalization of Nihilism: Twentieth-Century Responses to Meaninglessness.* New York: State University of New York Press, 1992.

Carson, D. A. *The Gagging of God: Christianity Confronts Pluralism.* Grand Rapids: Zondervan, 1996.

Carter, Stephen L. *Integrity.* New York: Basic Books, 1996.

Cave, Sydney. *The Christian Estimate of Man.* London: Gerald Duckworth, 1949.

Chafer, Lewis Sperry. *Systematic Theology.* 8 vols. Dallas: Dallas Seminary Press, 1947.

Chamblin, J. Knox. *Paul and the Self: Apostolic Teaching for Personal Wholeness.* Grand Rapids: Baker Book House, 1993.

Citron, Bernhard. *New Birth: A Study of the Evangelical Doctrine of Conversion in the Protestant Fathers.* Edinburgh: Edinburgh University Press, 1951.

Cohen, Jean L., and Andrew Arato. *Civil Society and Political Theory.* Cambridge: Massachusetts Institute of Technology Press, 1995.

Coles, Robert. *Children of Crisis.* 5 vols. Boston: Little, Brown, 1967-80.

————. *The Moral Life of Children.* Boston: Atlantic Monthly Press, 1986.

Collier, James Lincoln. *The Rise of Selfishness in America.* New York: Oxford University Press, 1991.

Connor, Steven. *Postmodern Culture: An Introduction to Theories of the Contemporary.* Oxford: Blackwell, 1989.

Coontz, Stephanie. *The Way We Never Were: American Families and the Nostalgia Trip.* New York: Basic Books, 1992.

Crittenden, Paul. *Learning to Be Moral: Philosophical Thoughts about Moral Development.* London: Humanities Press International, 1990.

Cushman, Philip. *Constructing the Self, Constructing America: A Cultural History of Psychotherapy.* Reading, Penn.: Addison-Wesley, 1995.

Delbanco, Andrew. *The Death of Satan: How Americans Have Lost the Sense of Evil.* New York: Farrar, Straus, and Giroux, 1995.

Dennett, Daniel C. *Consciousness Explained.* Boston: Little, Brown and Co., 1992.

Derrett, Duncan M. *Jesus' Audience: The Social and Psychological Environment in Which He Worked.* New York: Seabury Press, 1973.

Dertouzos, Michael. *What Will Be: How the New World of Information Will Change Our Lives.* New York: HarperCollins, 1997.

DeSilva, David. *Despising Shame: Honor Discourse and Community Maintenance in the Epistle to the Hebrews.* Atlanta: Scholars Press, 1995.

Diggins, John. *The Lost Soul of American Politics: Virtue, Self-Interest, and the Foundations of Liberalism.* New York: Basic Books, 1984.

Doherty, William J. *Soul Searching: Why Psychotherapy Must Promote Moral Responsibility.* New York: Basic Books, 1995.

D'Souza, Dinesh. *Illiberal Education: The Politics of Race and Sex on Campus.* New York: Free Press, 1991.

Dwight, Timothy. *Sermons.* 2 vols. New Haven: Ezra Read, 1828.

Eberly, Don E., ed. *The Content of America's Character: Recovering Civic Virtue.* New York: Madison Books, 1995.

Edwards, Jonathan. *The Life of David Brainerd.* Edited by Norman Pettit. New Haven: Yale University Press, 1985.

Eigo, Francis A., ed. *Christian Spirituality in the United States: Independence and Interdependence.* Villanova: Villanova University Press, 1978.

Ekman, Paul. *Telling Lies: Clues to Deceit in the Marketplace, Politics, and Marriage.* New York: W. W. Norton, 1992.

Ellul, Jacques. *The Technological Society.* Translated by John Wilkerson. New York: Alfred A. Knopf, 1965.

————. *The Technological System.* Translated by Joachim Neugroschel. New York: Continuum, 1980.

Elshtain, Jean Bethke. *Democracy on Trial.* New York: Basic Books, 1995.

Englehardt, Tom. *The End of Victory Culture: Cold War America and the Disillusioning of a Generation.* New York: Basic Books, 1995.

Erikson, Erik. *Childhood and Society.* New York: W. W. Norton, 1950.

Etzioni, Amitai. *The Spirit of Community: The Reinvention of American Society.* New York: Simon and Schuster, 1993.

Evans, Donald. *Spirituality and Human Nature.* New York: State University of New York Press, 1992.

Ewen, Stuart. *All Consuming Images: The Politics of Style in Contemporary Culture.* New York: Basic Books, 1988.

————. *Captains of Consciousness: Advertising and the Social Roots of the Consumer Culture.* New York: McGraw Hill, 1976.

Fairlie, Henry. *The Seven Deadly Sins Today.* Notre Dame: University of Notre Dame Press, 1979.

Farley, Edward. *Requiem for a Lost Piety: The Contemporary Search for the Christian Life.* Philadelphia: Westminster Press, 1966.

Fenn, Richard, and Donald Capps, eds. *On Losing the Soul: Essays in the Social Psychology of Religion.* Albany: State University of New York Press, 1995.

Fisher, Seymour, and Roger P. Greenberg. *The Scientific Credibility of Freud's Theories and Therapy.* New York: Basic Books, 1977.

Fitzgerald, Thomas K. *Metaphors of Identity: A Culture-Communications Dialogue.* Albany: State University of New York Press, 1993.

Fjellman, Stephen J. *Vinyl Leaves: Walt Disney World and America.* Boulder, Colo.: Westview Press, 1992.

Flanagan, Owen. *Mind, Morals, and the Meaning of Life.* New York: Oxford University Press, 1996.

Forsyth, Peter Taylor. *The Cruciality of the Cross.* London: Hodder and Stoughton, 1909.

————. *The Holy Father and the Living Christ.* London: Hodder and Stoughton, 1897.

————. *The Work of Christ.* London: Independent Press, 1938.

Foster, George M. *Traditional Societies and Technological Change.* New York: Harper and Row, 1973.

Fox, Richard Wightman, and Jackson T. J. Lears. *The Culture of Consumption: Critical Essays in American History, 1880-1980.* New York: Pantheon Books, 1983.

Fukuyama, Francis. *Trust: The Social Virtues and the Creation of Prosperity.* New York: Free Press, 1995.

Gamsun, Joshua. *Claims to Fame: Celebrity in Contemporary America.* Berkeley: University of California Press, 1994.

Gelpi, Donald, ed. *Beyond Individualism: Toward a Retrieval of Moral Discourse in America.* Notre Dame: University of Notre Dame Press, 1989.

Gergen, Kenneth J. *The Concept of Self.* New York: Holt, Rinehart, 1971.

————. *The Saturated Self: Dilemmas of Identity in Contemporary Life.* New York: Basic Books, 1991.

Gestrich, Christof. *The Return of Splendor in the World: The Christian Doctrine of Sin and Forgiveness.* Translated by Daniel W. Bloesch. Grand Rapids: Eerdmans, 1997.

Giddens, Anthony. *Modernity and Self-Identity: Self and Society in the Late Modern Age.* Stanford: Stanford University Press, 1991.

————. *The Transformation of Intimacy: Sexuality, Love, and Eroticism in Modern Societies.* Stanford: Stanford University Press, 1992.

Gilkey, Langdon. *Shantung Compound: The Story of Men and Women Under Pressure.* New York: Harper and Row, 1966.

Gilligan, Carol. *In a Different Voice: Psychological Theory and Women's Development.* Cambridge: Harvard University Press, 1993.

Gilmore, David D. *Honor and Shame and the Unity of the Mediterranean.* Washington, D.C.: American Anthropological Association, 1987.

Gitlin, Todd. *The Twilight of Common Dreams.* New York: Metropolitan Books, 1995.

Goffman, Irving. *The Presentation of the Self in Everyday Life.* Garden City, N.Y.: Doubleday, 1959.

Goldfarb, Jeffrey. *The Cynical Society: The Culture of Politics and the Politics of Culture.* Chicago: University of Chicago Press, 1991.

Gordon, Chad, and Kenneth Gergen, eds. *The Self in Social Interaction.* New York: John Wiley and Sons, 1968.

Griffiths, Morwenna. *Feminisms and the Self: The Web of Identity.* London: Routledge, 1995.

Grodin, Debra, and Thomas R. Lindlof. *Constructing the Self in a Mediated World.* Thousand Oaks, Calif.: SAGE Publications, 1996.

Grudem, Wayne. *Systematic Theology: An Introduction to Biblical Doctrine.* Grand Rapids: Zondervan, 1994.

Gurstein, Rochel. *The Repeal of Reticence: A History of America's Cultural and Legal Struggles Over Free Speech, Obscenity, Sexual Liberation, and Modern Art.* New York: Hill and Wang, 1996.

Hefner, Philip. *The Human Factor.* Minneapolis: Fortress Press, 1993.

Heim, Michael. *The Metaphysics of Virtual Reality.* New York: Oxford University Press, 1993.

Himmelfarb, Gertrude. *The De-moralization of Society: From Victorian Virtues to Modern Values.* New York: Alfred A. Knopf, 1995.

Hodge, Charles. *Systematic Theology.* 3 vols. New York: Scribner's, 1871-72.

Hoekema, Anthony A. *Created in God's Image.* Grand Rapids: Eerdmans, 1986.

Hoffman, Katherine. *Concepts of Identity: Historical and Contemporary Images and Portraits of Self and Family.* New York: Icon Editions, 1996.

Holifield, E. Brooks. *A History of Pastoral Care in America: From Salvation to Self-Realization.* Nashville: Abingdon Press, 1983.

Hopfe, Lewis M., ed. *Uncovering Ancient Stones: Essays in Memory of H. Neil Richardson.* Winona Lake, Ind.: Eisenbrauns, 1994.

Huber, Richard M. *The American Idea of Success.* Wainscott, N.Y.: Pushcart Press, 1987.

Hudson, Deal W. *Happiness and the Limits of Satisfaction.* London: Rowman and Littlefield, 1996.

Hughes, Robert. *Culture of Complaint: The Fraying of America.* New York: Oxford University Press, 1993.

Huizinga, Johan. *Homo Ludens: A Study of the Play Element in Culture.* Boston: Beacon Press, 1955.

Hunter, James Davison. *Culture Wars: The Struggle to Define America.* New York: Basic Books, 1990.

Jeffords, Susan. *Hard Bodies: Hollywood Masculinity in the Reagan Era.* New Brunswick, N.J.: Rutgers University Press, 1994.

Jenson, Robert. *Essays in Theology of Culture.* Grand Rapids: Eerdmans, 1995.

Jewett, Paul K. *Who We Are: Our Dignity as Human.* Grand Rapids: Eerdmans, 1996.

Johnson, Stephen M. *Humanizing the Narcissistic Style.* New York: W. W. Norton, 1987.

Jones, E. Michael. *Living Machines: Bauhaus Architecture as Sexual Ideology.* San Francisco: Ignatius Press, 1995.

Käsemann, Ernst. *Commentary on Romans.* Translated by Geoffrey W. Bromiley. Grand Rapids: Eerdmans, 1980.

Kaminer, Wendy. *I'm Dysfunctional, You're Dysfunctional: The Recovery Movement and Other Self-Help Fashions.* Reading, Penn.: Addison Wesley, 1991.

Kass, Leon. *The Hungry Soul: Eating and the Perfection of Human Nature.* New York: Free Press, 1994.

Kaufman, Gershen. *The Psychology of Shame: Theory and Treatment of Shame-Based Syndromes.* New York: Springer, 1989.

Kernberg, Otto. *Borderline Conditions and Pathological Narcissism.* Northvale: Jason Aronson, 1975.

Keyes, Dick. *Beyond Identity: Finding Your Self in the Image and Character of God.* Ann Arbor, Mich.: Servant Books, 1984.

————. *True Heroism: In a World of Celebrity Counterfeits.* Colorado Springs: Navpress, 1995.

Kilpatrick, William K. *Why Johnny Can't Tell Right from Wrong.* New York: Simon and Schuster, 1992.

Kohut, Heinz. *The Analysis of the Self: A Systematic Approach to the Psychoanalytical Treatment of Narcissistic Personality Disorders.* New York: International Universities Press, 1971.

Kolak, Daniel, and Raymond Martin, eds. *Self and Identity: Contemporary Philosophical Issues.* New York: Macmillan, 1991.

Kuhn, Reinhard. *The Demon of Noontide: Ennui in Western Literature.* Princeton: Princeton University Press, 1976.

Lasch, Christopher. *The Culture of Narcissism: American Life in an Age of Diminishing Expectations.* New York: W. W. Norton, 1978.

————. *Haven in a Heartless World: The Family Besieged.* New York: Basic Books, 1979.

————. *The Minimal Self: Psychic Survival in Troubled Times.* New York: W. W. Norton, 1984.

Lears, Jackson. *Fables of Abundance: A Cultural History of Advertising in America.* New York: Basic Books, 1994.

————. *No Place of Grace: Antimodernism and the Transformation of American Culture, 1880-1920.* New York: Pantheon, 1981.

Levin, Michael David. *The Opening of Vision: Nihilism and the Postmodern Situation.* New York: Routledge, 1988.

Lewis, Michael. *Shame: The Exposed Self.* New York: Basic Books, 1992.

Lunt, Peter K., and Sonia M. Livingstone. *Mass Consumption and Personal Identity: Everyday Economic Experience.* Philadelphia: Open University Press, 1992.

Luther, Martin. *Luther's Works.* Edited by Jaroslav Pelikan and Helmut T. Lehman. 55 vols. St. Louis: Concordia, 1955-86.

Lynd, Helen Merrell. *On Shame and the Search for Identity.* London: Routledge and Kegan Paul, 1958.

MacIntyre, Alisdair. *After Virtue: A Study in Moral Theory.* Notre Dame: University of Notre Dame Press, 1981.

————. *Whose Justice? Which Rationality?* Notre Dame: University of Notre Dame Press, 1988.

McClay, Wilfred. *The Masterless: Self and Society in Modern America.* Chapel Hill: University of North Carolina Press, 1994.

McCracken, Grant. *Big Hair: A Journey into the Transformation of the Self.* New York: Overlook Press, 1995.

McDannell, Colleen. *Material Christianity: Religion and Popular Culture in America.* New Haven: Yale University Press, 1995.

McKnight, John. *The Careless Society: Community and Its Counterfeits.* New York: Basic Books, 1995.

Malina, Bruce J. *The New Testament World: Insights from Cultural Anthropology.* Louisville: Westminster/John Knox, 1993.

Melanchthon, Philip. *Commentary on Romans.* Translated by Fred Kramer. St. Louis: Concordia, 1992.

Menninger, Karl. *Whatever Became of Sin?* New York: Hawthorn Books, 1973.

Messner, Michael A., and Donald F. Sabo. *Sex, Violence and Power in Sports.* Freedom, Calif.: Crossing Press, 1995.

Meyrowitz, Joshua. *No Sense of Place.* New York: Oxford University Press, 1985.

Milbank, John. *Theology and Social Theory: Beyond Secular Reason.* Oxford: Blackwell, 1990.

Miller, Donald E. *Reinventing American Protestantism: Christianity in the New Millennium.* Berkeley: University of California Press, 1997.

Moran, Gabriel. *A Grammar of Responsibility.* New York: Crossroad, 1996.

Morris, Leon. *The Testaments of Love: A Study of Love in the Bible.* Grand Rapids: Eerdmans, 1981.

Morrison, Andrew P. *Essential Papers on Narcissism.* New York: New York University Press, 1986.

―――. *Shame: The Underside of Narcissism.* Hillsdale: Analytic Press, 1989.

Mosse, George L. *The Image of Man: The Creation of Modern Masculinity.* New York: Oxford University Press, 1996.

Murray, John. *The Epistle to the Romans.* London: Marshall, Morgan, and Scott, 1967.

Myers, David G. *The Inflated Self: Human Illusions and the Biblical Call to Hope.* New York: Seabury Press, 1981.

Nathanson, Donald L., ed. *The Many Faces of Shame.* New York: Guilford Press, 1988.

―――. *Shame and Pride: Affect, Sex, and the Birth of the Self.* New York: W. W. Norton, 1992.

Niebuhr, Reinhold. *The Nature and Destiny of Man.* 2 vols. New York: Charles Scribner's Sons, 1964.

Organ, Troy Wilson. *Philosophy and the Self: East and West.* Selinsgrove: Susquehanna University Press, 1987.

Orr, James. *The Progress of Dogma: Being the Elliot Lectures Delivered at Western Theological Seminary.* London: Hodder and Stoughton, 1901.

Owen, John. *The Forgiveness of Sin: A Practical Exposition of Psalm 130.* Grand Rapids: Baker Book House, 1977.

Paglia, Camille. *Sex, Art, and American Culture.* New York: Vintage Books, 1992.

―――. *Sexual Personae: Art and Decadence from Nefertiti to Emily Dickinson.* New Haven: Yale University Press, 1990.

————. *Vamps and Tramps: New Essays.* New York. Vintage Books, 1994.

Patterson, James, and Peter Kim. *The Day America Told the Truth: What People Really Believe about Everything That Matters.* New York: Prentice Hall, 1991.

Paul, William. *Laughing Screaming: Modern Hollywood Horror and Comedy.* New York: Columbia University Press, 1994.

Peacocke, Arthur R. *God and the New Biology.* San Francisco: Harper and Row, 1986.

Pearlman, Moshe. *The Capture and Trial of Adolf Eichmann.* New York: Simon and Schuster, 1963.

Peck, M. Scott. *People of the Lie: The Hope for Healing Human Evil.* New York: Simon and Schuster, 1983.

Peristiany, Jean G., ed. *Honor and Shame: The Values of Mediterranean Society.* Chicago: University of Chicago Press, 1966.

Peristiany, Jean G., and Julian Pitt-Rivers, eds. *Honor and Grace in Anthropology.* Cambridge: Cambridge University Press, 1992.

Plantinga, Cornelius. *Not the Way It's Supposed to Be: A Breviary of Sin.* Grand Rapids: Eerdmans, 1995.

Postman, Neil. *Technopoly: The Surrender of Culture to Technology.* New York: Vintage Books, 1993.

Pritchard, G. A. *Willow Creek Seeker Services: Evaluating a New Way of Doing Church.* Grand Rapids: Baker Book House, 1996.

Putnam, Robert D. *Democracy and the Civic Community: Tradition and Change in an Italian Experiment.* Princeton: Princeton University Press, 1992.

————. *Making Democracy Work: Civic Traditions in Modern Italy.* Princeton: Princeton University Press, 1994.

Rice, John Steadman. *A Disease of One's Own: Psychotherapy, Addiction, and the Emergence of Co-Dependency.* New Brunswick: Transaction Publishers, 1996.

Rieff, Philip. *The Triumph of the Therapeutic: Uses of Faith after Freud.* New York: Harper & Row, 1968.

Robbins, Michael. *Conceiving of Personality.* New Haven: Yale University Press, 1996.

Roche do Coppens, Peter. *The Spiritual Perspective: Key Issues and Themes Interpreted from the Standpoint of Spiritual Consciousness.* Washington, D.C.: University Press of America, 1980.

Roiphe, Katie. *Last Night in Paradise: Sex and Morals at the Century's End.* Boston: Little, Brown, 1997.

Romanowski, William D. *Pop Culture Wars: Religion and the Role of Entertainment in American Life.* Downers Grove, Ill.: InterVarsity Press, 1996.

Rossi, Philip J., and Paul A. Soukup. *Mass Media and the Moral Imagination.* Kansas City: Sheed and Ward, 1994.

Roszak, Theodore. *Where the Wasteland Ends: Politics and Transcendence in Postindustrial Society.* Garden City, N.Y.: Doubleday, 1972.

Rouner, Leroy, ed. *Selves, People, and Persons: What Does It Mean to Be a Self?* Notre Dame: University of Notre Dame Press, 1992.

Rubinstein, Ruth P. *Dress Codes: Meanings and Messages in American Culture.* San Francisco: Westview Press, 1995.

Sandel, Michael J. *Democracy's Discontent: America in Search of a Public Philosophy.* Cambridge: Harvard University Press, 1996.

Sanders, Barry. *A Is for Ox: Violence, Electronic Media, and the Silencing of the Written Word.* New York: Pantheon, 1994.

Sartre, Jean Paul. *Being and Nothingness: An Essay on Phenomenological Ontology.* Translated by Hazel E. Barnes. New York: Philosophical Library, 1956.

Sarup, Madan. *Identity, Culture and the Postmodern World.* Athens: University of Georgia Press, 1996.

Schechtman, Marya. *The Constitution of Selves.* Ithaca: Cornell University Press, 1996.

Scheibe, Karl E. *Self Studies: The Psychology of Self and Identity.* Westport, Conn.: Praeger, 1995.

Schlenker, B. R. *Impression Management.* Monterey, Calif.: Brooks/Cole, 1980.

Schlesinger, Arthur A. *The Disuniting of America: Reflections on a Multicultural Society.* New York: W. W. Norton, 1993.

Schneider, Carl D. *Shame, Exposure and Privacy.* Boston: Beacon Press, 1977.

Schuller, Robert. *Self-Esteem: The New Reformation.* Waco, Tex.: Word Books, 1982.

Sherlock, Charles. *The Doctrine of Humanity: Contours of Christian Theology.* Downers Grove, Ill.: InterVarsity Press, 1996.

Shields, Rob, ed. *Lifestyle Shopping: The Subject of Consumption.* London: Routledge, 1992.

Sloan, Douglas. *Faith and Knowledge: Mainline Protestantism and American Higher Education.* Louisville: Westminster/John Knox Press, 1994.

Slouka, Mark. *War of the Worlds: Cyberspace and the High-Tech Assault on Reality.* New York: Basic Books, 1995.

Smedes, Lewis B. *Shame and Grace: Healing the Shame We Don't Deserve.* New York: HarperCollins, 1993.

Solovyof, Vladimir. *The Justification of the Good: An Essay in Moral Philosophy.* Translated by Nathalie A. Duddington. London: Constance, 1918.

Stephens, W. P. *The Bible, the Reformation and the Church: Essays in Honour of James Atkinson.* Sheffield: Sheffield Academic Press, 1995.

Stevenson, Leslie. *Seven Theories of Human Nature.* Oxford: Oxford University Press, 1974.

Stewart, David W., and David H. Furse. *Effective Television Advertising: A Study of 1000 Commercials.* Lexington: D. C. Heath, 1986.

Stout, Jeffrey. *Ethics after Babel: The Languages of Morals and Their Discontents.* Boston: Beacon Press, 1988.

Susman, Warren I. *Culture As History: The Transformation of American Society in the Twentieth Century.* New York: Pantheon Books, 1984.

Sykes, Charles J. *A Nation of Victims: The Decay of the American Character.* New York: St. Martin's Press, 1992.

Taylor, Charles. *Sources of the Self: The Making of Modern Identity.* Cambridge: Harvard University Press, 1989.

Taylor, John. *The Ethics of Authenticity.* Cambridge: Harvard University Press, 1991.

Tickle, Phyllis. *Rediscovering the Sacred: Spirituality in America.* New York: Crossroad, 1995.

Tocqueville, Alexis de. *Democracy in America.* Edited by J. P. Mayer. Translated by George Lawrence. Garden City, N.Y.: Doubleday, 1969.

Tomkins, Silvan S. *Affect/Imagery/Consciousness.* 2 vols. New York: Springer, 1963.

Touraine, Alain. *Critique of Modernity.* Oxford: Blackwell, 1995.

Toynbee, Arnold. *A Study of History.* 12 vols. London: Oxford University Press, 1934-61.

Twitchell, James B. *Carnival Culture: The Trashing of Taste in America.* New York: Columbia University Press, 1992.

Van Ness, Peter H., ed. *World Spirituality: An Encyclopedic History of the Religious Quest.* Vol. 22, *Spirituality and the Secular Quest.* New York: Crossroad, 1996.

Vitz, Paul. *Psychology as Religion: The Cult of Self-Worship.* Grand Rapids: Eerdmans, 1977.

Vorlicky, Robert. *Act Like a Man: Challenging Masculinities in American Drama.* Ann Arbor: University of Michigan Press, 1995.

Washington, Elsie B. *Uncivil War: The Struggle between Black Men and Women.* Chicago: Noble Press, 1996.

Wells, David F. *God in the Wasteland: The Reality of Truth in a World of Fading Dreams.* Grand Rapids: Eerdmans, 1994.

————. *No Place for Truth; or, Whatever Happened to Evangelical Theology?* Grand Rapids: Eerdmans, 1993.

Wiley, H. Orton. *Christian Theology.* 3 vols. Kansas City: Beacon Hill Press, 1940.

Wilson, James Q. *The Moral Sense.* New York: Free Press, 1993.

Witten, Marsha. *All Is Forgiven: The Secular Message in American Protestantism.* Princeton: Princeton University Press, 1993.

Wurmser, Leon. *The Mark of Shame.* Baltimore: Johns Hopkins University Press, 1981.

Wuthnow, Robert. *Christianity and Civil Society: The Contemporary Debate.* Valley Forge, Penn.: Trinity Press International, 1996.

————. *The Restructuring of American Religion: Society and Faith Since World War II.* Princeton: Princeton University Press, 1988.

————. *The Struggle for America's Soul: Evangelicals, Liberals, and Secularism.* Grand Rapids: Eerdmans, 1989.

Zaleski, Jeff. *The Soul of Cyberspace: How Technology Is Changing Our Spiritual Lives.* New York: HarperCollins, 1997.

Index of Names and Subjects